ANGELS, HERPES AND PSYCHEDELICS

Angels, Herpes and Psychedelics

UNRAVELING THE MIND
TO UNVEIL ILLUSIONS

BETH BELL

To my parents, who agreed to let me select them in
this lifetime to demonstrate unconditional love

To all souls wanting to ignite the fire within
and reveal the truth of who you really are

DISCLAIMER

The names of the characters involved in my stories throughout this book have been changed to protect the privacy of the individuals involved in my journey.

The many spiritual methods, modalities, and medicines referred to in this book are intended for educational purposes only. If you have a serious mental, physical, or emotional condition, please seek professional services from accredited providers. This also includes any reference to drug use of any kind. Only you know what resonates and is right for you on your journey. Please keep in mind the legal status varies in different countries and states regarding the medicines referred to in this book. Please listen to what your soul is calling in for you to experience.

ANGELS, HERPES AND PSYCHEDELICS
Unraveling the Mind to Unveil Illusions

ISBN   HARDCOVER: 978-1-5445-3058-1
       PAPERBACK: 978-1-5445-3057-4
       EBOOK: 978-1-5445-3059-8

CONTENTS

INTRODUCTION

My fiancé, Klaus, and I had left our Sunday brunch at a five-star hotel in India and were heading home with his ten-year-old son in the back seat. Cars, trucks, motorbikes, and tuk-tuks inundated the busy road as people, chickens, and cows dodged traffic. Klaus was an attentive, skilled driver. So when he swerved abruptly to the left, edging into the lane next to us, I assumed it was to avoid danger. This prompted me to glance over the back of Klaus's shoulders, just in time to witness a motorcycle slam into the back of the tuk-tuk next to us. I gasped at the sickening thud of metal on metal as the rider disappeared from view. Klaus had eliminated that narrow space between the cars where the motorbikes weaved in between vehicles. Was it intentional? No emotion showed on his face, not even when his son, echoing my thoughts, screamed from the back seat, "Dad! Did you do that on purpose?"

Klaus sped away from the scene, and I felt myself swallow my terror as my body began to tremble involuntarily deep within. I could no longer deny that I'd fallen prey to a con man with a devilish demeanor. This was the man who I thought was my soul mate and the love of my life. Fearing for my safety and wondering what else this man was capable of, I needed to find a way out of this nightmare. I was stunned that it was even possible that an educated, well-traveled woman like me could find herself in this situation.

*   *   *

PRESENT DAY—2022

When my parents read a draft of this book, they questioned—with compassion and concern—whether publishing it was a good idea. Around the same time, my boyfriend emphatically stated, "Why can't you just *be normal*, stop writing this book, and go back to a corporate job?" We broke up the next day, as he could no longer support my "alternate Universe."

I'd broken through and wasn't going to let anyone hold me back from showing others a way out of the old paradigm, where fear is greater than love. I'd spent years on my awakening journey, unraveling my mind and moving through the illusional veil. My time had come to share universal truths.

From the cast of characters on my journey, you'll see how deeply and blindly I loved. At times I unknowingly sacrificed my desires, soul, and self-expression to fit a mold created by beliefs. I was driven by the idea of having a confidant to build my life with, share my soul with, and count on for years to come. My life was running third-dimensional programs, and it wasn't until these beliefs and thought constructs started to dismantle that the illusions were unveiled.

Admittedly, the idea of writing a book about my life, successes, failures, shame, fears, and heartbreak was not something I'd ever dreamed of doing. My desire had always been to write a book on wisdom: the five pearls, three tips, or something profound based on experiential knowledge that could help others on their journey. Although my inner soul guidance was clear, it didn't stop me from shuddering when my mind surfaced with seeds of doubt. I would need to face my fear of sharing my most intimate life experiences and get beyond the concern of exposing my deepest and darkest moments. I realized that we all have an innate fear that the truth will be revealed and others will take advantage of our most vulnerable moments, especially knowing that these can easily be misunderstood, exploited, and twisted. We fear that we'll be standing naked while others throw stones.

One day, as if guided by the hand of destiny, the outline of the book flowed through my pencil effortlessly. I realized that if I didn't dare to share my rawest moments and lessons, I'd be missing out on a huge opportunity to reveal the insights I'd learned along the way. I finally knew that the point of all relationships is to help us awaken, and this includes knowing we're only here to heal our own minds. This doesn't mean we're not here to support one another; it means we allow others to learn their lessons and don't think we need to do this for them or protect them from their choices. Otherwise, we will remain in their suffering without transcending our own. I share my progression over the years to finally embrace this concept. It came in unexpected ways as I re-membered my connection to Source through the many blessings of people, healing modalities, and the power of plant-based medicines that helped me to unravel my mind. Up until the time of publication, my ex-boyfriend remained adamant that the book would destroy me, emotionally devastate me, and make me unemployable. His predictions haunted me and catapulted me forward in the final months of publishing.

Because every mind unravels differently, this isn't a "how-to guide" but rather an example of a life path to learn from. My lessons and awakening happen to be heavily weighted in romantic relationships. Others awaken through family drama, illness, the death of a loved one, business, or an accident, to name a few. The relationships you've brought into your life will be different from mine; learning how to harvest the pearls of wisdom from each one is the skill to mastering yourself so you can move beyond your deepest fears. This releases you from the constraints of the mind and the mental constructs the external world reflects, keeping you in the matrix. When you do, you'll recognize how you've intricately designed your life's journey to embody your soul, live through your innate wisdom, and break through to universal truths. You will be liberated from lower-dimensional programs where suffering, hard work, and heartbreak are prevalent. Embodying this freedom allows alignments to happen effortlessly, and life becomes easier. Now is the time for all of humanity to awaken. However, not everyone will heed the call.

My journey spans from an initial awakening kiss to transcending this reality to discovering and knowing the truth that lies within each one of us. The road has not always been easy, as my life-journey lessons came fast and some were harder than others. At times, I wasn't sure if I'd survive mentally, emotionally, or physically. As I moved through these life lessons, I realized that the acrobatics of the mind keep us distracted from knowing we are the dreamer of the dream. I share how angels, herpes, psychedelics, and the power of flowers have been some of my greatest teachers. All along the way, new possibilities are explored, and a multitude of tips, tools, techniques, and healing modalities are shared. You'll also hear how Mother Nature's magic can provide you with amazing shortcuts to unveiling illusions and understanding Truth.

The book isn't for the faint of heart, naysayers, complainers, or people who want to remain victims. It's for individuals who genuinely want to take responsibility for their lives by shifting the stories and inner dialogue the mind holds on to so tightly, releasing emotions of heartbreak, shame, guilt, and judgment, to name a few. It's about learning the lessons you've set yourself up for in order to see through a lens that brings greater peace, joy, and love. The awakening journey requires the unraveling of and detachment from the stories of "who you think you are" or "who you think you're supposed to be." Up until now, this has taken many people decades or lifetimes to embody. But it doesn't have to. The shift is happening now, and you only need to decide if you want to move into an easier way of living and loving.

My awakening has been the greatest gift to unwrap and is still in progress after twenty-plus years of accelerated deep-diving into expanded states of consciousness. I've repeated some lessons over and over until I finally embodied the wisdom of how to leverage my mind and let Spirit drive. Uncovering these intricately woven storylines allowed the facade of "who I think I am" to drop away and my inner wisdom to prevail. I see my relationships to the external world differently by recognizing that they are *designed by me* to allow me to learn great lessons. Sorting through the many experiences "called in" for growth requires deep inner work and bravery. It's an ongoing practice to be in this world, but not of it.

While most of us may not believe we were born to be like Buddha, Krishna, Jesus, or the Dalai Lama, I love knowing we can all wake up to this level of enlightenment. Not everyone has the desire to try, but if you're reading this book, I would guess you're intrigued by the path to healing and greater happiness. When we surrender to losing our minds as these masters did, we can "get out" of the circuitous loops of thoughts and release programs that hold us hostage to suffering.

Our value in the new world is how deeply we can love ourselves, shine our light, show the way, and share unconditional love with others. Love is the new currency. How rich are you?

* * *

PS: Getting past my initial resistance to writing this book, my soul also advised with humor, "Tell them about the things you said you would *never* do." So here they are—the things I said "never" to but have now done, except for one. You'll have to read on to find out which one is still outstanding...

- Move to New Jersey
- Get divorced
- Get breast implants
- Get a tattoo
- Take a cruise
- Leave my job for a man
- Move to India
- Take illegal drugs

* * *

**If we don't follow our inner knowing,
then we're just dreamers,
losing out on having the actual
life experiences we came here to live**

PART I

Initiating Awakening
and Soul Quickening

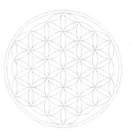

CHAPTER 1

My Knight in Shining Armor

FEBRUARY 1998

Exchanging wedding vows with Stuart in a small, quaint church in Corona del Mar, California, felt like a fairy tale come true. Our chocolate Lab trotted by our side as we exited the church while friends and family cheered us on. My roommate had introduced Stuart and me three years earlier, and our marriage seemed like a match made in heaven. We enjoyed many of the same interests: music, art, real estate, and travel, to name a few. Most importantly, our life goals were aligned, including a mutual desire to have children. He indeed was my knight in shining armor.

Around the time of our engagement, Stuart left his corporate job to start a furniture company, and I worked in sales for a large company in the pharmaceutical industry. I loved my job and had great success, even winning the national sales award, a coveted prize in the industry. This led to a promotion to become a district manager, covering Southern California and Arizona. I loved being in sales, but after about three years, I was interested in moving into a marketing strategy position. So when I learned of an opportunity within my company in the marketing department in San Francisco, I was keen to apply. The interview process went well and looked promising; everything was indicating I'd receive an offer for the position.

Unexpectedly, the global headquarters in Berlin announced that the marketing department on the West Coast would be moving to the main offices in New Jersey, bringing the sales and marketing teams together in one location. This put a kink in my excitement as I'd grown up in North Dakota and vowed to never live in the cold weather again, which meant New Jersey was not an option. Plus, I loved the ocean and the laid-back West Coast lifestyle, and I found the East to be a bit "hard and edgy." As a result, I declined to move forward with the position. But the seed had been planted, and I couldn't take my eyes off new postings for marketing positions; I felt destined to make a move into brand strategy.

Within the next six months, another marketing position was posted. It would be a promotion, and with Stuart working from home, we had the flexibility to move. After much deliberation, we both agreed and, surprisingly, exploring the big move to the East Coast invigorated us. It was only the beginning stage of learning that making "I'll never" statements often led me to do the things I said I'd never do. My sensitivity to the phrase "anything you resist persists" became heightened as I was prompted to look deeper at my passionate "never" and "no" reactions for any deeper meaning behind the resistance.

Stuart's company was in the early startup stage and jumping into a suppressed housing market in the hope of making extra money in real estate seemed like an advantageous thing to do together. Neither of us wanted to remain a one-income household, as we were eager to achieve our financial goals to keep ourselves on track with our life plan. Everything moved quickly. Our California household traveled across the US as we began house hunting from a temporary apartment in New Jersey.

We'd viewed fifty homes, if not more, when we walked into a run-down historical property in Morris Plains, New Jersey. It had been empty for a few years, was full of dust and disappointingly, the hand-crafted mission-style light fixtures were missing. However, both Stuart and I immediately saw it was a masterpiece. Built in 1913 and designed by Gustav Stickley, a well-known furniture designer leading the American Arts and Crafts movement, it had alot of potential. We both liked the same style of homes and immediately knew this was "our place." It would require significant renovation, but Stuart and I loved the idea of bringing back its unique beauty while also putting our personal touch on it. This home was a dream come true: it was 3,500 square feet and sat on an acre of land. Our furniture would fit in the large, open rooms encased entirely in gorgeous wood from floor to ceiling.

While our relationship seemed perfect in so many ways, there was an undertow of misalignment, which I conveniently ignored through the years. I didn't want to rock the boat and knew from my Midwestern upbringing that it was often easier to suck it up than speak my truth and share my feelings. In the earlier years of our courtship, I had returned to university and wasn't making much money as a full-time student, which made me feel that I couldn't ask for what I wanted because Stuart was paying for most of our purchases in those days. He would deny me little things, like a box of Jiffy corn muffin mix that I wanted to buy from the grocery store. Of course, I could have bought these things myself on the side, but instead I decided to let my desires go to please him. It's interesting how these "little things" can turn into big themes over time, in a way we don't even realize.

Our home renovation was finished by the end of 2004, and we felt happy and blessed. We'd gutted the kitchen and basement and added new furniture pieces and artwork. It took some searching, but we also found replicas of the original lanterns to maintain the mission-style theme and honor the property's uniqueness. The acre of land had been completely landscaped with multiple sitting areas, allowing us to bask in the summer sun and observe the vibrant fall colors. Although the winters were harsh, the six-foot-high stone fireplace provided an incredible "warm and cozy" experience as the snow fell outside. It was like having a mountain lodge in your very own living room as the wood fire crackled and popped.

There was no way I dared to complain about our incredible life; Stuart and I found ourselves living our dreams. Having the train station a block away was a bonus as a one-hour ride provided easy access to the heart of New York City. This made it convenient for us to meet up with Jessica and Jane (along with their spouses), two of my childhood best friends from North Dakota, who lived in New York.

Work was always busy, full of travel, and exhausting, but this didn't stop me from loving my job. It provided the new challenges I'd hoped for as I learned the complexities of marketing, expanding my skill set and my opportunity for career growth. This experience gave me an entirely new respect for all the strategies that had gone into the sales materials I'd received when "carrying the bag" and working in the field. What I loved most was the ability to inject my creativity into developing the strategies and then test the ideas with consumers and physicians to watch the ideas come to fruition.

Stuart continued working from home and had a comfortable life; online sales were increasing but not demanding, which provided him much free time. The upside was that he took care of everything around the house, including the cooking, which wasn't my strength. Having Stuart prepare his favorite pasta Bolognese, spicy chili, or his famous meatloaf was an asset that provided a warm welcome home after a long day.

We shared a love of wine tasting—so much so that we'd purchased a historical property in Paso Robles, California, a flourishing wine region. We envisioned many visits to this second home when our financial situation provided enough freedom that we didn't require rental income. I loved wine and carried a brown leather pocket journal to capture my tasting notes. This helped me remember the details of the vintage and grape varietals, along with my self-created scoring system for each wine experience. I enjoyed capturing these particulars, my experience of the wine's bouquet, and specific tasting notes on the front and back end of each sip. When we shared bottles of wine with our friends, I incorporated their experiences and asked them to autograph the bottom of the page. It took the wine tasting experience to another level, as I enjoyed discussing the particulars with others and referring to my notes.

Friends thought our life was idyllic. We had the houses, the lifestyle, and aggressive goals and milestones for our future together. However, our marriage had cracks that I continued to ignore. Now I was the primary breadwinner, yet Stuart continued to control what I could purchase. Some of what he denied me were silly things, like green apple dish soap and vanilla bean ice cream. Looking back, I recognized there had been earlier "rules," such as Stuart forbidding me to wear brown, stating, "You don't look good in it." I loved brown, and it was a trending fashion color at the time. Stuart caused many contentious issues extending beyond clothes.

Why I refused to recognize Stuart's controlling ways early on is a mystery. Maybe doing so would have meant making different choices in my life, like not marrying him. Looking back, we were great companions, but the deeper romantic soul connection wasn't ignited between us. Ignoring the fact that I wasn't speaking my truth for fear of confrontation made matters worse. This seems obvious now, but it was difficult to recognize when I was in the thick of it. It was only the beginning of the light being shone on the hidden patterns I'd come to realize were on my path for my spiritual growth and awakening.

About ten years into our relationship, our differences became more pronounced.

> I wanted to fully express myself and often felt like I had to fit his mold of me.

Before meeting him, I'd been more spiritually inclined, but I had let that drift away, as I wanted to please him with activities we could do together. Things like yoga were out, and gym routines were in.

Stuart also made it clear that he wanted me to agree with him, which meant following his wishes. His mother was always his biggest fan, but she'd gone a little overboard with the sun rising and setting on her son, thinking he could do no wrong. Perhaps he expected me to be more like her, a cheerleader on the sidelines. But this wasn't my personality.

Having my own strong opinions, I liked deep discussions and debates where my opinion was sought and considered. Speaking my truth and sharing my views in social situations with Stuart was difficult. If I said anything that Stuart felt was contrary to his beliefs, he would become upset with me, and upon our return home, he'd reprimand me for being disrespectful of him. My intentions were never to defy him or be confrontational; I preferred to be a united front. I couldn't quite grasp what Stuart thought was so disrespectful, and when I inquired further, he'd dismiss me with a curt "I've already told you, and I'm not going to explain myself again." My opinions and contributions at work were valued, and I felt heard when voicing an opinion or perspective. How could it be so different at home? I was beginning to see the cracks in the foundation of our relationship.

Stuart suggested I go to counseling, telling me I was the problem. I was open to the idea but suggested that we both go. When he resisted, I went alone. I believed that we could turn our relationship around, so I desired to find a way to understand each other better and get our intimacy on track alongside our life plan. Our larger plan to have a family kept me quietly distracted, and divorce wasn't an option. I anticipated living "happily ever after" in the dream life we'd created early on in our relationship.

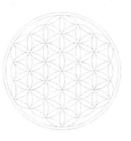

CHAPTER 2

Touched by an Angel

I'VE ALWAYS LOVED anything to do with self-help, development, or personal growth and was thrilled when my company selected me to attend a weeklong development course led by the Global Institute for Leadership Development in Palm Desert, California. The conference agenda included well-known inspirational speakers and personalized breakout sessions with business coaches. It would be a welcome bonus to be back in the California warmth and sunshine as the East Coast was moving into the deep chills of winter.

On the first day of the conference, lunch was held outdoors. The weather was spectacular, providing a nice break from the air-conditioned rooms. There were hundreds of people in attendance, providing a blurry buzz of noise in the background. I felt relaxed and happy to be silently soaking in the sun as I stood waiting my turn in the buffet line. My attention turned to two gentlemen ahead of me who were in a lively conversation, and I noted the confident stance of the man nearest me. A moment later, the conversation abruptly stopped, and he spun around. Our eyes met as we were about the same height and less than an arm's length apart. He offered a warm smile and enthusiastically asked, "Hi! What's your name, and where are you from?" His penetrating gaze jolted me with an infusion of energy as we quickly engaged in conversation. The self-reflecting thoughts in my head fell away, and I became incredibly present to him in that moment, responding, "I'm Beth, and I live in New Jersey."

He introduced himself as Robert, and the conversation that followed flowed effortlessly. His mannerisms came across as unpretentious, yet there was a dynamism in his voice. He looked northern European but said that he lived on the West Coast, owned a winery, and had brought a few members of his executive team to the conference. As we moved along the buffet line, we continued chatting. I commented on Malcolm Gladwell's session, where the author had shared insights on intuition from his book *Blink*, which had recently launched. Although I couldn't put my finger on it, there was something very familiar about this gentleman.

Because I started my career in sales, conversations with strangers were easy for me. But this was different; it didn't feel like an ordinary encounter or connection. I brushed it off until later that evening, when I left the outdoor team building event. From across the outdoor patio, I noticed the two gentlemen from the lunch line walking directly toward me. They were easy to spot: they were both tall, and Robert stood out with his blond, wavy hair and light complexion.

Our eyes met as we walked toward one another, smiling. This meeting seemed serendipitous, and we stopped to chat. Witnessing our easy flow, Robert's colleague asked how we knew each other, apparently not recognizing me from the lunch line. This prompted me to tease him by making up a story of how Robert and I knew each other from Neuchâtel, Switzerland. Out of nowhere, I found myself describing details like, "The 70 percent chocolate was wonderful and one of my favorites." As I looked at Robert to see if he would play along, he smiled as if encouraging me to say more. I continued: "and the white chateau and landscape were breathtaking." Robert nodded in agreement and seemed to be having fun with this ruse, eager to hear what I was going to say.

Even I wondered what would come out next. I wasn't typically a prankster storyteller; today, however, something was different. It almost felt like I was retrieving this story from an actual memory—although it didn't take long for me to break into laughter, admitting we'd all met in the lunch line hours earlier. We exchanged a few niceties, exchanged business cards, and parted ways. But I couldn't shake the feeling of familiarity and ease that came through as I continued to reflect on the encounter.

The breaks during our leadership seminars provided several opportunities to connect. There seemed to be a gravitational pull as we'd often find ourselves near one another, sharing insights regarding the recent session's content. Interestingly, we expressed similar viewpoints about the topics that were being presented. He asked me about my career, and we made some small talk about the pharmaceutical industry. Although it was highly confidential, I felt compelled to share that I was considering leaving my corporate life to work full time with my husband to build a wine cellar furniture company. What was it about Robert that compelled me to share details about this business idea that I hadn't yet even shared with family and friends?

Stuart and I had recently ideated this concept during a business trip to the High Point furniture show in North Carolina. While speaking with a potential Peruvian manufacturer, we quickly saw an opportunity to design unique wine cellar furniture with reclaimed gates from Peru. We were excited about it as it would allow me to work in a lifestyle business and would support my desire to begin our family. I loved my marketing career but didn't feel I'd be the mom I was dreaming of being if I continued to work long hours as a marketing executive in a high-profile corporate position.

Robert asked me some questions about distribution channels for the furniture, none of which I knew at that point but would soon have to figure out. Since Robert owned a winery, it was apparent that he would have some great insights to tap into as I created a business plan for this budding company. But for now, this was a side project, and I was dedicated full time to my pharmaceutical marketing career.

Eager to have some additional conversations with Robert, I hoped to see him at the closing banquet. Within moments of my arrival, he emerged from across a room filled with hundreds of people and walked directly toward me. With a disappointed tone in his voice, he said, "Unfortunately, I'm going to have to leave early and take my team home tonight." At that moment, I couldn't hold back, and expressed, "I'd hoped we'd have more time to chat." He agreed and said, "We know how to reach each other; let's be in touch." Our connection was noticeable, and I was attracted to his energy, but it didn't feel like romantic chemistry. It felt like we were old friends reconnecting, which was intriguing and left me wanting to explore. In these moments, I saw that we had some things in common and that he could provide some excellent business advice.

Upon returning home, I shared with Stuart about the wonderful connection I'd made with Robert. We were both enthusiastic about how his wine expertise and possible distribution connections could be of great value to our wine cellar furniture company. I remained eager to link up in the future.

A few months after I returned from the development seminar, Stuart surprised me with a new twist in our life plan. There weren't many things I recalled making deals on in my marriage, but we had agreed never to ask each other to move back to our hometowns in Oklahoma or North Dakota. I grew up in a town of twenty-five hundred people, and while Oklahoma City was much larger, we'd both said that neither place would be on our list of places to settle down. Now he'd somehow concluded, and was trying to convince me, that Oklahoma City was the *only* place we could live where I could quit my corporate job and start a family. The way Stuart presented this new idea made it seem nonnegotiable, and once again, I'd have to "suck it up" to fulfill my husband's dreams.

I worried that disagreement might cause an end to my marriage, and I wasn't ready for that to happen. I tried to keep an open mind about his desires, as being a good mom was heading to the top of my life's priority list. However, I'd quickly get shot down when I suggested other locations, which prevented me from being able to build a case that could counter his conviction for his hometown. In the back of my mind, I also knew I didn't want to trap myself in a situation where Stuart became the stay-at-home dad and I continued to work and pay the bills.

Meanwhile, I was still intrigued by my connection with Robert and looked forward to discussing opportunities in the wine business, especially realizing that I might be running the wine cellar furniture company sooner than expected. Robert felt like a kindred soul to me, but I didn't understand why, because I didn't know him that well. We'd been keeping in touch with brief notes via text and email, comparing calendars and dates to explore when we'd be in the same location and could connect.

Shortly before the holidays, I unexpectedly received a call from Robert. He was in New York City, passing through on his way back west across the US. He'd be flying out of Teterboro Airport in New Jersey, which was close to my office. He offered to delay his departure by a few hours if I could meet him for dinner. My heart pounded, and I thought, *Yes!*, but then I said, "Let me check with my husband, and I'll call you back." As I reflected on the situation sitting in my office, I decided it was best to decline. Although my conversations with Robert were not flirtatious, I realized I didn't know his intentions. I was also questioning mine, so I chose to go home for dinner and my nightly bottle of wine with Stuart.

Robert and I continued to casually write to each other, exchanging travel schedules and looking for opportunities to meet. Several months after the dinner invitation, we found we'd both be working in Los Angeles. I would be staying with friends over the weekend, so it was a perfect opportunity to meet for lunch on Saturday.

As my workweek in California ended, Stuart called me and requested that I divert from California to Oklahoma City for the weekend. He informed me that he'd signed a contract to purchase a home that neither he nor I had seen. I was caught completely off guard. We had looked at properties previously while on a holiday trip, but I still hadn't agreed to move to Oklahoma City, and I could not envision myself living there. But was the call from my husband making an offer on a home genuinely a shocker? Perhaps I was in denial all along, thinking I had a say in what his plans were for us. It wasn't the first time he'd steamrolled ideas through our relationship or his relationships with other people. Upon Stuart's request, I canceled my weekend plans, regrettably declined the opportunity to connect with Robert, and boarded a flight to Oklahoma the next day.

Stuart's parents picked me up at the airport, and we headed directly to the property. They were excited and glowing at the thought of us moving there. I was feeling conflicted, but I didn't want to burst the excitement bubble and disappoint everyone. Since Stuart had already signed the contract, a heaviness and a sense of anxiety weighed on me. Saying no would mean I was the one shattering everyone else's dreams. I quite liked my in-laws but wasn't interested in calling Oklahoma City home. Without a strong proposal for another option, I felt stuck. This situation didn't feel good because it wasn't a decision that my husband and I had discussed privately and decided on together.

Walking through the house with my mother-in-law by my side, I remember each step feeling like I was walking through quicksand. Damned if I do, damned if I don't. The house was light and bright, meeting one of my top requirements, but there was no feeling of "home," as my heart was nowhere to be found. Technically we were in a legally binding contract to purchase, although Stuart insisted that we could weasel out with the inspection if we had to. However, this approach didn't make me feel comfortable. I felt pressured to agree to purchase because any other option seemed doomed for divorce. I took a deep breath and said okay. My in-laws were thrilled, and we celebrated with a fantastic bottle of wine over dinner that night. This helped to dull the feeling that I'd not spoken my truth.

Six weeks later, we closed on purchasing the house in Oklahoma City. Instead of being excited, the pit in my stomach grew; I knew I was moving down the wrong road. But what was I supposed to do now? Around the same time, Stuart announced that he'd found a retail space that he wanted to lease for our new business and his current furniture company. Everything was moving fast, and it felt like a runaway train. My pharmaceutical career was buzzing with launches and success that garnered recognition as "best launch in the industry." I kept busy and distracted while plunging deeper into denial of the fact that I'd soon have to leave my job, where I felt valued, seen, heard, and appreciated.

Then, out of the blue, came another opportunity to connect with Robert. Our calendars put us both in San Francisco on the same weekend in May, only a few weeks away. My spirits lifted, and I was eager to explore ideas and reconnect through conversation that felt comfortable and inspiring. Perhaps it would help me get more excited about the wine cellar furniture business transition. I still wondered about the mysterious pull toward his energy as it went beyond business and a love of wine. At the time, I wasn't speaking in terms like "the Universe aligning." My soul seemed to be encouraging me to connect with him, and I was determined to listen.

A few days before my departure to California, I received a call from Robert. He would be passing through New York City on the day I planned to travel from New Jersey to San Francisco. Knowing this, he invited me to fly with him on his private jet, which would allow us to spend more time together. I shared my excitement with Stuart that night as we sat outside on our beautiful stone steps, sipping a bold glass of red. We discussed this as a unique opportunity to build a relationship for our wine business while flying with Robert across the United States. Stuart wasn't the jealous type and happily encouraged me to go. And so I did!

On the day of departure, Robert and I planned to meet in a coffee shop in New York and take a car service to the airport together. It was tricky navigating the small spaces, as I had a substantial piece of luggage and nervously fumbled around getting a table. Moments after I arrived, Robert was sitting in front of me, and magic seemed to enter the room. As we sipped our cappuccinos, we effortlessly engaged in conversation. Time passed quickly until our conversation was interrupted by a call from the car service alerting us that the driver was waiting outside to take us to Teterboro Airport.

Getting into the back of the car together felt familiar and comfortable, almost like we'd done it before. By the time we arrived at the airport, I was slightly disoriented by the intensity of our connection as we navigated through the protocol at the Million Air Terminal for private aircraft. It wasn't your typical curbside luggage check as the crew whisked us away without delay, escorting Robert and me onto the plane. Diana Krall, one of my favorite artists, played in the background, which set the tone for a magnificent trip. I quickly settled into the comforts only experienced on a private jet, including oversized seats, tables, and extra space. When I recognized that all the other seats were to remain empty, the plane turned into a cozy oasis in the sky.

Our conversation from the car continued as we delved into topics regarding corporate organizations, such as what we looked for in people when hiring and what we felt were essential attributes for leadership positions. I remembered thinking how refreshing it was to have business discussions with someone who seemed conscious and caring about others—something my husband and I always seemed to disagree on.

I was the mediator in my husband's business all through my marriage. He always had issues with people, and he'd often delegate me to clean up the messes he'd made. He had a pompous way of speaking to people, which almost always resulted in me having to salvage the task, project, or personal relationship. It became a daunting task because we were so misaligned in principles. I found it energizing to have open conversations about people and management styles on the plane with Robert.

There wasn't a moment of silence until, somewhere over the middle of the United States, while at thirty thousand feet, Robert leaned over and gently kissed me. I was stunned. I felt connected and attracted to him but was not consciously thinking anything romantic. I was married. Much to my surprise, I ever so naturally kissed him back, and my body reacted on a cellular level. Fireworks went off, lighting me up inside and causing a glow as sparks flew. I had no idea where this was going, but I knew there was no turning back. I could never unknow what this felt like or forget this moment, nor did I want to. I felt treasured, seen, and appreciated. It was a pure, magical, and unexpected connection.

Robert and I arrived at the hotel and settled into our separate rooms without any further romantic exploration. I was in awe of myself; I felt like a beacon of light. My world seemed to be cracking open as my mind began to unfold and reveal the most incredible clarity about my marriage. I wanted to believe I was romantically and spiritually connected to my husband, but I wasn't. I knew from previous relationships that Stuart and I hadn't come close to the intimacy I was capable of.

Now it was undeniable that I'd been lying to myself for a long time.

It felt like my guardian angels were singing praises that I'd finally seen the light.

At the same time, I was trembling. The facts were before me: I was married, and I'd kissed another man. Suddenly, it felt like a gavel had been slammed down, and I knew deep within my heart that I wanted a divorce. Having an affair with Robert to see if he was "my guy" before leaving my husband didn't align with my moral compass. I was long overdue to face the truth that Stuart and I never had the deeper connection I always needed and wanted. Starved for this level of intimacy, I was determined to experience the type of relationship I knew was my destiny. I no longer wanted to shut down my desires to live a life filled with love, laughter, and unconditional support. This was my new declaration.

My eyes were wide open as I lay there alone in my hotel room. The realization that I would be unexpectedly, yet somehow not surprisingly, getting divorced started to sink in. Memories I'd shoved away surfaced and began to stream through my head. The movie of my life provided great clarity now that I was paying attention to hear and see what Spirit had been trying to get through for years.

I remembered how Stuart had threatened several times throughout our marriage to leave me. The first time was on our honeymoon. I teased him about what his mother would think about him placing his bubble gum in the ashtray at our upscale bed and breakfast. He became angry, emphatically stating we'd made a mistake getting married. He was right, but I didn't see it that way at the time. This interaction resulted in us sleeping in separate rooms the first night of our honeymoon, which should have been an obvious red flag. But I had made a commitment "for better or for worse," and

> I sincerely believed that things would get better over time, *not* worse.

I knew marriage would have some bumps along the way, but the white picket fence I'd hoped for when I married Stuart had started with significant flaws that I'd stuffed down.

As I continued to lie there, sleepless in San Francisco, thoughts of getting a divorce brought up lots of anxiety and questions. We'd have to sell our three properties. Where would I live? What would we do with our dog (who, in some ways, I was attached to more than my husband)? I'd have to let go of my dreams of growing old with the person I married and would have to check the "divorced" box, and live with the stigma of a failed marriage. Ugh! Growing up in a small town, having friends with divorced parents was a rarity. People who got married stayed married; that's the belief system I was programmed with and was about to let go of.

Clear that I wasn't leaving my husband for another man, I was finally ready to speak my truth. Little did I know that this was the start of my accelerated awakening, which would lead me to understand Universal Truths about human existence on the planet. Although I didn't fully understand the concept of spiritual contracts at the time, it was evident that mine with Stuart was coming to an abrupt close.

The mystical energy continued between Robert and me the next morning as we walked through Fisherman's Wharf Market. The intensity of our chemistry and connection was astonishing. We wondrously and naturally flowed together as energy pulsed through my body like never before. It was as though we were old souls reconnecting, which seemed wild as he was a stranger by most definitions.

I didn't want our time together to end, but he needed to arrive home early on Sunday, and I needed to start work that evening. It was only one day and two brief nights, but better than only the dinner we'd initially planned.

> Distressed, I also experienced delight in knowing the
> Universe had aligned to allow this instrumental cracking
> open of my heart and soul.

The blinders were off, the veil was lifted, and for the first time I could clearly see the type of relationship I wanted and could have.

After Robert's departure, a deep emptiness emerged as I plummeted from a wonder-filled connection to feeling alone with all the unknowns ahead. Understandably, there was a longing in my heart for a greater comprehension of what had happened during this powerful time together. I wondered if I would spend the rest of my life trying to figure it out or if this would blossom into something more. Recognizing that my primary focus needed to be on cleaning up my life and moving forward, I welcomed opportunities to learn more about Robert and saw him as an eye-opening blessing in my life.

I'd have the day to process the rush of emotions I was experiencing before I needed to pull it together and give a presentation that evening to welcome the sales team to the conference. I thought that finding a park where I could breathe in fresh air might help clear my head, but I had no idea where to go. I hailed a taxi and asked the driver to recommend a place to sightsee. He responded, "How about a drive across the Golden Gate Bridge?" This seemed perfect. As we approached the base of the bridge, a beautiful park appeared. I noted this to the driver and requested he drop me there on our return.

As if in a movie, we glided across the historical bridge as I gazed out the window, viewing the gorgeous cityscape of San Francisco. There was no particular purpose for the taxi ride other than seeing the sights, keeping busy, and finding a park to sit in. Honestly, I was afraid of what my mind would conjure up next if I stood still.

Once back on the other side, I exited the car and stood in shock as I wondered what to do next. Wandering about, I noticed incredible fountains shooting water ten to twenty feet into the air surrounded by magnificent arches and old structures towering around them. This was the perfect spot to sit for a while, quiet my mind, and observe the beauty before me. Surprisingly, I felt incredibly peaceful, although I dipped in and out of this serenity, shuddering at the idea of what was ahead for me.

What if I don't find someone in time to have children?

What if this magical feeling is merely an illusion or a trick, and I wake up one day regretting this decision? What if I'm making a mistake?

I was always so hard on myself and wondered if I had worked enough on my shortcomings during the marriage.

As I sat on the grass and gazed up, an angel appeared—albeit a statue of an angel. It seemed to be peering down from the top of a monument as I sensed a Divine energy shining down on me.

> In my confusion and awe, I suddenly felt held and
> supported by a force much greater than myself.

I'd never experienced this feeling before. Time seemed to slow down as the breeze touched my skin and the rays of the sun kissed my forehead. My anxiety diminished as I continued to feel miraculously clear about moving forward with my divorce. Both Robert and the statue felt like symbolic figures from above, guardian angels of some sort, here to help me awaken to the illusional dream I'd been living. As I went to leave this peaceful park, I swiftly felt that my life was in fast-forward movement again as my thoughts swirled in anticipation of chaotic months that lay ahead.

I'd planned to meet my friend Candy, who lived in San Francisco, as we'd scheduled a late-morning coffee date. While sitting outside the café, the sun's rays provided a warmth that negated the cool spring breeze. I quickly burst into sharing all that had happened over the last thirty-six hours as my croissant remained untouched in front of me. Amazingly, she didn't appear to be stunned by my news and only smiled. Why wasn't she jumping on me and telling me I was crazy for cheating on my husband? She was so nonjudgmental about the affair, albeit it was only kissing. She listened intently to all I had to share about how my heart was bursting open, and then I began to dump my emotions about my marital woes on her. I'll never forget her saying, in her southern accent, "Girlfriend, life is too short, and you should follow your heart."

Before heading to my evening meeting, I called my mother and asked her to visit me the upcoming weekend in New Jersey. Stuart would be in Oklahoma City, which would allow me to deep-dive into the divorce news I was about to spring on her. I didn't want to do this alone and needed someone who loved me unconditionally to help me navigate this difficult time. My mom had always been such a good sport and so easy-going that my request to come for the weekend didn't seem to set off any alarm bells. I made it easy by telling her I'd buy the ticket, so all she'd need to do was get Friday off from work.

I couldn't predict how divorce discussions with my parents were going to land as I'd kept my marital struggles private. While my parents didn't have a perfect marriage, they stayed together through all their misalignments. Growing up in a small Lutheran church on the rural plains of America shaped my views on divorce; it wasn't an option unless you were beaten or abused. However, the door was opened, and I was determined to walk out no matter what might or might not happen with Robert. Everything felt irrelevant because I was clear about Stuart. Little did I know that this was only the beginning of the awakening that would transform my life forever.

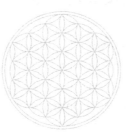

CHAPTER 3

The Exorcism

WHEN THE PLANE touched down in New Jersey, I had less than twenty-four hours before my mom's arrival. Everything seemed surreal as the car service dropped me off; I was realizing my life would never be the same again. Entering the house through the back kitchen door, the energy felt different. It was a harsh feeling knowing that I would no longer be walking into the fantastic aroma of garlic and onions sautéing in a pan as Stuart created one of his delicious meals. I felt a sinking feeling as a cloud of disappointment enveloped me. The hopes and dreams that my marriage was built on were shattered.

My thoughts quickly shifted to Stuart in Oklahoma City, finalizing the lease agreement for the retail showroom. He was eagerly waiting for me to sign the contract since he could not get financed without my income, which was also a point of contention. My divorce request would come as a shock on many levels, and I was scared to break the news. I planned to wait until I'd discussed this with my mother and had her by my side.

Although well-educated with significant life experience, both of my parents are quite traditional in terms of Midwestern culture. My mom was a registered nurse who had a way of listening without making me feel judged. My dad was an environmental scientist who was profoundly emotional yet practical. Even though my relationship with them was strong, this situation took us into uncharted territory. Asking for a divorce was a big deal, and I suspected that my mom wasn't going to let me off the hook quickly or without significant discussion. Telling her about Robert would be too much, and I needed to stay focused on the facts of why my marriage was failing and my newfound clarity to move forward.

Mothers always seem to sense when something out of the norm is happening with their child, and I hoped she wouldn't ask, "What's wrong?" on the drive home. I knew I'd easily break down if I started the discussion. Fortunately, she didn't ask me about anything on the way home. After we got her luggage up to her room, we quickly settled into the living room. I sat in my trusty rocking chair, where I spent each evening decompressing from a day of challenges and drinking the customary glass of wine with Stuart. This night was different. There was no wine and no husband in the room. Only my dear mother was sitting on the sofa, unknowingly about to receive what I thought would be the shock of her life.

My mom was often referred to as an "earth angel" at work because she has a compassionate and caring heart for others. Hearing me so upset would be difficult for her. Women from North Dakota have a remarkable toughness to endure almost anything. The mentality is that you get married, stay married, and figure out how to make yourself happy. I was embarking on a new path that would break a cycle of "enduring" that had been ongoing for generations. I'd not spoken with anyone regarding my troubled marriage throughout my ten years together with Stuart as I felt our issues should stay between us. Unfortunately, Stuart never wanted to talk through our issues because he believed all the problems were mine. Many people hadn't seen any obvious signs of struggle from the outside.

I tried to ground myself as I felt shattered yet clear at the same time.

My breath was shallow as I told my mom, "I'm getting a divorce." After that, our conversation was a blur, simply because what came next felt so painful to vocalize. I couldn't stop myself from screaming as my emotions flowed through me like a faucet turned wide open, sharing all the hurtful feelings I'd felt over the years. Stuart had threatened to leave me several times if I didn't change my ways. Now I felt bullied into moving to Oklahoma City. I hit on some of the early issues by reminding my mom about the many things that Stuart had forbidden, like using washcloths, buying items he didn't like from the grocery store, and wearing certain clothing styles and colors. If I did any of these, I was labeled "disrespectful." My mom nodded as I spoke. She knew the list was long and more profound than these simple examples.

There wasn't much room for her to chime in. But when I paused for a moment, she recalled a time when the three of us were driving up the California coast on a weekend trip. She reminded me that Stuart had declared, "Beth should become a pediatrician." The memory came flashing back as I recalled my mom responding from the passenger seat saying, "I don't recall Beth ever saying she wants to be a pediatrician." I sat quietly, listening from the back seat. At the time, I viewed his passionate opinions as his way of caring for me. I was a free spirit, straight from the womb, and I'm sure my mom always wondered why Stuart thought he had so much authority over me.

Over the years, I'd shoved down my thoughts and feelings about Stuart's controlling nature. I'd been so good at finding ways to accept this part of our relationship, but now my truth was coming out, and I was raging with anger, sadness, and disappointment all swirled together. I wasn't yelling at my mom; my emotions were just out of control as memories continued to surface. It felt like I had an exorcism that night; I hadn't expected to unleash so much repressed anger. Feeling safe and expressing my truth to my mom allowed me to feel these emotions on an entirely different level. As the pain poured out, the weight lifted and my heart began to open, allowing walls I'd built to start breaking down. I finally felt heard. My mom wasn't judging me, trying to change my mind, or telling me to "figure it out" as Stuart would often do.

Although she was shocked that I was taking the drastic measure of leaving my marriage, she could hear my clarity and remained supportive. I felt relieved. The last thing I needed was to be challenged as I began the daunting process of standing my ground with Stuart. It was apparent she'd quietly witnessed our disconnect and our clashes over the years. Recognizing it was late, we both paused. Our attention shifted to my adorable chocolate Lab, looking at us with inquisitive eyes. Now I hoped for a good night's sleep, as I planned to call Stuart in the morning to announce my divorce request.

As the sun rose the following day, so did my anxiety. Sitting down at my husband's desk in our home office, I took a deep breath and dialed his mobile number. As he said, "Hey, Babe," electricity pulsed through my veins. My heartbeat pounded out of my chest, and I immediately proceeded to tell him I would not be moving to Oklahoma City nor signing the retail contract he'd negotiated. Then I emphatically stated that I wasn't interested in working on our marriage any longer. He was speechless. After a momentary pause and with surprise in his voice, he asked, "You want a divorce?"

I responded with confidence: "Yes."

Complete silence hit the line, and you could have heard a pin drop. It felt like a communication standoff. I waited, having nothing more to say. I was almost breathless, and my heart was still pounding. He finally said, "I'll be on the next flight home." Another jolt of emotion flowed through me as fear set in, and I wondered how he would handle this situation, which was out of *his* control.

The next day, I dropped my mother off at her departure terminal, and we hugged goodbye as I held back tears.

> I didn't want to be in this movie any longer, but there was
> no way to stop the frames from rolling forward.

My body felt numb as I headed toward Stuart's terminal, only a few minutes away. I saw him standing at the curb and felt no emotion toward him and nothing for us. I jumped out to open the back of the vehicle, and after he placed his luggage inside, he hugged me, cried, and pleaded for me to not give up on us. I was emotionless and wanted to stay strong. I calmly reminded myself that I had tried to discuss many of our issues throughout our marriage, specifically regarding his condescension and lack of communication, only for him to reiterate that I was disrespectful of him. I was determined not to turn back on my decision.

On the ride home, Stuart was eager to talk and was suddenly all ears, which I wasn't used to. When we arrived at home, I was exhausted and chose to remain guarded and stoic, not wanting to be coerced into a conversation. That night, he slept in our bedroom, while I slept in the guest room. I felt stunned, and while emotions were high, I was trying to hold it all together and not lose my focus.

Thankfully, I had a work trip to Las Vegas the next day. I was eager to remove myself, not wanting to stay in the house with him. I'd never stood my ground with him like this before, and I was scared. I wasn't afraid he would physically harm me but that he would somehow emotionally manipulate me back into the marriage. I'd put my desires aside too many times and knew I wasn't emotionally strong enough. I didn't want to be guilted back into working on the relationship. I'd been down that road too many times already.

Clarity was my freedom, and I didn't want to lose sight of this or start discussions that couldn't be resolved.

> My deep "knowing" that I was moving in the right direction was driving me, but the truth was that I could've unraveled emotionally at any moment.

Many days I was hanging on by a thread. I needed to stay the course and process on my own as my life moved into massive disarray. I had significant corporate training for handling difficult situations with employees, but I didn't have any training for navigating divorce. I was riding off the empowerment I received while emptying my heart with Mom, and the fire remained in my belly to be me, not who *he* wanted me to be.

My mind continued to swirl with repetitive questions, like *What if I am single forever? What if I don't find a partner in my childbearing years? What if Stuart drags this on and becomes nasty as he did in other relationships?* and *Will I find a place to live that makes me happy?* These questions, and more, haunted me as I went from having a well-thought-out life plan to an unknown future. At the same time, an indescribable energy seemed to carry me through these new and unfamiliar waters. I didn't know exactly what it was but was grateful for this feeling of support, which made me feel more optimistic. It was me, myself, my mind, and this mysterious Angelic energy that enveloped me and supported my every move.

I mentioned to Robert that I was divorcing my husband, but we didn't talk about it in any detail. It was clear that I was on my own throughout this process, which was okay as I didn't need to take on anyone else's feelings, emotions, and opinions or over complicate my own. I had enough to juggle in these early days and would face many difficult decisions in the days ahead. We kept in touch via text and email, giving each other updates on our lives. He was living his glamorous life, and I was shattering mine.

On the plane to Las Vegas, I prayed for help from the mystical power and God-like presence I felt was surrounding me. I wasn't sure how long the strength from my mom's visit would last, and I didn't want to weaken or let my clarity become clouded. As I sat on the plane, a voice began subtly speaking to me through my thoughts, which inspired me to capture the messages coming through. Pulling out a pen from my handbag, I flipped over my boarding pass to write down the wisdom that flowed so quickly. What appeared onto the paper were three simple questions intended to guide me and keep me focused on moving in the direction of my highest good. These became my new rules for decision making.

If I make this decision,

1. Is it aligned with my soul's purpose?
2. Will it help me expand and grow?
3. Will it protect me or harm me?

These questions came out of nowhere and seemed to have some miraculous grounding that made my life easier to navigate throughout the difficult situations to come. When asking these questions, I remained in my truth and could feel my light shining brighter. It seemed the easiest way to let Spirit lead the way—whatever that meant.

Of course, I secretly wanted Robert to scoop me up and make everything alright, and for us to live happily ever after. Who wouldn't? However, I knew deep inside that he was a catalyst, a guardian angel of some sort. Whatever role he would play in my life was yet to be determined. The only thing I knew for sure was that I wanted to enjoy each moment and not worry about the future. I recognized that this was easier said than done.

When I shared my divorce news with a dear friend who lived near me, she and her husband offered to let me stay with them after I returned from Las Vegas. As soon as I got back to New Jersey, I packed the most oversized suitcase I owned and filled my car with clothes and shoes, as these were the only things I wanted or needed. I was prepared to walk away from everything I had associated with my identity at the time: a fairy-tale marriage and a historic home with décor we'd collected from around the world, the finest dishware, and all the trappings of a beautiful life. I was willing to leave it all behind and walk toward freedom and liberation into the unknown. This was a tradeoff and a risk I was willing to take.

I shared the news with my childhood friend Jessica days after returning from my work trip. It was a gorgeous sunny day in May, so we planned to meet at the outdoor tables behind the New York Public Library. As we sat down, I announced, "I'm getting a divorce!" Her eyes popped open, and she burst out with an unexpected gasp, followed by a nervous laugh. Then her expression turned to a slight smirk and she appeared relieved. My announcement gave her the liberty to unleash how she'd felt about Stuart, and it wasn't complimentary. She had been tired of his controlling ways too and had felt separated from me for years; she longed to have our close friendship back. She'd wondered many times, when trying to make plans with me, why she couldn't get a straight answer out of me. She said she'd often pondered if she'd done or said something wrong. She'd had no idea about my marital problems, but everything made sense now. We hugged each other and looked forward to diving deeper into our friendship to make up for lost time. I felt bolstered with Jessica by my side. Although Stuart was contesting my divorce request, the future seemed bright in spite of the darkness that inevitably lied ahead.

Next on my list was Jane, my college friend from North Dakota who was living nearby in Hoboken. Her reaction resembled Jessica's, and she was not at all disappointed to hear I was leaving Stuart. She quickly reminded me of times when he had not impressed her and gave explicit details that I was surprised she could recall. One example she provided was when we'd all gone to a Prince concert together at Madison Square Garden. Stuart had complained, saying the music was too loud and tried to coerce me to leave. Fortunately, I chose to stay in the stadium with them to enjoy the concert while Stuart stood outside in the hallway.

Jane was married to a lovely gentleman, a born and raised New Yorker. She had divorced her first husband years prior and was eager to share her friendly advice. I distinctly remember her saying, "This will be a difficult time. Find a place that makes you feel good, and pay more money if you have to." She emphasized that the importance of finding a home that would uplift me and support my emotional needs was more important than pinching pennies. Before we left one another, Jane looked at me with a tender expression and said, "Everything around you may crumble a few times, but you'll make it through." She hugged me tightly, and I was on my way.

Although I didn't grasp the magnitude and reality of what she'd said at that moment, her advice made a huge difference in my life. Without it, I may not have widened my home search and would have most likely stayed in the suburbs in an apartment tucked between homes with baby strollers or retirees to save some money. New York City wasn't feasible because the commute would be too long, but the Jersey side of the Hudson River had some vibrant up-and-coming communities to explore.

Miraculously and quickly, I found a flat in Jersey City that over-looked the New York City skyline. Energetically this felt like the perfect location as the area was vibrant with people, along with new high-rise buildings, and yet had a small-town feel thanks to its many small busi-nesses and restaurants. Jessica and Jane would be an easy subway stop or two away. I hadn't spent much time in this area or neighborhood, but there was a sense of "knowing" that this was perfect for me. The only problem was that I couldn't see the actual apartment before signing the lease; the agent had told me, "It has a great view, and they go quickly." I trusted my gut, followed my heart, and signed the lease without seeing it. I never looked back and felt excited about building my new life.

I was grateful to my friends for letting me stay with them, but I was more than ready to have my own space. I have a vivid memory of the day I moved to Jersey City: I drove to my new apartment with my clothes, a few household items, an air mattress, sheets, and pillows. All I could think was, *Please, let this feel right,* hoping it would feel like home. I was desperate for a safe place to fall into, where I could cry, laugh, or scream if I needed to. As I opened the door, I instantly felt at peace in my heart. Home truly is where the heart is, and I'd finally listened to mine.

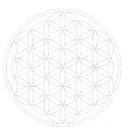

CHAPTER 4

New Beginnings

I'D LEFT MY dream home and its acre of land for a nine-hundred-square-foot apartment and wondered how I'd feel walking into my new space on the thirty-third floor. As I walked into the living area, the hollow echo could have reeked of loneliness. However, it felt full of love, opportunity, and possibilities. Instantly loving my new space, I knew size truly didn't matter. The expansive views across the river and the height of the building provided me with the perfect oasis for my new journey in life. I had no furniture other than an air mattress, so I decided to inflate it in the middle of the living room. I pushed it up against the floor-to-ceiling windows that first night, which allowed me to connect to the vibrancy of the skyscrapers and city lights. I stared at them until my eyelids couldn't stay open any longer, like a kid that doesn't want to fall asleep on Christmas Eve.

After work over the next several days, I painted every wall in my new apartment in my underwear and felt elated to be on my own. I don't know why my underwear, but I suspect I didn't have any jeans I wanted to splatter paint on. Listening to jazz music, I would enjoy one of my favorite bottles of Zinfandel from Paso Robles as I balanced my glass in one hand and a paintbrush in the other. At any given moment, I would glimpse over at the New York City skyline and feel elated with my new freedom to express myself.

The divorce proceedings were in progress, and I was moving through the emotions of building a new foundation for myself. At the same time, Stuart wasn't willing to let me go so easily. He pleaded for me to talk through our issues and suddenly wanted to hear about my discontent in the marriage. He suggested couples counseling, but the reality was that I'd been trying to communicate and grab his attention for years, and I was done. There was nothing left to work on, and I continued to repeat this to him. His character and our relationship weren't healthy for me. There hadn't been any depth to our romantic connection, and I realized the driving factor behind the relationship had been the illusion we'd created about what we thought our marriage *should* look like. He was a good companion, and we enjoyed similar activities, but he was not my soul mate. I wanted kisses, hugs, and affection that made my heart beat faster.

On the weekends, I'd savor the scent and taste of hot Jiffy cornbread muffins fresh from the oven. I knew their nutritional content was less than optimal, but they tasted like freedom and were feeding my soul. I was able to do, think, and feel without any judgment from Stuart. This energy of coming back into my own self-expression, along with the daydream that Robert might come to visit, was helping to catapult me forward.

Robert and I stayed in touch and continued looking for opportunities when our schedules would align again. I was especially interested in connecting now that some of the initial divorce dust had settled. Shortly after moving to my new apartment, I had a work trip to San Francisco. The following weekend, Robert had planned to host a small group at his nearby winery and invited me to join him. This was perfect timing as I could easily delay my return to New Jersey to partake in the festivities.

We were both thrilled for this opportunity to spend some time together, reconnect, and see what magic might swirl between us.

It was late on Friday afternoon, and Robert was scheduled to pick me up outside my hotel. As I stood curbside, awaiting his arrival, a twinge of nervousness came over me. It felt like a dream that we'd finally have an opportunity to spend time together. I was far from divorced but had been making all the necessary movements to start over on my own, and I felt my soul blossoming more each day. My excitement grew when I saw his car approach. He was smiling as he stepped out and came around the back of the car, giving me a gentle kiss on the lips, followed by a brief, yet warm embrace. His calming energy surrounded me once again as he swiftly placed my luggage in the trunk.

As he drove away, he immediately reached for my hand, caressing and gently squeezing it, which set off sparks between us. It was clear that our physical intimacy was about to be ignited as the chemistry between us was undeniable. Now there were no limits to what we could physically explore together. Within moments of our arrival at Robert's home in the city, we melted into a soft yet passionate kiss. The Universe seemed to swirl around us.

We shared a beautiful bottle of champagne and continued to talk and embrace one another. Time stood still. Since he'd made dinner reservations at one of his favorite restaurants in the city, we needed to peel ourselves off one another to go freshen up. Moments later, the phone rang. Robert came back to the bedroom with a concerned look on his face. Stuart had called Robert's secretary looking for his "wife" and inquired if Beth Bell happened to be there. I had not told a soul, not even my mother, that I'd be spending the weekend with Robert, nor had I shared the details about my location with anyone. While the unexpected call was shocking, it was par for the course of what would be coming in the days, months, and years ahead with Stuart. He was heartbroken and determined now more than ever to influence me, get me back, or perhaps try to destroy any future relationships. Robert and I recognized the intensity of the situation, yet we weren't going to let this spoil our time together. In moments like this, my heart hurt for my destroyed marriage, but being away from Stuart's controlling energy continued to catapult me forward.

Early the next morning, we were off to Robert's winery, where we'd stay in his vineyard home for the next few days. As the driver pulled up to the gates of the estate, I was stunned by the majestic archway, which provided a grand entrance, showcasing the beauty of the rolling hills in the background. The winery was perched at the top of a hill that provided magnificent views of the large lake below and the vineyards that spanned for miles. I had looked at the website photos but had no idea it would be so breathtaking. Everything felt dreamlike as we walked through the property and experienced the magic of Mother Nature that surrounded us.

Moments later, Robert's guests arrived. We all gathered at the entrance for a brief meet and greet before embarking on the winery tour. The sun was shining with a cool breeze that swirled through every so often as though guiding us through the grounds of the estate. Once inside the tasting room, we experienced some of the most exquisite, award-winning wines as Robert shared intimate details about the winery and its origins, successes, and struggles over the years. Our senses were heightened as we viewed the most stunning artwork, VIP rooms, underground cellars, and secret places that were not part of traditional public tours.

As the tour came to a close, we found ourselves at the terrace restaurant overlooking stunning and expansive views. The beautiful table that had been set for the group appeared to be a scene straight out of a food and wine magazine. I was excited to chat with this new circle of acquaintances. Conversations ensued quickly as Robert's prized wines were being poured alongside a fantastic array of cuisine.

Robert walked away to attend to something, and at that moment, my mind paused, and the thought of Stuart's phone call began to disturb me. How did he know I was here? I had a pit in my stomach, thinking Stuart might walk through the arches of the winery entrance at any moment. What would he do? What would he say? After a few moments of reflection, I reminded myself that I was living my truth and taking all the necessary steps to dissolve my marriage amicably. My intentions had been made clear, and I'd already taken up residence outside of the marital home. Quickly tuning out of this self-talk, I eased back into the conversations around the table.

The magic continued the following day with a gourmet lunch during which the staff and chef had left no detail unattended. We dined under a large canopy between the vines as the breeze gently blew through and the leaves danced along with our conversations. As I watched Robert entertain the group with his stories, my admiration for all his accomplishments grew. As he glanced at me and took my hand along the way, our connection was glowing. I appreciated the style and generosity of his hospitality; he wanted to do everything he could so that others would have a great experience. We seemed to both find joy in helping others be happy. I thought of Stuart and reflected on how refreshing it was that I didn't have to be a mediator in social situations.

The weekend seemed to end quickly as we found ourselves arranging departure details for the next day. Waking up the following morning, I had a heart-wrenching feeling similar to the first time Robert and I had parted after our magical time in San Francisco. I'd spent years being single prior to my marriage and wasn't the type that always needed to be in a relationship. So this pull toward Robert was unexpected. Maybe the reality that I'd be going from this magical bliss to being alone back home dealing with my divorce drama was setting in. I loved being married and having a confidant by my side; I'd just chosen the wrong person. Truth be told, I wasn't looking forward to being on the dating scene again. I desired nothing more than to spend more time with Robert and yet knew I needed to continue to put together the pieces of my new life.

Fortunately, our schedules aligned so that we could meet in spectacular places over the next several months, including Dallas, New York City, Barbados, and Philadelphia. The highlight for me was having Robert visit me in my Jersey City apartment. Although my place was about the size of his bedroom closet, he seemed thrilled to be with me and enjoyed the views of New York City. Having him in my space was lovely, and it allowed us intimate time to connect, away from the world's distractions and chaos. We easily hopped on the PATH train for the five-minute journey direct to Manhattan, where we spent the day taking in the sights and enjoying a lovely dinner. I was mesmerized by how safe, relaxed, and comfortable I felt being in Robert's presence. Although we never talked in detail about our connection when we were together, I always felt a current of energy run through my body when I was around him. It was a feeling of aliveness that left me supercharged, awake, and aware of the fascinating flow of energy between us.

It seemed mutual, and I didn't doubt he was experiencing the same thing—until he'd leave and I felt our connection rip apart over the distance. Only then would questions start popping into my mind, causing me to wonder if he felt the same way I did. Was it just me feeling the magic and imagining it all? I'd wake up alone and look out at the beautiful skyline of New York City, wanting to share the moment with him and wanting us to be a part of each other's everyday lives. However, it was clear that he was a very busy businessman. At the same time, I knew that if you want to be with someone, you find a way. Robert certainly had the means to make anything happen. Although we weren't deeming ourselves exclusive, I often wondered where I stood in his life and desired to explore our connection further.

Because I was actively in the process of getting a divorce, I wasn't interested in telling many people about my relationship with Robert. I didn't want the added complication of being judged. Surprisingly, sharing about my divorce with my friends and family triggered many people to reach deep into the truth about their own relationships. This accentuated their emotions and opinions around the concepts of the "right thing" to do and whether they thought I was doing it. People started asking themselves, "Am I happy? If you're getting a divorce, should I be?"

People who love you try their best to ensure that you are really "done" with the relationship. Others hope they can help you fix it. The problem is that they don't know what's behind the curtain. Other people saw my relationship with Stuart primarily through their lens of life experience. I didn't want to air our dirty laundry or make Stuart look bad, so I stayed quiet. This was especially difficult when Stuart's mother left me a voicemail saying, "We all go through these times; please call me!" I wanted to talk to her more than anything at that moment. However, recognizing that she believed her son could do no wrong, I worried my feelings would most likely fall on deaf ears if I spoke out, and I couldn't bear to hear her disappointment. The thought of not having our family get-togethers, where we had so much fun eating, drinking, and laughing together, made me sad. It was hard to let go, although I knew wallowing in the sadness wouldn't help me move on.

Months passed, and I found myself wanting more with Robert but wasn't in a position to expect it, as I was still sorting out my life. I had to stay focused on my healing while quietly struggling with divorce delays that were getting old and tiring for me. At the same time, my soul was miraculously quickening and my consciousness was expanding as new concepts were stimulating my mind and lighting up my brain.

I continued to bounce back and forth between healing my old wounds, expanding into new perspectives, and wanting to understand what creates connections between people. A real, scientific explanation would have been great—something that explained why I was so intrigued with the connection I felt with Robert. What had created this sense of familiarity with him early in our relationship? Of course, one could simply say I was infatuated by him. He was dynamic, wealthy, and successful, and his sphere of influence was vast. Who wouldn't want to be with someone like this? But I sensed something more because his worldly wealth didn't attract me; as my mom used to always say, "money is the root of all evil." I didn't necessarily agree with her, but it wasn't a priority in a mate. If anything, it made me feel inferior because I wasn't making anything near his income. I just had a sense of "knowing" with Robert, since our connection felt so comfortable. I wondered if we'd known each other in a previous life, even though I wasn't sure I believed in that concept at the time.

I was intrigued by all that was happening in my life and became increasingly interested to learn more about the human spirit and what creates this sense of connection with others. Communication with Robert unexpectedly began to fade, causing my curiosity to heighten around why we weren't destined to explore our relationship further. He was texting less, phone calls weren't happening, and opportunities to meet weren't being planned. I wanted more, not less. I didn't understand why and didn't have the guts to ask. Maybe I didn't really want to know but remained optimistic that this fairy tale would have a happy ending.

Despite, or maybe because of, my growing disappointment, I delved deeper into my spiritual awakening that facilitated an extraordinary flow of energy through me. My life became so fascinating as I started understanding more about the guidance that is constantly available to us. This made me want to listen more and deepen the connection. I'd be at work or in a conference and, while on a break, I'd find a quiet space to read a chapter in a book like *Conversations with God*. From all the books I was reading, I learned that the interconnectedness of science and spirituality was proven and had data supporting it. How was it possible that this wasn't plastered all over the news?

More than a year had passed since I'd left Stuart, and there continued to be no end in sight for my divorce. I was so frustrated. From a spiritual perspective, I wondered why I'd be calling this drama into my life. Stuart had moved on from being Mr. Nice Guy, who'd begged me to work on our relationship, and was back to being the guy I knew while we were together. His past behaviors—being condescending, being self-serving, steamrolling others, and ruining relationships—were back in full force and focused on me.

The divorce proceedings continued. Most of the time, I felt helpless in the face of the court process and attorneys draining my bank account. I'd married a man to build a life plan and create a secure future with, knowing that we'd take care of each other. I knew he "loved" me, but it was an ideational, conditional type of love in which he suffocated my spirit and pushed me to break away to express myself. All the years we were together, I wanted to believe that his controlling ways were due to his love for me. But now I recognized I'd allowed him to treat me that way.

I couldn't help but think about how different I felt with Robert. Sadly, a lot was left unsaid between us. It became clear that he had other priorities when our opportunities to connect all but disappeared. Needing to move on, I sent a request out to the Universe that if Robert wasn't for my higher good, I wanted him to be taken completely out of my life. The in-between and not knowing why he wasn't interested in more was not serving me. Still yearning for the magical feelings we'd experienced together, the phrase "what you love the most, you must set free" came to mind. Perhaps my biggest disappointment was that it felt like a love left unexplored.

Soon after this, my answer from the Universe came and was painfully clear. I'll never forget exactly where I was sitting. After a long day at work, I'd run an errand at the shopping mall and decided to grab something to eat at California Pizza Kitchen. As I sat at the counter bar to order my pizza, I pulled out my phone. In my hustle and bustle, I hadn't heard my phone ring. I saw Robert's missed call and voicemail. I listened to his voice relaying that he would soon be a father. Hearing his enthusiasm for this new chapter in his life, I felt my heart drop and shatter on the floor. Our story was unwritten, and there was so much more I'd hoped to share and discover with Robert. It was a difficult pill to swallow that, after a sixty-second message, everything had changed and he was no longer available to me. While I was devastated that the possibility no longer existed, I'd received precisely the clarity I'd requested.

I'd woken up on so many levels, but at the same time, many emotions were pushed back down. I continually questioned whether I'd misunderstood my connection with Robert. If he had felt the same way I did, there was no way he would have ever let me go. Heartbroken and embarrassed, I wanted to move on from the illusion I'd constructed in my mind about the potential for this relationship. I was determined not to sit around and cry about it, so I carried on as best I could. This was a challenge as articles about his winery appeared everywhere, making it difficult to forget him. I began to use these situations to transform my thoughts into happiness instead of spiraling into sadness and despair. When I did, it seemed to help me transcend, and I started feeling something shift in my soul.

As my spirituality strengthened, my curiosity about what had happened in my initial interactions with this earth angel didn't fade. When looking for a partner, I vowed not to settle for anything less than how I felt with Robert. The spark of our relationship inspired me to read about soul mates, twin flames, and previous lives as I continued to try to understand the greater purpose of him coming into my life. I knew that over time the stories I'd built in my mind would fade and become fond memories I would cherish for a lifetime.

My awakening was well on its way, although emptiness and loneliness remained in my heart. I decided to keep my eyes wide open and trust in the power of the Universe. I felt there was still a great mystery about relationships: ones that fall apart and others that catapult you forward. While I was okay being alone, I longed to be in a romantic relationship and was certain my guy would be coming soon. I was eager to apply all these great learnings and lessons with a partner and build a future together.

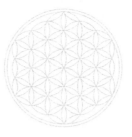

CHAPTER 5

Mind Monitoring and Flower Meditation

I WROTE IN MY little blue journal almost daily in junior high, back in the eighties. Many secrets were disclosed and secured behind a lock and key to preclude anyone from reading them. If you could see the quality of the lock and key, you'd know how young and naive I was at the time. I wrote a lot about life's happenings and my daydreams about romantic interests. Where else but my trusted journal would I want to share secrets about my crushes on guys? This all changed one day when my mother snuck into my room, dug around for my coveted blue book, and read it. I promptly tossed it out and thought I'd never journal again, and I'd certainly never trust *her* again. Being a teenager, I was unable to understand the value of profoundly caring parents who would become my most trusted confidants.

Decades later, journaling became a beloved tool that helped me sort through circuitous loops of thoughts in my head. When I wasn't traveling, my free time was filled with deep reflection and learning, which I loved. My Jersey City apartment felt cozy, and gratefulness enveloped my heart in the comfort of my home. I was also eager to meet new friends and neighbors in the hustle and bustle on the streets below. Serendipitously, a woman from work named Patricia approached me and said she'd heard I'd moved into the building right next to hers. Her smile was warm and inviting as we made plans to meet up back in our neighborhood. I soon learned she was starting a side business centered around wine, so we had a lot to talk about, became fast friends, and enjoyed meeting for impromptu dinners.

Patricia called one Saturday morning and invited me to her apartment to share a cup of tea. As I sat on her sofa, I noticed a book on her coffee table. The title popped out at me: *Spiritual Divorce* by Debbie Ford. I was a little perplexed as Patricia had never been married, and I was curious why she had the book. Upon inquiry, she said, "If you asked about it, it was meant to be yours." Grateful for such a generous and caring friend, I happily took the book home, eager to learn more.

Later that day, I delved into the book and found so much good advice. The author talked about learning to love yourself while accentuating the point that it's one of the most extraordinary tasks in life. She wrote, "It takes the compassion of an innocent heart and the dedication of an Olympic athlete." Naively, I felt that I was up for the challenge. There was an energy in this book, a purpose that the information served. I loved it and was hungry for more as I desired some logical structure to this mess called divorce. Yet I knew it was all about following my heart. Appreciating the guidance coming through, new concepts and ideas continued to open my mind and my view on life.

Sometimes my mind swirled feverishly and my thoughts seemed endless. I realized the only way to stop my mind from racing and building stories was to "mind dump" into my journal. I always felt lighter and clearer afterward as writing things down permitted me to let the thoughts go and stop pondering the same ones. Writing a question and allowing the pen to transcribe the answer was even more impactful. It was like having a crew of angels providing wisdom to all my unanswered questions. When reading the following day, I'd often wonder, "Who wrote this?"

This technique of Q and A journaling sessions accelerated my writing and wonderment. It seemed to shift my mind out of the equation and let Spirit speak. Sometimes the questions were basic, like "Why do I feel so sad?" and I'd be guided through the pen in my hand. The more I wrote, the calmer and more peaceful I felt amidst many unknowns. This guidance from my guardian angels, guides, and higher self was helping me sort through the chaos in the early days. These journaling experiences helped me understand what "remote writing" meant, as it allowed information to flow through and taught me how to access my inner wisdom.

I'd suffered a broken heart before, but this time seemed different because the magnitude of the implications was so vast. It felt like a double heartbreak parting from a marital commitment and losing Robert. I had moments when I wavered on the "whys" and wondered if I was doing the right thing. My mind was active with thoughts and judgments about my every move. At these times, I often wished someone would unequivocally tell me what to do. I knew it didn't work that way, and that I needed to do my inner work, be responsible for my decisions, and navigate whatever lessons I'd called in for my growth.

One day, I received a Divine intervention of clarity I'd never experienced before and will never forget. I had agreed to stay the weekend in our marital home, where Stuart lived. He would be out of town and needed someone to care for our sweet dog, Kaile, whom I missed tremendously. Although it would be difficult to be back in the home we'd shared, I loved our dog and wanted to spend time with her, so I agreed.

Arriving at the house after work, I relaxed on the sofa in front of the fireplace reading a book focused on relationships called *Creating Love* by John Bradshaw. While I was engrossed in my book, a bizarre energy rushed into the room. It startled me, causing me to hesitantly raise my gaze over the top edge of my book. Five figures appeared, standing by the doorway to the kitchen about ten feet away from me, and I felt my entire body go numb. There was a mix of men and women all wearing flannel shirts and blue jeans. They all appeared slightly translucent, not solid as humans would appear, yet I could see them clearly. They looked to be in their thirties and were glowing, with luminous energy around them.

A soft yet stern voice said, "You're doing the right thing; keep going." Then I felt a big swoosh of energy sweep through my body, moving from my head down through my toes as I remained lying on the sofa with my book in my hands. All the fear I had initially felt was washed away as an enormous sense of peace, joy, and love flowed through and over my body. It was almost an unexplainable experience. It all happened so fast as the figures quickly dissolved away, only giving me a glimpse of their human characteristics. I checked my surroundings and glanced at Kaile on the floor. She looked back at me, also bewildered and trying to compute what had just happened.

The experience seemed Divinely guided as I'd been contemplating my intense spiritual awakening a few days prior. Even though I had the clarity to leave, I wished it could be different and kept wondering why our loved ones don't awaken with us at the same time. Why couldn't I miraculously shake Stuart awake? Then we could make all the necessary changes to live happily ever after. I believe it was these questions that encouraged the energies to show up, as though they'd heard my calling and inquiry about the challenges coming my way. But who were they?

Immediately I dismissed the entire experience as my imagination going wild, although I knew it hadn't. The last thing I wanted to do was tell anyone. How could I expect someone else to believe me? I could barely explain the experience myself. I wondered, *Was I hallucinating?* I hadn't taken any medicine, so this was not a possibility. I wasn't expecting what looked like people to show up in the living room, and I wasn't thinking about angels when this energy appeared.

Although it felt wonderful, having spirits show up was one of my worst nightmares.

I'd always disliked being home alone. I was less worried about someone coming through my door and more concerned about the unknowns of spirits in other realms visiting me. And now five of them had appeared right in front of me! Little did I know that this would only be the beginning of my encounters with the other side.

It became clear that we all have many guides and are never alone, although I often felt a sense of loneliness. As these unique experiences started to occur, they catapulted me toward expanding and immersing myself in more books and topics regarding Angelic realms, energies, psychic encounters, quantum physics, conscious breathing, archetypes, soul contracts, and so much more. This was surprising, as I rarely read anything other than what I had to for work. Typically, I'd fall asleep as soon as I cracked open a book. Now I couldn't stop reading. You name it, and it was on my shelf, fully read, highlighted, and underlined with comments noted in either the back of the book or the margins.

Louise Hay, a famous self-help author, caught my attention when I heard about her book *You Can Heal Your Life*. Her concepts were progressive back in 2005. Over a few years' time, her teachings became wildly popular as she created a movement around the idea that our thoughts create our lives and influence everything that happens to us. She had become so successful that her company, Hay House Publishing, was becoming mainstream along with many books that had become bestsellers. Admittedly, I was skeptical reading her book as I'd come from a science-based background where clinical trials are the gold standard. However, what Louise wrote about made so much sense, and the idea that our thoughts create our reality was of great interest to me.

Adding another layer to this concept, I was intrigued by the mind. I wondered how we could use our imaginations and abilities to create detailed dreams at night and apply this to our waking state. Around the same time, the book and movie *The Secret* launched, catapulting the law of attraction into the mainstream. Determined now more than ever, I wanted to master my mind and use it to create my life. I must have ordered more than one hundred books as my soul quickened and my mind thirsted for knowledge. The titles and topics of the books I read were fascinating as my desire to understand the link between science and spirituality almost became an obsession. I now recognized that explaining God was possible, and religion had nothing to do with it.

Admittedly, my Christian upbringing was being challenged during this time, as my definition of God and ideations around religion and spirituality were emerging and changing. I started to see similarities in how Jesus, Buddha, Krishna, and many others were human representations of enlightened beings. My curiosity heightened as I saw how religions became constructs of the mind that gave structure to their teachings. In many ways, scriptures had become flawed. Some flaws stemmed from the original scribe, and others from religious leaders and organizations. Deeper faults crept in over time due to interpretations expressed by influential people, formation of societal norms, and agendas that use fear to control and manipulate humanity. Zealously wanting to step out of this paradigm, I read even more.

I began questioning whether my subconscious mind was a sponge for everything happening in my external world or if I was projecting everything out into the world for myself to observe. As I explored this further, I didn't want to infiltrate my mind with media and realized that television was not my friend. The news and popular programs were planting seeds of ideas and creating constructs in my mind that didn't help me feel happy. Programs like *Seinfeld* were great, as it could inspire me to laugh at myself and the silly things I do or encounter. But other programs, such as *Friends*, had an undertow encouraging one to compare themselves to others in the external world. This can have an impact as the subconscious mind may plant the seed of separation about not being a part of an "in crowd" that meets at a location like Central Perk Coffee Shop. While the show was lighthearted, it could also create a sense of loneliness, as not everyone has a group of friends like the ones on the show or experiences of popularity and belonging. I wanted to be focused on the inward journey, not what the media and society wanted me to think I should be doing.

As a result of this realization, I decided to no longer watch TV or have one in my home. There was no need for this subconscious programming and participation in the collective consciousness. It was the first of many steps I would take to progress out of the matrix in which popular programs were planting seeds not aligned with my expansion. My life already had enough drama. Exposure to ideas that would bring more peace and less chaos became my priority. This resulted in a commitment to honoring this practice indefinitely. The value of having my home as a sacred space with no "programs" running in the background was priceless.

Eliminating TV gave me the idea to begin practicing what I lovingly referred to as "mind monitoring." The intention was to bring awareness to my daily thoughts. According to the National Science Foundation, the average person has about twelve thousand to sixty thousand thoughts per day. Of those, 80 percent are negative, and 95 percent are repetitive thoughts. This made me curious, and I wondered what I was saying to myself.

The more I observed my thoughts, the more I realized they were filled with questions and uncertainty that created unnecessary stress. Identifying disparaging thoughts allowed me to promptly replace them with positive and constructive ones. Often a simple twist of words could quickly change the trajectory of optimism or pessimism about a situation. This helped me detect that most of my negative thoughts were based on a past negative experience or association, not the current situation. Reframing circuitous loops that spiraled me down a rabbit hole became critical to helping change the course and outcome of life situations that were taking place. This empowered me to create my life and not fall victim to negative thought patterns. The best way I knew to monitor myself was in my daily journaling practice, where I reflected on the thoughts I'd had throughout the day. This ultimately led me to identify and release ideas and beliefs that were not serving me. The less cluttered my mind became, the more peaceful I felt.

As I experienced more serenity with my mind quieting, I began obtaining information and receiving "downloads." Ideas would start streaming in through my thoughts but didn't seem to come from me; they just appeared. The guidance came from a place of pure love, not fear. This helped me call out silly fear-based ideas coming from the ego-mind. I became happier and happier as the mental clutter dissipated. This catapulted a desire to experience these more profound levels of tranquility and a heightened state of mindfulness.

Everywhere I turned, it seemed people were recommending meditation, meditation, meditation. Who had time for this? The problem was that I couldn't do meditation effectively, and journaling wasn't always possible. Yet I knew meditation would help me maintain peace of mind and prevent chaos from quickly creeping back in. It would frequently end up being the fifteen minutes I couldn't get back, leaving me pondering how I could have used that time to complete other to-do items. But something deep inside continued to encourage me to keep focused on trying. If only I knew how!

I needed a break from work and the craziness of everyday life, and a holiday to Hawaii seemed perfect. A few weeks before my departure, I was inspired to buy a good camera. At the time, phone cameras were nowhere near the quality they are today. I'd been working within the limitations of a small point-and-shoot camera, and this seemed like a perfect time to upgrade. Being an avid yet casual photographer of architecture and landscapes, I was very interested in photographing the beauty Hawaii had to offer.

As I exited the airplane in Maui, all my senses were heightened. Many fragrant scents permeating the air, the humidity, and the sunshine made me sigh. This immersion in Mother Nature's magic put me into a relaxed state almost immediately. After checking into my hotel room, I was determined to inhabit a lounge chair near the ocean. As I walked down the pathway, flowers appeared all around me, drawing my attention toward them. Their fragrance emanated as though someone had gone before me spraying a light floral perfume. As I gazed at the many flowers next to the walkway, the beauty of an orchid pulled me in. At this moment, my fascination with observing and photographing flowers began.

Viewing the flower up close, the details became mesmerizing. The deepest part of the flower illuminated and created a bright vortex I couldn't stop staring into. I'd rarely paused with such intention to examine a flower so closely. My new camera took incredible close-up photographs, which kept me observing longer as I stood for what felt like hours photographing several orchids. I saw something different in every moment, as each angle provided a new way to view nature's masterpiece. A twinkle of light or a gentle caress of wind would move the flower ever so slightly. The longer I observed, the more I experienced incredible peace, enticing me to photograph more. The experience was magical, as if I were being transported to another place where time and space didn't exist. Eventually, I made it to the beach, after a worthwhile delay, and I repeated a similar saunter throughout the day!

After that trip, I carried my large Nikon camera everywhere, always making time to photograph flowers. Realizing the camera provided me an opportunity to quiet my mind, I believed it was the Universe's sneaky way of helping me truly experience the benefits of meditation. I'd tried so hard to sit and be still and believed there would be advantages to doing it, but I wasn't really getting it.

> Now the flowers were drawing me in, and my mind was naturally quieting so I could finally *feel* the power of stillness.

This peacefulness led me to go beyond the flowers as I fell in love with nature, experiencing a whole new appreciation for its magic. I found myself feeling called toward the twinkle of the sun shining between each petal or leaf as it beamed down to the ground below.

Returning to California to visit a friend, I kept disrupting our walk to stop and photograph the many flowers calling me toward them. This was frustrating for her, as she was hoping to get a workout. To make it up to her, I created a mini album filled with the photographs of flowers captured on our walk together. She loved it, which led me to ask the question, "Should I make these to sell?" Many months later, this contemplation became the genesis of my first product, the flower bouquet photo albums.

Mysteriously, the flowers seemed to be teaching me how to remain peaceful and calm during any storm. I needed this peace of mind as my divorce started to become even more unpleasant. Unexpected situations would catch me by surprise as the proceedings continued to be delayed due to Stuart firing one attorney after another. This challenged my ability to remain grounded because things seemed to be dragging on for no good reason. Stuart's behavior continued to validate the reasons why I left the marriage; observing my own behavior provided critical keys to my growth.

I quickly learned that flowers had a mysterious power to bring me right into the "now" moment. As a result, issues in the outer world lost their emotional charge. Flowers were helping me to recenter and obtain clarity with greater ease. The more I observed them, the more I saw and learned. My life was flowing together in mystical ways, helping me realize there are no mistakes, but there are new choices to make. I knew everything was in Divine order and I simply needed to trust in the magic of life. Sometimes this was easier said than done, but if all of Mother Nature could trust in this enchantment, I believed I could too.

My insights expanded to a greater awareness of the biological network of flowers and trees as they communicate and demonstrate the interconnectedness of life. My appreciation continued to grow as I recognized we're all guided by a force larger than each part. The parables that nature was offering to human life provided wisdom about living in ease and grace. Each jump in life could be like a tiny drop of water that had no fear of falling.

While I still struggled, many things seemed to either miraculously fall into place or blossom naturally, reinforcing how life could be blissful without the constraints of fear. This made me ponder what it would be like to simply enjoy the ride instead of continuing to worry and trying to control outcomes. What would existence be like without decisions and actions that feel like freefalls? Perhaps quite dull, as many humans like to live on the edge of life's possibilities. I, too, was determined not to let life pass me by.

Trusting my intuition now more than ever, even after a few life stumbles, was my practice. At the same time, my values and my corporate training to have a plan, a strategy, tactics to implement, and contingency plans were still deeply ingrained in me.

> I was nowhere near ready to let go of these ideas, but I recognized that taking intuitive risks and making big jumps was my destiny.

My focus remained on strengthening my readiness and willingness to trust whatever would come my way as a result. Ignorance can be bliss, but not forever as I felt called to embody wisdom, not ignore it.

As I read more books on quantum physics, it became apparent that science was filling in the blanks of how we are all connected and never alone in the Universe, despite the fact that I still felt lonely. Topics such as the Holographic Universe blew my mind and helped me dive deeper into understanding spiritual concepts from a scientific perspective. On top of this, my mystical experiences with nature allowed me to feel a connection to Source energy beyond the concepts I read about in books.

Life's mysteries captured me and created a desire to understand the more profound, philosophical concepts of how to remain in this energy. However, its elusive ways made wrapping my head around it and staying connected challenging. Still fearing the unseen, ominous spiritual realms, I desired to better understand the unknowns, not run from them. At this time, I didn't know why I had this ingrained fear, but I would find out much later as I became more open to the mysteries of other realms.

I longed to find a human guide, a teacher of some sort who understood broader concepts of how the Universe works, someone who could guide me on my journey. At the same time, I was very particular about "who" because I didn't have any desire to follow a guru or join any spiritual organizations.

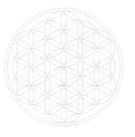

CHAPTER 6

A Course in Miracles and Archetypes

W HO KNEW THAT the plot of *The Matrix* was real and that we're constantly being faced with a choice of the blue pill / red pill scenario? Unplugging from the ideas of the matrix by taking a pill seemed too good to be true—and it was. But life was offering a way to do it that could be just as easy. I think it was my upbringing, which instilled the idea of working hard, that often made me take the long road home. However, I wouldn't really understand this for another decade.

My life felt like a romantic comedy, with some scenes of complex chaos and others of incredible alignments as unanticipated moments unfolded. I felt physically and mentally strong, but my body had a weak spot in my lower back that I'd struggled with for years. Now the pain was at an all-time high. A chiropractic adjustment in my early twenties had caused the space between two disks in my lower back to collapse, and inflammation continued to cause problems. Fifteen-plus years later, the doctor pointed to the x-rays and said the only thing they could do was fuse my vertebrae to give me relief. This wasn't an option in my mind; I was hoping for another modality for healing when a serendipitous event occurred.

I was in New York City for a weekend and called my friend Candy, from San Francisco, as her job as a flight attendant often had her popping into New York. She didn't have a layover planned, but our conversation led me to mention my severe back pain. She immediately responded that she "knew a guy" in the city who could heal me, and his name was Axel. I laughed when she texted over a photo of his business card displaying a cartoonish image of a yellow Buddha character holding a phone. This seemed a little out of the ordinary, but I trusted Candy's opinion. Without delay, I dialed the number, only to find he was out of town. I scheduled an appointment for a few weeks later, when he would be back.

Interestingly, Axel didn't work at a spa but out of a tiny apartment in the East Village. When I called Axel to book an appointment, he suggested we meet at a local coffee shop called Kudo Beans near First and First in the East Village. I hadn't been to that part of the city since the late nineties when a friend took me to a famous drag club. Recalling that area to be a bit dodgy, I wondered how this would unfold. The idea of showing up at an apartment with a man I didn't know and taking off all my clothes under the guise of massage felt odd, to say the least. Even though Candy was adamant that Axel was safe, I decided it was best not to go alone and invited my friend Patricia along. Luckily, she said yes.

It was a beautiful, sunny Saturday morning when Patricia and I met to take the ferry across the Hudson River together. Once on the other side, we jumped into a taxi, and minutes later we arrived and ordered a tea, awaiting Axel's arrival. Moments later, Axel came strolling in. You couldn't miss him: he was over six feet tall, had gray hair with big curls, blue eyes, and a wide smile on his face. We still weren't exactly sure where this massage would take place, but he said "nearby." When he mentioned he was originally from Wisconsin, our Midwestern connection started to make me feel better about him. After some small talk, it was obvious to us that he was a kind man, and our safety concerns diminished. He laughed a lot as he spoke, which helped us let our guard down. So when he asked, "Who's my first victim?" Patricia and I both smiled. To my surprise, she eagerly said, "I'll go first," which allowed me an opportunity to journal and clear my mind.

After about an hour and a half, they appeared arm in arm, very cozy with each other. It was apparent she had been crying from the depths of her soul as her eyes were puffy. At the same time, she had a big smile on her face and sparkles in her eyes. They both laughed and joked that a new angel had been born. Honestly, I was skeptical and might have taken an out if I could have come up with something quickly. This wasn't my thing, and I was perplexed by the whole situation. I preferred a more traditional, lavish spa-type experience.

Although I prefer silence during a massage, Axel spoke the entire time. Amazingly, I wasn't annoyed by it. He seemed to be touching my soul with messages from a place of wisdom, stating things like "only love is real" and "this is all an illusion." As he spoke, my mind suggested this was all hippy-dippy crazy talk. But I couldn't deny that there was some type of energetic shift happening, and my soul was hungry to hear more. Axel used his healing hands and kind words while I lay on the table in a relaxed state, allowing me to completely surrender and receive. This wasn't always easy for me, but I melted right into the table that day. As he continued with the massage, my mind calmed, and a softer side of myself started coming through. The "get it done to-do list" mind chatter was gone. More loving realizations, like the power of connection between people, were coming through. I don't mean romantic connection; it was a more familiar feeling of trusting another.

I had a relatively good life, so I didn't consciously fear many things. However, Axel's words brought an awareness that in many ways I was functioning based on fear instead of love. As we talked through life's experiences, it became clear that if I wasn't feeling love, there was likely fear lurking in the background. He opened something in me that day that I couldn't explain but felt grateful to have experienced.

As the massage ended, Axel mentioned that he was a student and teacher of *A Course in Miracles* (also referred to as ACIM or the Course). I didn't understand all the intricacies of the messages he shared that day, but they resonated with me. Before I left, he offered me a copy of a big, heavy blue book that looked like a Bible. Sensing that it contained profound information, I eagerly accepted his gift and was excited to start exploring the Course.

While reading over the next few days, I found it more challenging than expected and was often left puzzled. Sometimes I understood the concepts, but many times I did not. Axel suggested starting with the lessons in the back and then intermittently dipping into the book. I often could only read a paragraph before calling Axel to discuss. Even when I had no idea of the underlying meaning, I felt a sense of peace that kept me coming back for more. As I sorted through life's curveballs and tumultuous, never-ending divorce proceedings, the Course soon became a saving grace. Conversations with Axel became a daily occurrence, and I fondly began referring to him as my "spiritual healer."

The lessons in the book often felt impossible to comprehend, and I felt silly doing them at times. For example, Lesson 1 had me repeating, "Nothing I see in this room means anything." While I didn't understand this at the time, Axel continued to encourage me to trust the process. So I continued with the lessons and would randomly open the book, looking for topics that appeared relevant at that moment.

I still struggled with references to God in the Course. As I continued to study the material, it became clear that God was referred to as Source energy and was very different from the fearful or judging God depicted in many religions. Eventually, I learned that the book's authors were both atheists but described the teachings to be coming directly from Jesus as they channeled as scribes. Hearing that Jesus was involved gave me some comfort in knowing the material came from a highly conscious place and from a character familiar to me.

Reading the words and absorbing the vibration of the concepts created a shift within me, and I could feel my vibration rise. My mind was attempting to grasp the information, connect the dots, and fill in the blanks as I worked to overlay the content with my more scientific and quantum physics books. While I wasn't performing miracles quite yet, I continued to be interested in seeing life through a different lens. It grounded me in a way nothing else had ever done.

At one point, I wondered if I was getting involved in some type of cult. But it didn't take long to see that this book had nothing to do with organized religion. The Course began bringing to light the various mental constructs I'd been indoctrinated with at a very young age and was now playing out as an adult. It started with the concept of "I" and how my self-identity was influenced by my external environment, parental programs, and the community that raised me. As a result, I'd constructed an ideation of my life that was well articulated regarding who I thought I was and what I was here to do.

The societal mental constructs of right and wrong, and good and bad began to unfold. It was clear that I'd assigned meaning to everything as a result of building these associations. This prompted me to circle back to the first lesson in the Course, which encourages us to drop judgments and the meaning we place on interactions and experiences. It became apparent that circuitous loops of gibberish take place in our minds, building limiting beliefs and repetitive thought patterns. Today's experts refer to this as the "default mode network." My interactions with the external world became more pleasant as I shifted along with my environment. Taking away the emotional charge of what I thought the world and all people, places, and things represented allowed me to understand my mind's power to create.

Another "aha" moment was realizing that we're all programmed to believe we are separate from one another. It became evident I was spending my life trying to be somebody, build my résumé through my career, and have a unique identity as a person. These attributes are fine as long as we're not attached to the character identity we create. In many ways, it felt odd to be dismantling these ideas and programs I'd learned in childhood about my existence and how the world worked. Some thought programs were helpful, while others created limiting beliefs about myself and could hinder my ability to flourish. For example, a phrase as simple as "Do you have time or money?" implied that I should do it myself to save money, and "Don't count your chickens until they're hatched" taught the exact opposite of the law of attraction rules. My mom's frequently used phrase "Money is the root of all evil" was obviously a limiting belief that had planted seeds suggesting that making a lot of money would corrupt me. I knew my parents had instilled these programs to help me succeed, but now I wondered what life would be like without them.

The Course talks about the fact that we're already healed and whole, which was a challenge to conceptualize when I was still experiencing back pain. Although I believed the goal was to re-member back to the innate innocence of our Divine birthright, I desired to know it, embody it, and live it with confidence, like Axel did. Many people gathered in groups to talk about the concepts of the Course. However, I felt this was a very personal, inward journey and wasn't interested in attending groups or joining with others aside from Axel. The learnings were individualized, and the interpretation seemed purest between Spirit and me. The more the ego-mind filter gets involved, the more we unknowingly create story lines and complicate our perception of reality. My focus was to gain clarity and answers to life's quandaries. I felt my tribe was in the books I was reading and the authors writing them.

I searched for chunks of time when I could immerse myself more into my spiritual learning. The possibility of taking a break from my job came to mind, although this wasn't something I thought was feasible. To satiate my love of learning and take a mini-break, I decided to check off another "never" on my list and take a cruise. It wasn't your typical cruise and booze vacation. It was a unique trip filled with a series of seminars featuring Hay House Publishing's most popular authors. When I saw the promotional email, it was an instant yes, which prompted me to immediately book a spot and request vacation time from work. Even though my schedule was hectic, I knew this was a unique opportunity to hear authors I loved in person. Suddenly, one of my "nevers" became a dream come true as I looked forward to being aboard a ship filled with thousands of high-vibe people.

I'd placed a request to share a room because staying in a cabin by myself seemed less exciting. The events team quickly matched me with an Australian woman named Tara, who wanted to bring her thirteen-year-old daughter. I hesitated to respond yes, as the rooms on a cruise ship are already small, but I was willing to explore the idea. We spoke on the phone and immediately hit it off: our excitement was a mutual match, and all other concerns dropped away.

In the spring of 2006, I boarded the cruise liner leaving from the port of San Diego for five days at sea. As I approached the check-in line, I quickly found Tara and her daughter, Suzi, several people ahead of me. The trip was starting out very serendipitously, bringing us within a few feet of each other amongst hundreds of others checking in. Then while boarding, a gentleman in front of me turned around and started chatting. He mentioned he'd signed up for the series focused on speaking to loved ones on the other side. I found this interesting as I didn't know there were programs other than mine taking place.

Approaching the ship's welcome table, I decided to inquire about adding on the "speaking to loved ones" series of sessions and was thrilled to find out I could join for only an extra $250. I booked it and was eager to learn more about the speakers, many of whom were unfamiliar to me. This would likely mean I'd have no free time on the ship while we were out at sea, as I'd be attending seminars for over eight hours a day. Several stops were planned as we navigated down the Mexican Riviera, but I was more interested in immersing myself in the sessions and had little interest in the shore excursions. When all the passengers were touring, I planned to take advantage of some quiet time at the pool, reading and journaling.

After my check-in, I proceeded to find my room and connect with my roommates from down under. I was thrilled that our connection on the phone over thousands of miles was reinforced in person. While we waited for the ship to depart, we spent the afternoon soaking in the San Diego sun and checking out the notorious cruise ship buffets. The passengers quickly found our language differences quite funny as they provided fun ice breakers so we could get to know one another. Before we knew it, the cruise liner's horn was blaring and we were pushing away from the shore just in time to see an amazing sunset.

I loved every minute of my all-day sessions, and I found that each speaker delivered fascinating and insightful information. To start out the day, I'd go to the gym for my workout before the sessions started. One morning, I ran late and had to go directly from the gym to the session. Upon arrival, I could see only one empty seat and quickly made my way to it, since the session had begun just moments prior. The workshop was about self-hypnosis and was being conducted by an esteemed practitioner, Brian Weiss. Having had several mind-bending hypnotherapy sessions with a therapist back home in New Jersey, this topic was of great interest to me. I'd also read several of Brian's books discussing soul mates and previous lives, and I was curious to learn more.

At the beginning of the session, he guided us into meditation to relax our minds and experience what he would be talking about regarding hypnosis. He asked us to find someone nearby, but not someone we knew. To my right sat a lovely woman in her late sixties or early seventies, and we agreed to be partners. We listened to Brian's instructions as he asked us to exchange something with our partner, suggesting that jewelry or something metal would be ideal. She gave me the gold band from her finger and placed it in the palm of my hand. Having come directly from the gym, I was still in my workout clothes and wasn't wearing jewelry or accessories. I gave her my sneaker, as it was the only item I could remove for her to hold. Luckily, it wasn't stinky!

We were asked to close our eyes and focus on our partner's item that we were holding. As Brian began, he spoke very slowly and suggested we relax into a tranquil state. Since meditation was still a challenge for me, I was surprised it didn't take long to quiet my mind from racing thoughts. Almost immediately upon closing my eyes, I could vividly see the gold band in my hand. Within seconds, my mind's eye saw it turn into a ring of fire.

As Brian continued to guide us, I saw several symbols flowing in front of me as though I was watching them on a movie screen. A beautiful waterfall appeared, then a silver rose moved closer to my face, accentuating its detail and color, followed by the Statue of Liberty. While this figure emerged, there was an emphasis on the torch as the word *freedom* showed up across my visual screen, all while my eyes were closed. All the images disappeared as I felt a presence near my hand holding the ring. I heard myself say in my mind, "What's your name?" and a male voice responded, "George." Surprised to hear myself asking this unknown energy/entity a question, I was stunned when I received an answer. I'd never talked to dead people before. Or had I? I wondered, yet again, who the five people who showed up in my living room months prior had been.

Brian asked us to share exactly what we saw with our partner, but not what we thought about it: only the images, words, or feelings that came to mind. I was a little embarrassed, as I had no idea what all these symbols meant and wondered if the woman would think I was silly. But I also had great curiosity because everything I saw was so clear! As I proceeded to reveal the details, her eyes opened wider and wider. As I described feeling a presence that prompted me to ask their name, she looked at me with intensity. When I shared that a male voice had responded, saying "George," she began to sob.

Now I was all ears, eager to hear *anything* she was willing to share. She went on to say that early in life, she had a relationship with a man who she felt was her soul mate, but for various reasons they'd been forced to part ways, and they'd married other people. Her husband was now in an assisted living facility and didn't recognize her, even though she visited him daily, as he'd had Alzheimer's for several years. A few years ago, she'd reconnected with this soul mate and they'd rekindled their deep love for one another. Then, unexpectedly, he passed suddenly from a heart attack less than a year ago. She stated the reason she was on this cruise was in the hope of connecting with him. In between tears and with a quivering chin, she said, "His name is George."

I cried. How could I not? But it didn't stop there. Every symbol and word communicated had significant meaning to her. They'd spent a lot of time at a particular waterfall, and he always gave her silver roses. She believed he was trying to tell her to reclaim her freedom and not feel guilty about not visiting her husband. He wanted to assure her of his presence next to her from the other side. Now she had the answer to the question that had brought her to the cruise.

I was astounded and found this to be a life-changing moment for me. I'd never done this before and felt honored to bring this information through for her. The energy of my sneaker didn't seem to carry as much information, as my partner didn't receive many visuals. She said she'd seen snow and a feather during the meditation, but I wasn't sure what this meant. Maybe it had something to do with my upbringing, surviving the snow. The feather brought to mind Native American headgear, but neither of us knew. I was content and found that my experience with her was the gift from the session. Now that I'd felt what it's like to channel a being on the other side, I believed and hoped this would only be the beginning.

Before the cruise, my exposure to psychic mediums was limited, and I had a healthy level of skepticism. Knowing I could tap into this realm, I had no doubt that the information the psychic mediums were channeling from loved ones who'd crossed over was legitimate. I believed we could all do this to some degree and was eager to witness more miraculous events. Heightening this gift within me would require focused intention and practice to gain more knowledge and insights, although speaking with spirit realms still made me anxious, knowing everything on the other side isn't Angelic. I still felt naive and scared of spooky things that happen in crazy movies like *Poltergeist*. Perhaps the expertise of these authors would help calm my mind and allow me to find ways to learn more about communicating and attracting paranormal experiences.

I was keen to attend the sessions with Sylvia Browne, a talented and respected psychic medium. The first half of her session delivered broad-reaching information, while the second half was allotted for individual readings. Participants would approach the microphones in the aisle and be allowed to ask her a personal question. Her goal was to provide everyone in the room with a psychic reading, which meant she had to respond quickly. Many were asking if they should leave their job, and to all of them, she said no and stated specific reasons why they should not. This was also my question, and I became timid to ask, anticipating the same response. I didn't necessarily want to quit my job; I wanted to take some time to delve deeper into my soul quickening as I craved to learn more.

Even though I was floating in the ocean on the other side of the North American continent, I was worried about confidentiality. I didn't want anyone to know I was considering leaving or taking a break from my corporate career. I was in a high-visibility position at work, so I could easily be identified without recognizing other employees. Pushing through these concerns, I nervously went up to the microphone and provided a brief background on why I was contemplating leaving. The funny thing was that I could tell she didn't care about the details of anyone's stories. Once she understood a person's question, no other information was considered, as she received an answer from her guides immediately. She was focused on listening to them instead of everyone babbling on about the particulars.

Immediately Sylvia said, in her scratchy yet stern voice, "Yes, you'll leave your job in the next three to six months. You'll find a storage unit for your items for about a year." Then she abruptly said, "Next!" I sat down in my chair, numb with disbelief. She'd told everyone else to hold on to their jobs, and I wasn't expecting her to advise me any differently. It was exactly what I wanted to hear, and yet the thought of it was a bit frightening, as she confirmed I was destined to take some time off. A year? I wondered if that was possible. I was making good money and knew the successful product launches I'd been working on would lead to new opportunities, not leaving my career. However, my accelerated soul quickening was my priority, and I decided to trust in the Universe and look for guidance along the way.

As the cruise ended, I felt full of new ideas and concepts. Some material from all the reading and journaling I'd done had been solidified, and other information provided new avenues of exploration, which I felt immensely grateful to receive. As I began packing up my things, sadness hovered at the idea of having to say goodbye to my Aussie friends, although I was confident we'd meet again somewhere in the world. Having no time to linger in San Diego, I soon found myself back at work in New Jersey.

The marketing department restructured a few months later, and I was promoted to a director-level position, managing a team responsible for creating sales materials for a portfolio of products. I was excited about this, even though I knew there were some significant challenges from the start, as the team I'd acquired consisted of a group of inexperienced people. The team was under-resourced and lacked support on many levels: financial budgets were low and we had an inadequate headcount to accomplish the tasks and milestones at hand. On top of this, the professional marketing agency we had working on the brands was not the strategic partner we needed and wasn't producing adequate results. No one seemed to be happy. This, along with my ongoing divorce drama, must have created the perfect storm of complexity for what happened next.

It was mid-morning when one of my colleagues, Sally, approached me in my office and asked if she could talk with me. I knew this person quite well, as I'd reported to her in my previous position for several years. From the look on her face and the way she shut my office door, I knew she had something serious to discuss. She sat down at my desk and said, "You know I'm a registered nurse?" as she looked directly into my eyes. I responded, "Of course, I remember," but had no idea where this was going.

She went on to say, "I've observed warning signs indicating you're suicidal." I was shocked by this comment and wondered if this was a joke; my first reaction was to laugh. She didn't crack a smile, and there was an indescribable tension between us. Then she said, "It's common for people to be in denial." I was stunned. My body went numb; I realized how serious she was and yet had no idea why she would be approaching me with this idea. I didn't think it could be any worse until she continued, saying, "I'm requesting that you seek psychiatric counseling, and I'll be following up with you on this." You could have heard a pin drop.

Now it felt like I was hearing her every word in slow motion while my mind was racing, trying to pinpoint what could have given her this impression. In that moment I had an inner dialogue going on and I was in a complete quandary. At the same time, I wondered what my reaction looked like from the outside. I suddenly became very conscious of what my face might be saying and how she might interpret it.

Finding this accusation utterly ridiculous, I gently pressed her for examples of how she had concluded I was suicidal. She mentioned an interaction we'd had while passing in the hall a few weeks prior. In this brief discussion, she'd stated to me, "We should fire the agency," referring to the one working closely with my team. I agreed but said the timing wasn't right and "I'd slit my wrists" if we let them go now. For me, losing the agency's historical memory, product knowledge, and marketplace experience when my team was so green and underperforming wasn't realistic without significant internal support and resources—which we both knew weren't available.

I understood the seriousness of this conversation but was stunned that she would think this is something I'd take my life over. Granted, my statement might have been dramatic; I was simply trying to protect my team. They were already suffering from the pressures of being over-whelmed with responsibilities. Taking away their entire support system would not have been feasible for anyone leading this team, and I was using a figure of speech to reflect the serious implications of her rec-ommendation. When asked for a second example, she didn't have any details but said, "There have been many signs."

I tried to reassure her that although a lot was going on in every aspect of my life, I was *not* suicidal. That didn't cut it. She reiterated, "It's com-mon not to admit it." If she only knew that the previous two years had been such an intense spiritual awakening and that I had great clarity, knowing my soul was eternal.

Not learning lessons in this lifetime would only mean I would reencounter them in the next, which confirmed suicide to be a futile endeavor.

Trying to escape the lessons I came here to learn on a soul level was nowhere on my radar. Why would I want to start over and repeat what I had already worked hard to learn in this lifetime?

She left my office abruptly, and all I could think was, *How am I going to get out of this situation?* I shut and locked the door, staring at the wall, waiting for the numbness to go away. I wanted to burst into tears but was worried it would be perceived as another sign. Then I wondered who might be watching me. Would she be outside my door, documenting my next move? Chances were that someone would soon be knocking on my door. How would I respond when they asked, "Why all the tears?" I couldn't possibly tell them I had been accused of being suicidal. That's not a topic you want to share with many people, if any.

I did my best to lay low until later in the afternoon when I quickly snuck out, hoping not to encounter anyone. My mind continued to race all the way home, searching for a reason why she would be saying this to me. Why was this happening? What was her motivation? Our recent restructuring had brought two new senior managers to the department who didn't know me or my work ethic from a hole in the wall. Was she trying to take me down and break me in front of these new guys? Was she insecure that they'd see more value in me than in her? None of that made sense, as she was a strong player and had supported me, or so I thought. Feeling completely violated and misunderstood, I called Axel on my way home. Keeping it simple, I asked if he could be at my apartment in time to have dinner. Luckily, he was available.

How would I walk back into the office and not be completely freaked out, wondering whom my colleague had told and who would be observing me for more "suicidal signs"? My thoughts were nowhere near peaceful as I searched for meaning and reached for solutions as to how I was going to navigate this situation. Upon my arrival at home, Axel and I sat down for dinner. I explained the situation by recapping the story and then asked only one question over and over: "What the hell is happening?" It felt like I was in a movie, but I didn't remember auditioning for this role.

Axel listened to my desperation for understanding, then looked at me with a peaceful face, laughed, and asked in a calm voice, "What archetype is she playing out?" Surprised by the question, I paused for a moment to think. In the previous months, I had been extensively studying material on archetypes. Carl Jung, the Swiss psychologist, was the first to introduce the concept formally, and modern authors like Caroline Myss had written books on this topic. I had read many of them because I wanted to understand deeper aspects of myself and others better.

Knowing the basics of archetypes, I saw them as personality traits or patterns reflecting a character description. Some of the most familiar archetypes include the Queen, Victim, Hero, Sage, Saboteur, or Prostitute, to name a few. I'd hung my archetype cards from Caroline Myss's deck next to my door to further my learning. This way, every morning when I left for work, it provided a reminder to live in the light and acknowledge how the dark impacts my interactions. But at this moment, my mind was still spinning, and I could barely think, let alone respond.

"The Caretaker," Axel said. Then we began discussing the dark and light sides of the Caretaker archetype. He explained that she was most likely coming from a place of caring. Through her lens, my life under these circumstances wouldn't be manageable, and she wanted to help. This was not what it felt like she was trying to do because this accusation was causing me more strain. However, I had a whole new perspective of the situation, and luckily my paradigm shifted.

As a result of our lengthy discussion that night at the dinner table, I saw everything clearly. Honestly, if I hadn't had these revelations and seen this situation differently, it might have taken me under. My colleague's attempt to help me was one of my biggest professional hindrances at the time, especially because I didn't need another issue on my plate. Thanks to Axel's assistance, it became an opportunity for me to practice a spiritual lesson I'd called in to learn.

Walking back into the office each day, I focused on seeing the caring behind her ways. I completely deflected the insanity I should've felt by transforming it into loving and compassionate energy toward her. This simple shift in perspective saved me from emotionally overreacting and helped me to see things from a greater spiritual perspective. It also became clear to me that she was reflecting her fears. Perhaps *she* would be feeling suicidal if she were in my shoes. Interestingly, she never mentioned the topic of suicide to me again. There was no follow-up, and no one came to admit me to a mental institution. Thank God.

I realized so clearly that we are in relationships to help us heal our wounds by acting as a mirror for others. It doesn't matter if they are friends, colleagues, or romantic lovers. The important part is recognizing that everyone is here to support each other in their growth, despite how it may feel in the moment. The truth is that hurt people hurt others. I worked on staying above the fray and not getting so deep into the storylines, as I wanted to continue to shine light and not allow others to dampen mine.

All my relationships at work started to take on a whole new meaning as I began to see people differently. Realizing that I'd called them in for a reason, I wanted to learn the lesson from each of them, and this came at the perfect time to apply all my learnings about archetypes. The archetypes I was playing out were the only things I could change. I wanted to leverage this information so I could move through any situation by mastering myself.

Sylvia's voice from the cruise continued to provide a gentle nudge that leaving my job was a real possibility. At the same time, I didn't see *how*; I still had a lot to accomplish in my life and many bills to pay. All I knew was the corporate career path. Plus, I didn't want to find myself in a situation where I couldn't leave something because I wasn't making enough money. Freedom to make choices seemed heavily tied to financial income, and I wasn't so keen to give up my love of clothes, shoes, and jewelry anytime soon.

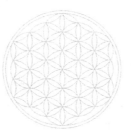

CHAPTER 7

Homelessness and Rebirth Sabbatical

T HE CHAOS HAD reached an all-time high with unsuccessful mediation sessions beginning the third year of divorce proceedings. Divorce court was imminent. I was feeling discouraged that we hadn't achieved a simple settlement and were going in the opposite direction, and the proceedings were becoming increasingly complicated as Stuart requested alimony. I was happy to sell the marital property to him, but he insisted on acquiring it far below its market value. Unexpectedly one day, he announced that he'd be moving out of the house and back to Oklahoma in defiance. This seemed odd, as I'd been paying the mortgage and many of the bills; he lived there almost free. Maybe he thought this would force me to agree to his unfair requests.

This was during the coldest winter months, and the massive historic property couldn't be left empty. This presented a challenge: I was still committed to my apartment lease for another six months, and the property was an hour's drive away. However, I didn't want to take a risk on one of the most significant assets we had and decided to work on getting out of my lease. At the same time, I asked Axel if he'd be willing to come and stay with me in the house. He was a trusted confidant who felt like a family member I could rely on as a steady stake in the ground. The reality was that I didn't have time for all the attention the house needed for maintenance on top of everything else I had going on. Thankfully, Axel agreed, and he helped with many chores while I worked late nights and traveled extensively.

The first item of business was to sell the property. However, Stuart refused to sign the listing agreement. Inspired to find solutions, I decided to create a website and market it myself. This was a massive undertaking in 2006 because there were no easy templates or platforms like there are now. I contacted every influential newspaper and magazine to target the tri-state area of New York, New Jersey, and Connecticut for potential buyers, along with historical societies that I knew would appreciate its historical features.

A significant breakthrough happened after several attempts to get newspapers and historical societies to cover the story of the home and promote its sale. A representative from the *New York Times* called me expressing interest in writing an article about the historical aspects of the property in their home section. I was beyond thrilled as I knew this would help attract a buyer who would cherish and care for this unique historic home. Weeks later, the perfect couple, curators of a famous museum in New York City, made an offer on the house. Stuart had no choice but to agree to sell the home. I was elated knowing that the house would be in good hands and that this chapter was finally complete. My heart felt at peace and grateful for this beautiful alignment.

As I cleared out the house in the final days, new challenges presented as I would soon be homeless and unsure of what I would do next. I believed a significant movement and transformation were approaching, which led me to put my belongings in storage and rent a room from a friend living close to my office. She was flexible and seemed happy to have me until I could get myself sorted. Although I was relegated to a storage unit and small bedroom, I was grateful for the optimism I still had about my life.

Several months prior, I'd seen advertisements regarding a new high-rise in development that was a block over from my Jersey City apartment. I loved living so close to New York City and decided to use my portion of the proceeds from the sale of the marital home as a down payment on a unit in this new building. However, the building wouldn't be finished for one to two years, and I still had no place of my own to call home.

Now that I was free of massive expenses, I suddenly had a deep desire to take time off from my job.

> Resetting, rejuvenating, and reviving myself was vital as I quickly recognized that no one else could do this for me.

In addition, I was keenly aware that if I didn't pay attention, the Universe might find a less desirable way to make me take some downtime. I didn't want an accident or illness to force me to pause. The question "How and when would it be a perfect time?" seemed to be imminent.

My new role continued to take a toll on me as the team was still under-resourced, and I couldn't compensate for the missing skill sets and massive gaps. The fun factor was fading, and appreciation for the team's work continued to be compromised by others in the department. I was used to working with high-performing teams, yet I couldn't obtain traction to move this one in the right direction.

While walking up the stairs at work one morning, I felt great resistance to being in the office and knew it was time to make a move. I recognized that leaving a steady income and benefits was not something that made much logical sense, as I was still in the middle of a divorce. (Yeah, I know this damn thing is getting old!) I was also in a contract to buy my condo on the edge of the Hudson River and would need significant income to obtain a mortgage. The future couldn't have been more uncertain, but it was clear that the time to make a jump was imminent. The question remained where to go. I threw this request out to the Universe, and within days, three people gave me the unsolicited advice to go to Costa Rica.

I remember so vividly sitting on my bed that Saturday morning, wanting further validation that this was the right location. I told myself that if it was reasonably priced and easy to travel there, I would just do it. Pulling up my favorite airline's website, I discovered a direct three-hour flight. How could it be so simple? I hit the purchase button and said, "Oh shit, now I have to quit my job!" There was no turning back. I don't remember calling anyone to tell them, as my focus was on what I would say to my boss on Monday.

Women hate to cry at work, but men hate women crying in their offices even more. It's so uncomfortable. When women burst into tears, I think many men's first reaction is to try and figure out if they caused the problem. Once they are relieved to know they aren't the problem, they can quickly turn to their natural state of finding a solution. And that's precisely what happened.

I walked into the department head, Karl's, office, sat down, and although I'd planned exactly what I was going to say, all I could do was cry. That sucked. Lips quivering, I couldn't speak the words. Awkward, awkward, awkward. I'd worked my entire career to be competent, and now I felt like a vulnerable mess. I wanted to walk out, shake it off, and start over. But I couldn't. I was there, and now I had to say what I came to say.

Eventually, I spit the words out. "I need to leave." With great compassion, Karl listened and then offered, "Take a month, take two or maybe even three, but don't quit." I felt a sense of relief at his support and then was a bit shocked by the words of encouragement he shared next: "Go to a Buddhist monastery or whatever you need to do; just come back." I was incredibly grateful and agreed to check in after one month to revisit my situation, even though I felt in my heart I would be gone longer.

Miraculously everything seemed to align, as I had minimal possessions, and they were already in a storage unit. I'd pared down to a very select number of things, and there was still room in storage for what wasn't going with me to Costa Rica. I loved my career, and to be honest, it was the only thing I really had in my life at the time. I was single, still trying to finalize my divorce, and was dumped by the one guy I'd admired and felt a connection to. Work was a great distraction in so many ways, and it paid the bills, which relieved a lot of stress. The idea of leaving my life and the comforts of a corporate career behind was not easy.

As I counted down the days until my departure, it was almost like I was living two different lives because I didn't tell anyone other than my boss and his boss about my leave of absence. Maybe I was in denial or worried about the questions people would ask that I didn't want to answer. Nor did I desire to share my feelings and process others' emotional responses regarding my situation. As a result, I waited until the last day to tell my direct reports, and then I walked out the door.

The heaviness of the decision to leave dissipated as I sat on a plane headed to Costa Rica. A deep knowing that I was following my heart and taking intuitive risks along with big jumps was my inspiration to journey onward. I didn't have a place to stay lined up, or even an air ticket to my final destination, but the Gemini in me was always up for an adventure. I was notorious for taking last-minute trips and finding amazing accommodations upon arrival. My plane ticket would get me to San José, and from there, I planned to decide on my destination—an approach not recommended for the fainthearted traveler. Admittedly, I was relying heavily on the *Retiring in Costa Rica* guide I'd purchased at a New Jersey bookstore, hoping for guidance on local insights instead of tourist traps. I'd identified three areas but wasn't sure which one was the right place for me. The pressure was on to decide, as I needed to have a hotel room before nightfall.

As luck would have it, I was upgraded to first class. Little did I know, this was the last luxury I would see for a long while. I was optimistic that whoever was seated next to me would have some insights regarding the ideal spot to go. As it turned out, the Frenchman seated to my right was going to visit his girlfriend and knew nothing about the country.

After landing in San José, I navigated over to the domestic terminal to look for flights leaving to the three locations on my list. Deciding to let fate choose, I planned to take the flight scheduled to depart first. Peering up at the board, I saw that a flight to Tambor, on the Nicoya Peninsula, was departing in about an hour. This was perfect, as I could go to Malpais, a small town near Santa Teresa, a location on the top of my list.

As I approached the counter, the attendants looked troubled by something, but I wasn't sure what. I asked to buy a ticket, and they informed me the aircraft was tiny and they were apprehensive about the weight of my luggage. Luckily, it came in under the plane's maximum weight limit, and I was booked to go. While waiting at the gate, I struck up a conversation with two ladies who I recognized from my flight. They seemed friendly, and I hoped they might have some insights on Malpais. They planned to meet up with a fellow New Yorker friend and said they'd be happy to give me a lift to town, which was over an hour away.

A short flight later, the six-seater plane started its descent and I realized we were not landing at a typical airport. It was simply a short, narrow concrete strip on the ocean's edge in the middle of a thick jungle. We swayed back and forth as we approached the landing strip. As I peered over the shoulders of the two pilots, I felt like I was in a movie, and I was disappointed I hadn't thought to keep my camera in hand. The beauty and the simplicity before my eyes were beyond breathtaking and it would be difficult to describe this magnificence to anyone.

There was nothing around this jungle strip except for the five passengers on the plane and a few cars. There was no taxi stand or even a building, only a beat-up asphalt parking area big enough for a few cars. As we went one by one to collect our bags, I felt incredibly grateful that these ladies would give me a ride. Seeing them connect with their friend, I started walking toward them. As they turned around, I could tell there was a problem, and my heart sank. They said they couldn't give me a ride because their friend had planned a few stops along the way. At that moment, I felt scared, vulnerable, and alone. The only other options were a few guys with vans shouting, "Taxi!" What was I to do? Out of nowhere, another woman appeared and offered to let me share her taxi, which I could then take on to Malpais. Appreciative of her kind offer, I jumped in.

It was a brief twenty-minute drive to the resort where she was staying for a friend's wedding. Before she hopped out of the vehicle, I asked her if we could exchange phone numbers in case of an emergency. No one knew where I was or was going, and neither did I. Suddenly, I realized how foolish I'd been, as this was different from dropping in to an accessible European city. Trusting that I would make it in one piece, I waved goodbye and said that I'd text her upon arrival in Malpais. Honestly, what was she going to do if I didn't?

The countryside was green and plush with palm trees all around. I loved the jungle feel even though the shocks on the van and the potholes in the road didn't facilitate a smooth ride. Along the way, we saw small collections of cows, homes, chickens, and people that appeared alongside small clusters of houses. Interestingly, the driver would wave as though he knew all the locals along the way, and a few times, we picked people up from the side of the road. Since I didn't speak the language, it wasn't clear to me if they knew each other.

The first time this happened, I was a little concerned, thinking they could be planning an abduction. Movies like *Proof of Life* and stories of kidnappings were coming to mind. After a few different people came in and out of the car from one town to another, I realized it was a friendly taxi-type opportunity. This made me appreciate that it was a friendly community and perhaps not as concerning as my interactions in the airport in the city where taxi drivers were aggressively approaching me to take my luggage, vying for me to hire them.

It was early afternoon when we arrived in Malpais. Everything was dusty and dirty and didn't look anything like the pictures in the guidebooks. My driver didn't speak English, and my Spanish was almost nonexistent. Luckily, my translation dictionary was able to help us communicate, and he quickly understood our mission was to find a clean and safe place for me to stay. We drove down the two-lane dirt road and made several stops at places he thought might work for me. Eventually, we found a small property nestled within the palm trees of the jungle that appeared clean and safe.

After checking in, the stress lifted from finding a place, and I suddenly realized I wasn't feeling that great. I'd taken my antimalarial medication earlier that morning and hadn't drunk enough water, causing severe dehydration and a tumultuous headache. It would be dark soon, so I wandered down the dirt road to find a market to purchase a few things. Not knowing how safe it was for women traveling alone to wander the streets, I was lucky to find a store only a block away. Upon my return, I collapsed onto the bed and was asleep before the sun fully set.

The following day, I woke up early to the sounds of the jungle and was eager to start the search for a one-month rental to call home. Walking the dusty dirt road, I headed toward the town, which consisted of a small collection of buildings spread along the main road. It wasn't long before I stumbled upon a real estate office, only to find they didn't do short-term rentals. I asked the gentleman if he'd allow me to use his phone to make a local call. Jessica had given me the number of her friend's sister, who lived there. He smiled and said yes, and a lovely young woman named Jenny answered the phone. She was more than happy to help me find a place and wanted to know where I was staying so she could come to pick me up. In my wonderment, I had forgotten the name of my accommodations. As I started describing it, she said, "Oh, the place near the soccer field?" That was exactly it.

Jenny picked me up the next day and took me around to some local expats who she thought might have a room or home to rent. We didn't have much luck, but at our last stop, the woman said her property was full and asked, "What about Lena?" Jenny called Lena to inquire and found her happy to meet us in thirty minutes to look at her oceanside property.

Upon arrival, we learned that she had two houses as we parked between them. One was on the oceanfront and the other was a back house next to the road. I was disappointed when Lena started walking toward the back house, saying, "This one's available." It was small, a few feet from the road, and rickety; not what I had been manifesting. We walked inside, and the dust from the road was piled high on all the furnishings.

Costa Rica hadn't had much rain, and the dust from the roads often created a choking hazard. People on motorbikes had bandanas over their mouths and, in some cases, goggles over their eyes so they could see. Being near the dust was not my cup of tea, nor was the road noise. I also wondered about the challenges regarding pest control, as many dead scorpions were lying around. My attention quickly turned to the oceanfront home, and I inquired about its availability. Lena said it was being rented by a German family and wouldn't be open for another week. Seeing my disinterest in the back house, Lena ended up making a deal to let me move into the oceanside cottage upon the family's departure. She'd clean the back house so I could move in the next day.

The following morning brought a downpour of rain and stormy skies; thunder and lightning woke me from my slumber. This eliminated the dust on the road, but now I struggled to keep any part of my luggage dry as I hauled it down from my room to the front driveway. On time, Jenny picked me up to take me to Lena's property. As we arrived at the property, Lena ran over to my window and hastily said, "Get in my car." I looked at Jenny, a little shook up by the abruptness, and wondered what was happening.

My mind swirled with questions. Why was this woman pulling me into her car and not opening the doors to the place where I was supposed to stay? Jenny didn't have much of a reaction and calmly smiled at me as I hesitantly got out of her car. Once the luggage was transferred into Lena's car, she explained that she thought the back house was too dusty, too noisy, and not good enough for me to stay in. She went on to say that she had a dentist appointment in San José and would be gone over the next few days. If I was willing to take care of her two dogs, she thought it would be best for me to stay in the guest room of her home until the oceanside cottage was ready. Going with the flow and feeling grateful, I agreed.

As we pulled up to her property, I was happy to see that she had a proper home, which created the feeling of an Airbnb. The fact that this wonderful woman in her sixties was taking me in felt like a dream come true after all the uncertainty and vulnerability my lack of planning had caused. I realized that traveling as a single woman had some downsides in countries where most people didn't speak English and the ease of first-world systems was relatively nonexistent.

Lena and I quickly burst into conversation, delighted to become acquainted with one another. She shared stories about her Swedish heritage and moving from Oregon to Costa Rica after her husband passed away. From there, it was one story after another as we shared about our life's experiences and bonded as though we were long-lost Scandinavian relatives.

While I unpacked my library of books that I hoped to read during the month, Lena looked on. Since she seemed interested, I'd show her the covers, and with each one, she smiled and said, "I know that book" or "I know that author." She seemed especially fond of my Osho books, as I think he was a trendy guru in her tribe. When I showed her *Physics of the Soul* by Amit Goswami, she asked if she could take a closer look. Knowing this spiritual journey all too well, she could see I was at full throttle with mine.

As evening approached, Lena invited me out on her porch for her nightly sunset-gazing. She crawled into her hammock and motioned for me to sit in the rocking chair next to her. Then she announced she'd be partaking in her nightly herbs. "Herbs?" I wondered naively. I didn't know what she was talking about until I saw she was about to smoke a joint.

I've always been against drugs, and now I'm staying with a woman who smokes pot? I had tried it with a roommate many years prior in the privacy and safety of our home. However, this encounter didn't go well for me, as I felt super paranoid with only one puff. This solidified my strong aversion to drugs. I had a strict rule about not being a part of any situation involving mind-altering substances other than alcohol. If they showed up, I would immediately leave. *What should I do now?* I couldn't leave. I decided to break my rule and let it be. It was her house, her routine, and her rules. While I didn't partake in any aspect of her herb smoking, I quickly got over my judgment and felt okay being in her presence. She enjoyed this activity each night, and all I needed to do was position myself in a spot where the smoke would go in the other direction.

Before my trip, I'd read Ram Dass's book and was intrigued by the insights he'd harvested from his LSD trips. In my discussions with Axel, he'd also spoken about expanded states of consciousness with LSD in the seventies. While I admired both gentlemen's insights, my strong stance against psychedelics wasn't going to change. I couldn't figure out how anyone would want to lose control of their mind!

Seeing my Ram Dass book prompted Lena to share her experiences and stories of how she and her husband journeyed on LSD trips together. Trying not to appear shocked, I listened intently as she spoke fondly of how it changed their lives. Our conversations were fascinating, and she opened my mind to ideas and insights that shifted me to not make quick judgments about people's choices. My certainty that I'd *never* try them momentarily flip-flopped as she spoke about shifts in consciousness that I was desiring to experience and embody. I thought to myself, *If I have the right guide, a shaman, or someone whom I trust, maybe I would consider...* That was a bold thought coming from my anti-drug mentality, but I was not interested in welcoming an opportunity.

Lena was gone and back from the dentist in what felt like the blink of an eye, and it was time to move into the oceanfront property. The cottage on the ocean's edge was exactly what I had been manifesting while in my room back in New Jersey. I was blown away by the level of detail in this incredible spot that matched what I'd visualized back home. Now it was right in front of me, with palm trees surrounding the home and a little isolated alcove where ocean waves were crashing about two hundred steps away on the beach. It was far from glamorous and more like five-star camping, as the house was rickety and had hinged windows made of wood that required a rope to secure them open.

Lena continued to remind me to close and lock all windows and doors. Crime was an issue, and she warned that even if I was upstairs, any open window below would put me at risk of inviting in any robbers who were watching the house. I appreciated the warning, but this didn't make me feel at ease living by myself. Many stories of break-ins were being shared around town, making me nervous and uncomfortable. I soon found out it wasn't only robbers who wanted to steal my stuff; so did the animals. One day a bird perched on my kitchen windowsill and swiftly grabbed an entire loaf of bread, hauling it out for a tasty meal as I looked on from my rocking chair in awe of how quickly he did it.

Since I didn't have a car or motorbike, getting to any amenities required a thirty-minute walk to town. Luckily, Lena would often pop by on her way in to ask if I wanted a ride or if I needed anything. She frequently picked up people she saw walking by the side of the road and offered them a lift to town, like the taxi guy who drove me from the landing strip. One day we picked up a gentleman who looked a little rough for my liking. When she dropped him off, I saw her slip him money. This had me curious, and so I asked who he was. She exclaimed, "The town thief!" Wow, it seemed crazy that she was giving him a ride and paying *him* money. I learned that day the meaning of "keep your enemies close." She said it's important to be kind, and voluntarily giving him money kept her off his list so he wouldn't rob her.

I was enthusiastic about my drastic change in lifestyle, as it seemed I needed to remove myself from my corporate life altogether.

> Interestingly, Costa Rica was offering me the time I needed to disconnect, deconstruct, and design my future—or at least scratch the surface of going deeper and getting in touch with my soul on a whole new level.

Each morning I woke around 5:00 a.m. to the sounds of Mother Nature, the animals, waves crashing on the beach, and to sunlight popping through the cracks in the boards of my house. I had to admit, it felt bizarre to go through the day and not have any emails to check, phone calls to take, or questions to answer from people waiting at my office door. I didn't even have Wi-Fi to surf the internet unless I went into town. My identity had been wrapped up in who I was at work. Now the question was, "Who am I without a job?" I wasn't sure but was certainly willing to find out.

I wondered what my response would be when people asked me what I did. Surprisingly, people didn't care, and during my entire time in Costa Rica, no one ever inquired about what I did for a living. Everyone was in the present moment, sporting a tropical beach bum look; mainly wearing shorts, T-shirts, and swimsuits all day and into the night. There wasn't one day when I said to myself, "I miss my high heels, business suits, and jewels."

During my time in Costa Rica, I took self-development seriously and often forgot to have fun. I loved my time rocking on the front porch in my squeaky wooden chair, watching the animals, journaling, or reading. If I went out, I'd return before dark and be off to bed around sunset. This was a drastic difference from my life in America, where I'd be lucky if I was home from work before dark. I was also eager to shut my doors and windows before dark. Otherwise, the bats would fly in, circle my bed, and swoop down around my head. Lena tried to teach me her system, using the broom to swat them away, but it didn't work so well for me. They knew I was scared and would dive toward me, which I despised. I cringed in fear at the thought of them attacking my hair as I'd seen in movies.

In the morning, the sounds of Mother Nature's orchestra complemented the extraordinary sunrise views. I enjoyed being in tune with nature and following the cycle of the sun rising and setting at the same time every night. But I couldn't deny that the nights often felt cold and lonely.

One evening while Lena and I were eating together at a small local restaurant, she bumped into a nearby neighbor. She introduced us, and we made small talk. He seemed like a lovely gentleman, and his beautiful blue eyes were captivating. He was an American named Tom. He had been living on the peninsula for quite some time and was working for a small electrical company in town.

After we left the restaurant, she inquired with a big smile on her face, "Any interest in him?" I smiled back and said no, thinking he wasn't my type. I liked to date CEOs, not the town electrician. As I laid my head on my pillow alone that night, I thought, *Wait, why not? He'd make a great friend.* I didn't know many people and was eager to have another local show me the ropes; it didn't have to be romantic. It didn't take long for him to become one of my trusted companions for most of my time in Costa Rica. We spent a lot of time together swimming in the crystal blue ocean, watching sunsets, drinking vodka and cranberry juice, eating together, and having conversations about love and life. Needless to say, we got along well and enjoyed each other's company.

I was in my third week away when it became clear that I wouldn't be ready to immerse myself back into corporate life. My flight back to the US was imminent, but the inner work I had done was barely the tip of the iceberg. Torn about making a life-changing decision, I vacillated about the three months' leave of absence my workplace had offered. Waiting was the most logical choice, but it didn't seem fair to my team; they deserved a leader to help buffer the intense workloads. Believing and trusting my heart to make this jump seemed necessary, and delaying it felt misaligned with my integrity. Waiting would have only benefited me, not my team, and I was confident there was still so much to explore on my inward journey.

While at the internet café in town, I reached out to my dear friend Katarina, who'd moved to Germany only a few months prior on an expat assignment. I talked through my situation with her and mentioned the possibility of coming to Europe. She was quick to invite me to stay with her in Germany if I decided not to go back to work. Something about this felt right, and within days, I'd purchased a ticket to depart a week after I returned to New Jersey.

Writing my letter of resignation was a tough endeavor. Deep inside, I had great clarity that my soul journey was my priority, but I was nervous about cutting myself off from the securities of my corporate life. I went through many drafts before deciding to delete much of the content. I kept it simple by thanking them for their support, let them know I wasn't ready to come back, and stated my preference to resign from my position.

It was my final week in Costa Rica, and the rainy season was coming on stronger and stronger each day. The roads were muddy, and the locals started talking about the possibility of road closures. I hoped the main road leading to the airport wouldn't wash out before I caught my flight. My friend Tom graciously offered to drive me to the international airport in San José, which was a three-hour trip each way. This would be wonderful, as I wouldn't have to take the tiny aircraft from the landing strip at Tambor, where flights were unpredictable.

Anxious about the weather, we decided to go early and spend a few days at Arenal Volcano before my departure. I was sad to be leaving Lena, yet I anxiously anticipated arriving back in the US. It was an awkward ending saying goodbye to Tom at the airport after all the time we'd spent together and the life stories we'd shared. We hugged and smiled, and I felt grateful and sad, knowing we would most likely never see each other again. The ease and safety of the US were pulling me forward, along with the knowledge that it would be only days before I'd be back up in the sky, headed to Europe.

As I walked into the international arrivals area in Newark Airport, I felt a rush of excitement seeing the US flag on the wall. I was surprised; I'd never felt so patriotic upon reentering the US, but I was happy to be back to some of the comforts I'd taken for granted. I wanted to see people and share my experiences, but I was only able to have a quick dinner with a few friends because time was limited to repack my bags from my storage unit and prepare for colder weather.

Management had emailed me back, accepting my resignation and wishing me well, which encouraged me to move on. My attorney thought I was crazy not to take the two extra months of paid leave, but I didn't want to lead them on or take advantage of the situation.

What a drastic change it was arriving in Berlin and settling into Katarina's neighborhood in Prenzlauer Berg. Everything was clean, neat, and tidy. No bugs, no bats, and no dusty roads. My most significant risk seemed to be getting hit by a bicycle on the sidewalks. Each day, numerous adventures and errands allowed me to explore the surrounding community while Katarina was at work. I enjoyed finding fun restaurants and logistical places, like dry cleaners and groceries, to help Katarina get familiar with her neighborhood.

Interestingly, Berlin was the hometown headquarters of the pharmaceutical company I'd worked for before resigning. I'd never made a work trip there, and now as a tourist, I'd be able to visit the head office and see many of my German colleagues. Everyone was asking, "What are you doing now?" That was difficult for me to answer. I'd deconstructed my identity in Costa Rica and had been designing my life and dreams for what was to come, but there was no clear-cut answer I could share.

> I had no idea what would unfold, and not having a life plan pushed me way out of my comfort zone.

Perhaps becoming more content with the unknowns could be exciting along with the deeper lessons this may bring.

It was clear that this time in my life was all about practicing the freedom and flow I'd grown to love, which didn't require a plan. While in Germany, I decided to get a third tattoo, of the kanji symbol representing love, inked over my heart by a local German artist. Tattoos had been on my "never" list until I was inspired several months earlier by Masaru Emoto's description of the energetic effects of positive words and symbols on water crystals. Realizing that the body was over 60 percent water, I was inspired to have high-vibrational symbols on each chakra. The first tattoo was my initials, and the second was the symbol of the Tao, which means "the waterway," evoking the flow of life.

Germany provided a remarkable opportunity to ground myself and spend some time with my dear friend before heading out on my next adventure. The next stop was England, where I'd stay with my friend Ella's parents in Newcastle for several days. After this, Ella's mom had offered to take me to a Buddhist monastery in the English countryside to attend a silent retreat. I guess the head of the department at work was right; he must have known what I needed, as I wasn't considering this idea at that time. Ella's parents toured me through the rural areas that linked small, quaint towns where sheep roamed among the rolling hills. There were many wonderful little pubs and restaurants along the way. We had fun popping into a few places where we shared great conversation and good food.

Soon after arriving at the monastery, I realized silence was not my specialty. While I'm naturally an early bird, getting up at 4:00 a.m. to chant without any hot beverage to start the day took some dedication. It felt strange not being allowed to introduce ourselves verbally to one another. This provided interesting moments sitting at meals, looking at each other and not talking. All communication took place through our eyes, body language, and the movements we made. This facilitated a new way of communicating by being fully present with others. Every moment felt very intentional, and although it was quiet, I still struggled with quieting my mind. Keen to take my meditation skills to another level, I persevered. Realizing that silence was golden, I worked to achieve more stillness each day.

I reflected on the time when I'd first met Axel; he was always in the flow. He often didn't know where he would be living, how he would receive money, or whom he'd be with. I remembered thinking, *Please, dear Lord, do not make me a vagabond or make me wear Birkenstocks and look like a hippie.* Ironically, I was now doing a slightly sophisticated version of this as I flowed on my spiritual path. However, I was far from giving up my comfortable lifestyle and amenities. For now, I was finding my way even though I had no income, attorney bills still coming in, and more unknowns facing me than ever before. I was grateful to have savings that allowed me to explore my soul's journey in a way that felt compatible with my desires, although "frugal" often felt like my middle name.

It was around this time that the deeper meaning to the phrase "jump and the net will appear" sank in and I understood what trusting in the Universe felt like. I cherished the small things in life, like a warm bed, healthy food, and good friends. Most importantly, an abundance of love seemed to be surrounding me at every turn. I wasn't comfortable with the idea of spending my savings, but I knew living in Spirit was learning how to trust that my every need would be met.

Axel was staying with some friends in Barcelona, so I stopped in to visit him before heading to the East Coast of America. I planned to change out the contents of my suitcase again, a routine I never thought would become comforting, especially since I had to do it in the hallway outside my rented storage unit. I switched out clothes for warmer weather, as my mom needed to have knee surgery and had asked if I would come and help her recover in Arizona. I proposed attending a Wayne Dyer conference in Maui together the week before her surgery and she happily agreed. I had been an admirer of Wayne's teachings and his life's work for years, and it was an excellent way for us to spend time together.

Robert owned a home on Maui, and even though we hadn't been in touch, I decided to ask if we could stay there as a friendly favor. I'm not sure why I felt this bold request was appropriate, other than the fact that he was always generous and happy to help. Communicating via email, he said yes, and everything fell into place as the details of the trip magically aligned.

As we arrived at Robert's vacation home, I felt grateful that we'd maintained a friendship. The oceanfront master suite was the obvious place to stay: it had wide-open ocean views. But I couldn't convince myself to sleep in this room and recommended to my mom that we stay in the back guest room. It was kind of silly to miss out on the gorgeous views, but it seemed inappropriate, as the closet contained a few personal items, including his partner's shoes. I guess it was still hard to fully acknowledge that he was with someone else. Despite this, I had a sense of peace knowing he was happy with his partner and child.

My mom and I had an incredible time at the conference. Wayne's optimism and teachings set us up for the perfect mentality to work through the grueling knee surgery she'd be facing ahead upon our arrival back in Arizona. During the seminar, Wayne invited us to join him for a Bikram yoga class. We were interested in attending because neither of us had experienced this style before. I worried about how my mother was making it through, as the intensity was high and required serious mental stamina. As we stepped outside, a rush of energy flowed through us in a way neither of us had ever experienced before. Amazingly we both felt we'd received a cleansing renewal, although we'd barely survived the high heat and twisty turns of the yoga moves. It felt torturous while inside and yet we were so refreshed afterward that we went back the next day!

Returning to Arizona, my mother went under the knife, and we worked through the recovery together. It was late in November, and I'd planned to stay in Arizona through the holidays as my dad would soon arrive from the prairies to start his snowbird season with my mom.

While partaking in Christmas festivities, I received a call from Sally, my colleague who had accused me of being suicidal. She was recruiting me back for a position at the pharma company I'd resigned from. Even though we'd remained friendly over time, I was surprised to hear from her. She'd been promoted to vice president and offered me a job in her department to lead a brand team that had high visibility and importance within the organization. While I was flattered that she felt confident in me for the job, I expressed my gratitude and said I had to decline. It was a promotion for me, but I was still on my soul journey. I didn't know when it would end, but I knew the time was not now and continued to trust in a much bigger plan than I could comprehend. Enjoying the holidays with friends and family was a perfect way to close out the year. Numerous alignments were happening, and my heart was full of gratitude.

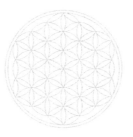

CHAPTER 8

The Journey
Down Under

I DON'T RECALL SETTING any New Year's resolutions for 2009; I was living my dreams and it felt like there was no stopping me. I'd been in touch with my friend Tara from the cruise and had explored making a trip down under to fulfill my promise to visit her and her daughter in Australia. I'd also had a deep desire to experience Bali. Now seemed like the perfect overlay to visit both since they were geographically near one another.

A few days before my departure from LAX, I received another call from Sally, recruiting me back for a different role in the marketing department. This time she wanted to discuss a position leading a new product launch. Building new brands and launching them was exciting and challenging. But I wasn't sure about going back for this opportunity.

When I learned that the role would involve participating on the global brand team as the US representative, my interest was piqued. I was tempted but also confident that my inner journey was still in progress. I told her I wasn't planning to be back in the US until at least April. She said, "Think about it; we have time."

Upon my arrival in Sydney, I found my way to our hotel in the heart of the city to meet Tara and her daughter for a long weekend. Reconnecting was so much fun as we walked, talked, and shopped our way around town. The opera house was grand, breathtaking, and wonderful to finally experience in person after I'd seen so many photos and postcards over the years.

Unexpectedly, I received another phone call regarding the job offer. She informed me the timeline had shortened and they would need to know quickly if I was interested in the position. Suddenly, "take your time" turned into "hurry up and decide." Tara and I talked for hours about whether the timing was right to make this commitment. She was familiar with being in the flow of life but was still grounded in the value of a corporate career, as she was a professional résumé writer, specializing in job placements for candidates. After hours of discussion, I felt clear that going back to corporate life wasn't my path at this point. Anticipating that it might take some time to write a thoughtful email to decline the offer, I decided to wait until Monday and not further interrupt our time together.

On our last day, we were strolling along in the area near the Rocks. As we explored, we found a lovely cobblestone street filled with small air-conditioned shops and street vendors. Tara and I were both drawn to a shop that seemed to call us in energetically. It was filled with unique, eclectic items such as crystals, new age books, cards, and music that made the store feel magical.

Tara was intrigued by a sign promoting tarot card readings. I had no interest in tapping into the unknown energies of these cards or whatever might be lurking out there in the other worlds. Yes, I'd had some paranormal experiences with the spirit realm, but they felt like Angelic encounters. Tarot cards made me think of Ouija boards, and I was uncomfortable with the idea that they might taunt darker spirits. I used angel cards almost daily, but they provided positive guidance and light-filled inspiration.

I realized Tara was serious about booking a reading when I overheard her ask the store clerk about available slots. There were a few openings, and she turned to me, asking, "Are you okay to wait thirty minutes?" followed by, "Or maybe you should get one too?" In that moment, my hesitation stepped aside, and I thought, *thirty minutes wasn't necessary, but fifteen minutes couldn't hurt.* I heard myself say, "Okay, only fifteen minutes," and felt a newfound curiosity about what might happen. I didn't have any questions, as I'd solved the job dilemma by talking to Tara ad nauseam before making my final decision. Since there were many unknowns in the coming months of travel, I was intrigued about what magic might unfold and was open to receiving insights.

Walking up the creaky, narrow steps to the first landing, the strong scent of incense came wafting out of rooms filled with crystals, hanging ornaments, and feathers. I remember thinking, *What the hell am I doing?* After climbing the second flight of stairs, I approached the tarot room and saw a tall, masculine, pleasant-looking man sitting at a desk waiting for me. He had a friendly smile, disheveled hair, and one partially missing finger. It was all a bit questionable, but I was intrigued. I knew one thing for sure: I was not going to share any personal information. I'd do my very best to hold a poker face so I didn't give him any clues. I wanted to be open to whatever he was going to tell me but didn't want to lead him on or give him any information. My skepticism was at an all-time high.

He began by telling me he was an architect by day and a part-time card reader on the weekends. Somehow this made me feel better, as I'd been enrolled in the department of engineering and architecture for the first two years at university before switching my major. This loosened me up, but I still wasn't going to share. He proceeded to tell me he would need my name and my birthdate. I thought this was harmless enough, so I provided it. Instantly he started telling me attributes about myself and specific personality traits. Everything was true. How did he know I was stubborn, goal-driven, and impatient? I wondered if he said this to everyone and watched for a person's reaction to cue him on. But the level of detail and specifics he gave described me perfectly. He said everything matter-of-factly and didn't seem to care about my response or reaction, which sparked my curiosity more. Don't get me wrong; I still had my radar on for bullshit. I didn't want to be gullible to whatever he was going to throw my way solely because he got a few things right in the beginning. I wondered if my appearance gave it away and he was fortuitously reading my body language. But the reality was that I was dressed very differently from my usual attire; he had to be seeing something more than what meets the eye.

He shuffled the card deck and pulled three cards, laying them down between us. When he turned the first card over, he said, "You have a job offer on the table." I was shocked and thought, *Keep your poker face, and don't react.* I remained motionless while he provided more details. The second card was flipped over, and he said, as if surprised himself, "You should take it!" Again, I unassumingly listened with open ears while trying to prevent my eyes from widening. It was undeniable at this moment that he was tapping into something particular to me. Nothing of what he said was general information. Now he was looking at me with curiosity, anxiously awaiting a response and curious to hear if any of what he said made sense to me. Again, I said nothing, smiled, and waited for the third card. Once it flipped, he mentioned seeing a new home and wondered if I was buying a property.

Everything he was saying made perfect sense to me, and I could feel the energy in my body saying yes to the job offer I'd received, which felt so out of left field. Of course, the irony was that this was the opposite of the decision I'd made while talking it out in the days prior. Suddenly I was keen to share. I blurted out what was happening in my life while the fifteen-minute session was ticking down. I wanted clarity on his insights; they were too profound to ignore.

He found my sharing helpful because it filled in a few blanks, allowing him to connect the dots in what he was seeing while channeling information through the cards. I told him about the job, the condo I'd signed a contract on, and whatever else I could fit into those few minutes. So much for my poker face and not sharing any personal details. Without hesitation, he responded to each situation at hand with specific guidance.

The buzzer rang from the front desk downstairs, telling him my session was complete. It suddenly felt like a race against time to obtain clarity on a major life decision. I could see the compassion in his face and the desire to help me when he said, "Don't worry about the buzzer; I'm here to help you work this out." We stayed overtime, and then, out of respect for his time, I thanked him and closed our conversation in disarray as I collected my things. He offered his number and said he'd be open to helping me, if needed. I told him I couldn't call out internationally from my phone. He said, "If you give me your number, I'll call you, no worries." I jotted it down for him and proceeded to walk down the creaky stairs in dismay, confusion, and excitement.

Hustling back to the hotel to checkout, Tara and I talked nonstop, sharing what came through for each of us. There was an urgency within me to quickly work this out in my mind. I sat in the hotel lobby to ground myself as we waited for our car service to the airport. While I was still spinning from the reading, my phone rang, and it was the card reader. He expressed concern; he wanted to make sure I was okay and asked if he could assist me further. He felt responsible for shaking up my whole plan and wanted to make sure I could process it all. Agreeing that it was a lot for me to take in, I reassured him I'd be fine. Simply knowing he was available for any additional questions made me feel supported. I thanked him again, and we were off to the airport. Tara and her daughter were headed back home to the Sunshine Coast, and I would be flying to Bali.

As I sat in my seat, my mind kicked in, creating chaos, and nothing felt clear. I wanted to get my head around this, so I started writing a pros and cons list. I figured this would get me out of the emotion and into the logic about what to do. I scribbled away in my little black Moleskine journal, listing all the pros of going back to corporate life. There were so many positive reasons pouring onto the page that my excitement grew.

Then I listed all the cons. I could only come up with four. Amazingly, the card reader had addressed every single one of them, making them nonissues. Boom! My clarity was back as I shifted to a new level of confidence and was clear that I wanted to go back into corporate life. During the second half of the flight, I drafted an email to Sally communicating that I'd be thrilled to accept the position. I added the stipulation that I wouldn't be back until April, which was only a few months away. I hoped they could wait that long and looked forward to her response.

Miraculously, in one afternoon I went from being completely skeptical of tarot cards to seeing them change the trajectory of my life. I look back fondly on this time, as having that reading seemed to have been Divinely guided. If I hadn't been inspired to have the session, my life would have unfolded in a completely different way. To this day, I love pulling and reading cards for myself and seeing psychic mediums. Sally responded via email, excited that I wanted to come back to lead this new team. She said that April was fine and that she'd be back in touch shortly with the contract and details regarding salary.

I was scheduled to arrive in Bali late in the evening. To avoid unnecessary stress, I had booked a few nights in a hotel in Seminyak. Because this was a popular tourist area, I believed most people would speak English, making it easy for me to navigate upon arrival. I certainly didn't want to find myself in a vulnerable situation like I'd experienced in Costa Rica.

As I deplaned and walked through the jetway, the warmth and humidity seeped through the cracks. Balinese music played in the terminal, and the air smelled of incense with a hint of mildew. It was the first time I'd stepped foot in Asia, and I felt very far from home. Once I had my visitor's visa in hand, getting through customs and picking up my luggage was easy. However, figuring out transportation was a bit more perplexing. After I provided the taxi service with the hotel's name, they pushed back a slip of paper, and a few moments later, a driver arrived on foot. As I blindly followed the taxi driver through a dark parking lot full of minivans, my mind ran wild wondering about my safety. He seemed friendly enough, but I was happy to arrive safely at my hotel in less than twenty minutes.

The next day, the animals woke me up before the sun. As the light shined in, the details of the traditional Balinese-style hotel began to be revealed. Arriving in the breakfast area, I found a fantastic display of fruits, Balinese banana pancakes, and eggs in all forms. Excited to see the beach, I inquired about directions at the front desk. This led to a complicated conversation, partly because of her Balinese accent but mainly because she was rattling off street names like Jalan Kerobokan, which were impossible for me to pronounce or remember. It seemed best to approach finding the beach as an adventure.

I made a few twists and turns before I caught the road that led directly to the beach. It was only 7:00 a.m., which provided a quiet and serene stroll past many hotels and properties. A beautiful hotel caught my eye, and I was enchanted to explore it as I entered through their beach access pathway. I thought this was worth checking out, as it seemed like the perfect place to have a glass of wine at sunset. Near the swimming pool, an employee was stocking a hotel bar in anticipation of a busy day. Out of curiosity, I inquired about the room rate. The Balinese staff smiled and encouraged me to sit while calling someone to assist.

A few minutes later, a well-dressed gentleman emerged and introduced himself as the general manager. He sat at the bar with me, and after only a brief hello, he said, "May I offer you a coffee? Latte? Or tea?" I was keen to have a coffee, but I had intentionally left my wallet back at the hotel. I had no idea if there was a risk of being robbed. Admitting I hadn't brought any money, he reassured me he was offering me the coffee with no intention for me to have to pay for it. It was a glimpse into the generosity of the culture that I would soon grow to love.

Jumping into a conversation, I asked him about the room rates because I wanted a backup if I needed to stay a few more nights in a hotel. He immediately offered me a great deal on an extended-stay rate. However, my goal was to live like a local expat and integrate myself into a community. I didn't want to be a tourist; I wanted an immersion. I thanked him, telling him that it was more than what I wanted to pay and I preferred a private residence. Since I was living off my savings, I also wanted to conserve cash. Admittedly I was also thinking about how much David Yurman jewelry I could buy in place of the monthly rates he'd quoted! A few moments later, it sunk in, and he said, "Oh, you want a villa?"

Without hesitation, he called his wife and said, "I have a lovely American woman here. Do we know anyone who has a villa to rent for a month?" He said he'd get back to me, as his wife was "connected," and he was confident she could come up with something. But in the meantime, he suggested I head down a little further to his friend's four-star hotel, suggesting that he might know of options for private villas on his hotel property. I thanked him and said I'd be back for a glass of wine at sunset.

I continued my exploration down the beach and found his friend also eager to help. Although the property was primarily a large grouping of standard hotel rooms, he offered one of the private villas they had for rent across the street. Out of curiosity, I decided to have a look. It was gorgeous, and as we walked in, he introduced me to the private butler who would be servicing the villa. I hadn't even thought of this as a possibility. A private butler? That seemed terrific, and of course, the price reflected this extra attention and service. I hadn't set a budget, but I could feel that this was not what I wanted to splurge on and thanked him for his time.

Even though I was declining to stay at his property, he was still eager to help me find the perfect place. He said, "Let me call Samantha; she has some beautiful new villas with private pools."

Samantha and I immediately hit it off. We had lunch together, and then her driver took us to her stunning villas. They were incredible inside, but unfortunately had no views. They were surrounded by tall, gray brick walls and were nowhere near the beach. Explaining my desire to be connected to nature and preferably rent a private residence, she nodded with enthusiasm, saying, "I have an idea." She knew of a jeweler planning to be out of the country for the month and offered to reach out to his business manager to inquire if the house might be available to rent.

By now, it was midafternoon, and the shops were open, which inspired me to take another walk to explore the main street storefronts.

It was a good thing I'd worn my most comfortable flip-flops, as the side-walks were barely meant for walking. They consisted of large, cracked concrete slabs that were occasionally missing, exposing the murky drain water below. Falling into the sewer was not an experience I sought. I quickly realized walking wasn't the preferred way to get around; motor-bikes and taxis were bombarding me, their drivers yelling out "Taxi?" It was a bit unnerving; I wanted to watch where I was walking and see the shops and restaurants, but all I could do was tell people no and shake my head.

The sun would set around 6:00 p.m., and happy hour was fast approaching. Having a glass of wine while looking out at the ocean from the hotel bar where I'd had morning coffee seemed like a great way to end this spectacular day. This time my camera was in hand as I journeyed through the property. I became entranced by the beauty of the lotus flowers in the ponds along the path. I arrived just in time for sunset, as the waves broke along the beautiful sandy beach. I paused in appreciation, excited for all that this adventure would entail.

The sun rose around 5:00 a.m., and the Balinese people were already bustling around amongst the orchestra of animals. I loved this and found the smiling faces of the locals to be refreshing; we seemed to share the excitement and anticipation a new day brings. They were lovely people who had a genuine desire for visitors to have a miraculous experience on their island, and this allowed my fears of traveling alone to dissipate quickly. Samantha called me back, excited: the jeweler's villa was avail-able. She offered to pick me up and take me there whenever I was ready.

> I recognized that feeling of being in the flow which allowed the magic to happen instead of making it happen, which I'd been so programmed to do growing up in the Western world.

We turned off a busy street and onto a long, narrow driveway as we approached the villa. Tucked behind several buildings, I saw a sign for Villa Narnia. The staff eagerly greeted me with excitement, ready to show me the property. The intricately hand-carved wooden doors provided a grand entrance. The details of the villa displayed a magical mix of Balinese design and unique Westernized flairs of elegance. The estate seemed endless, as buildings sprawled on both sides of the pool, and another guest house sat near the river's edge. Who could know this unique property existed beyond the hustle and bustle of a busy road?

This villa was perfect! The only misalignment was that it had six bedrooms, and I only needed one. As luck would have it, the owner would soon be leaving for London and wouldn't be back until a day or two after my scheduled departure date. We worked out a great deal since it was all last minute and no one was booked to be there. The villa included a few luxuries, including a private butler and a cleaning lady. Anticipating all the enchantment to come, I couldn't wait to move in a few days later.

Since I had a few days without a booking, I decided to go to Lovina, on the northern tip of Bali. I'd heard it was known for dolphin watching, which piqued my interest, as I've always been fascinated with these intuitive mammals of the sea. Locals described Lovina as a relaxed, uncommercialized area of Bali with black sand beaches to explore.

Although my upcoming job back in the US seemed like a slam dunk, a new twist presented itself while I was in Lovina. I had only a verbal agreement with the hiring manager that we were moving forward, and I'd received a call that the department head, Karl, had requested to speak to me before they could move forward with the offer. This would be an important call requiring a good internet connection. This was a challenge; the connection on the north shore of Bali was incredibly spotty back in 2009. There was an internet café with limited hours, and my Skype call was set for 4:00 a.m. to accommodate business hours for the East Coast of America. Hotels didn't have Wi-Fi, the internet café wouldn't be open that early, and the routers weren't even left on at night. The day before, I explained the situation to the internet café staff and begged them to leave their Wi-Fi on during the night. It was a pay-per-minute program, so I could use my prepaid credit.

The moon and sun were transitioning as I sat outside on a stone picnic table. I prayed the Wi-Fi had been left on overnight as I opened my computer. I was relieved to see a connection appear, albeit a very low signal coming through the wall. Although it was early, the background sounds included the Balinese sweeping with their brooms, motorbikes buzzing, birds chirping, and roosters hollering at the top of their lungs. I hoped this wouldn't impact the serious conversation I was about to have with corporate headquarters in New Jersey.

I hadn't spoken to Karl since the day I'd left the company, and hearing his voice felt a bit surreal. Almost seven months earlier I'd been crying in his office. Now I was at a remote location with animals in the background, trying to participate in a job interview. His first question was "Why do you want to come back?" He followed this up by expressing concern that he didn't want me gallivanting off to go back on the road, as this position leading the product launch team was essential to the portfolio. To gain reassurance, he asked me to make a verbal commitment that I'd stay for at least two years. I felt good about this, and with clarity that had come from my time in Sydney, I confidently said yes.

A few days later, I was back in Seminyak, ready to move into Villa Narnia for the month. The first morning, the butler, Gede, made me his banana pancakes, which were delicious. They tasted similar to French crepes but were fluffier. They reminded me of the Norwegian-style pancakes my grandmother used to make. The fresh papaya juice and melon made it even more delightful. It was fun to watch Gede giggle with pride when I'd rave about his breakfasts. Although there was a proper dining room, he set up the table next to the swimming pool each morning. The glistening sun would sparkle off the water as I sat in my swimsuit eating breakfast.

The grounds were serene and, for the most part, provided a zen feel—with the exception of the geckos, which took some getting used to. They were disturbing when they'd call out with what sounded like them shouting, "F—k you!" The rooms were not sealed, allowing many animal noises to slip through the cracks. The roosters were crowing, the ducks quacking and splashing, and the bugs were buzzing and humming their way through the gardens.

The villa contained a small jungle of green, blessed by ponds and planters of flowers everywhere. I often spent my days photographing the flowers on the property and reveling in all the incredible photos I'd taken in Australia. While I was visiting the botanical gardens, the energy that Mother Nature emitted was spellbinding, as it displayed unique flowers I'd never seen before. Now, in Bali, the lotus flowers captivated me; it was hard to ignore how they effortlessly blossomed from the depths of the mud. They simply follow the guidance of the sun's rays, which illuminate the way through the water, miraculously unfolding into a beautiful display of art. The blossoms were grand and breathtaking, and I couldn't get enough of them. My growing flower photo collection kept me busy as my connection to Mother Nature's magic grew stronger. The flowers inspired me and continued to be among my greatest teachers.

Before leaving for Australia and Asia, I'd been looking for a manufacturer for my flower bouquet photo albums. Since giving the first one to my friend and seeing how much she enjoyed it, I'd been inspired to produce them in quantity to sell. Finding a manufacturer who'd place the intention of love on them during the assembly process was important to me. I realized the beautiful Balinese were heart-centered people, so they seemed to be a perfect match to assemble the albums. But could they meet Western standards?

Gede appeared resourceful, so I asked if he knew any manufacturers that could make my 2.5 inch × 2.5 inch albums containing the collection of flower photos. His eyes lit up, and within hours he'd arranged for a manufacturer to meet me at the villa to discuss and provide a price quote. Excited about this partnership, I designed seven different albums following the colors of the chakras. I quickly moved into production, not realizing that being on time wasn't a strength of the culture. Unfortunately, my order wouldn't be finished before I left the island, which meant I'd either need to ship them to the US or perhaps come back to pick them up.

It was hard to know that the Balinese I grew to love by day went home to minimal living standards at night. This quickly sensitized me to the issues that disparity can bring between foreigners and locals. I floundered a lot with the discrepancies in financial status and often felt naive about the currency exchange. It was challenging at times to determine fair prices for products and services. Sometimes I got ripped off because I didn't understand the zeros, and other times I intentionally overpaid, and my generosity humbled them. It was even more complicated when they'd say, "Up to you" when asked "How much?" One thing was for sure: they were eager to take others into their family and stay connected forever.

The days were flying by, and it would soon be time to head back to the US. I'd be starting my new position shortly after my arrival and needed to find a place to live, as my condo wouldn't be finished for another year. My excitement began to amplify as I looked forward to corporate life and the simplicities and conveniences of living in the US. I wasn't sure when Bali would be calling again but had no doubt that my love affair with this mystical island was just beginning.

As much as I loved the idea of psychics predicting my future, I wouldn't have been able to wrap my head around what the Universe had in store for me and what would bring me back to Bali many times to come. And I wouldn't have believed the island would be positioned to provide me with the most miraculous healing blanket in several years' time.

My ticket home had me flying through the Sydney airport. While walking to my gate, a pair of high-heeled shoes in a store called Witchery caught my eye. They were ostentatious, glamorous, and probably not the typical shoe most would wear to the office, as they were silver-gray with lots of shimmering beads draping over the front. They were stunning and perfect. I loved shoes and always looked for the most unique, sleek, and classy designs. I hadn't thought about anything other than flip-flops and flats for the last nine months. Now I was enthusiastic about going back to my corporate suits, big jewels, and high-heeled shoes.

As I zealously toted my new shoes and struggled with all my luggage, my attention turned to the sound system, which was playing Michael

Bublé's hit song "Home." The lyrics evoked unexpected emotion, and my eyes welled with tears. I realized that I was ready to be off the road and was ready to *go home.*

> Even though I had no home and no man to go back to, and my divorce was still not complete, everything felt perfect as I boarded the plane to New York.

The lessons I'd been learning during my travels were simple yet profound. Happiness was, in fact, the key to life and could be found deep within myself, not in something or someone else. It was important not to believe the internal chatter of my mind, which was often harsh, judgmental, and eager to make comparisons. By trusting my inner guide, I was able to feel into the energy that allows abundance to flow and alignments to happen effortlessly. Most importantly, it was clear that I was responsible for listening to life's opportunities and making choices that resonated in balance with my heart and mind.

> I no longer believed in bad decisions; I knew there was always another choice to make on life's journey.

Recognizing that new options were available in every moment, I wanted to maximize my life experiences by exercising them. There's always a way, and if I let Spirit guide me, I'd be supported every step, one lantern at a time.

Although I hadn't planned my self-created sabbatical to be nine months long, it was coincidentally similar to a gestational period—almost suggesting a rebirth and reset that no business plan could have ever unfolded with such ease and grace. Coining the phrase "intuitive risk-taking," I continued to practice utilizing this gift in my everyday life. Living in the flow with Spirit in the driver's seat was much easier than trying to follow the ego-mind through judgment and suffering. I had a whole new appreciation for having a home and a job where I felt valued and was grateful to be living out my dreams. Reflecting on Sylvia's prediction from the Hay House cruise, I realized that she'd been spot on about me leaving my job. All this unexpected wisdom and guidance from other realms also sparked curiosity and intrigue in me. I wondered what other unanticipated events might unfold.

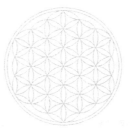

CHAPTER 9

My Plan vs. THE Plan

EVERYTHING HAVING TO do with jumping back into my corporate life felt easy and yet surreal. My previous apartment building in Jersey City seemed the perfect place to reestablish myself. It was familiar, and I loved living there. Reintegrating into Western living happened swiftly, as everything aligned wonderfully.

While it was fun sharing stories of my adventures, my focus quickly shifted to my core responsibilities of launching a brand from the ground up. The first big challenge was to hire a team to build the brand and prepare it for the marketplace in time for the Food and Drug Administration (FDA) approval. It was exhilarating; I loved creating strategic plans and watching them blossom. Participating on the global brand team in the Berlin headquarters, working with different challenges and perspectives worldwide, was also a highlight.

In record time, the core team had been hired and was synergistically building the brand strategy, messaging platforms, and sales materials for the product we'd be launching in less than a year. Committed to not falling back into the soul-sucking traps of corporate life, I concentrated on bringing a higher vibration into the workplace. I was determined to maintain a better life balance for myself and the team. Together, we built an environment where we supported one another instead of being engrossed entirely in the tasks we had in front of us. We were all dedicated to maintaining a positive attitude and not letting others in the department spin us around with their agenda, which helped make work more efficient and fun.

After almost five years (yes, I said years), the never-ending divorce drama was also about to come to a head. Stuart had brought his father with him on a previous court appointment with the judge, which made me wonder if his father would be attending for the trial date. I had gotten along well with Stuart's dad over the years. He was a compassionate man, and I'd wished his son was more like him. However, this time it was only me, my attorney, and Stuart's attorney in the courtroom, and Stuart conferenced in via speakerphone from Oklahoma City.

The judge listened to the attorneys make their cases and then he adjourned to his chambers. I anxiously awaited his ruling. Upon his return, he went through every point, awarding all assets fifty-fifty and denying the alimony request. My heart opened with emotion. This was all I'd ever asked for, and now it was finally settled. Thinking we were finished, I was surprised when the judge continued, "I'm awarding Ms. Bell attorney's fees, as Mr. Bell has been unreasonable and unrealistic about what was due to him." My heart pounded in disbelief, and I finally felt validated for not giving in to all his demands and unfair requests. The judge knew Stuart had a PhD and was fully capable of making his own money. My attorney and I walked out of the courtroom, hugged, and parted ways. I called my parents as I walked to the car, barely getting out the words "It's over" before bursting into tears. Many emotions ran through me, but joy prevailed; I felt that the chains were finally off.

Soon after this grand divorce finale, I met a British man named John at a dinner with a group of colleagues in New York City. This added a much-needed twist of fun into my life. We hit it off immediately, as he opened the conversation with flirtatious, witty British banter. Due to time constraints, our first encounter was brief; he had to head back to England the next day. Although international long-distance dating wasn't ideal, I was eager to explore this relationship and experience the magic of romantic chemistry in my life again. It's such wonderful energy and a great reminder of how connection can catapult us by providing an unexpected excitement for the potential of something new.

John seemed to have an equal interest in me, and neither of us could deny our whirlwind connection. In a matter of days, he'd booked a flight back to New York the following weekend so we could spend time together. The Universe appeared to be on our side, aligning numerous opportunities personally and professionally for us to become acquainted with one another. Another bonus was that we'd both be in Paris for a meeting in a few weeks.

I thought back to my weekend trip to Lovina, in the north of Bali, and a memory came to mind about my visit to a local village healer. When I'd questioned if there was a man in my future, he had told me, "You'll soon be in a relationship with someone you already know." I enthusiastically looked through the address book on my BlackBerry, trying to identify who it might be. Having no luck, I dismissed the healer's comment. Fast-forward to the present, and it occurred to me that John and I had briefly met years prior. He worked for the same company in Europe but in a different department. At that time, we had no reason to exchange contact information, so he wasn't in my contacts. I continued to find it fascinating that all these healers and card readers were spot-on regarding details that were unfolding before me. Their gifts gave me great inspiration to channel more information for myself and heighten my intuition.

My romance with John began to swirl as we maintained seeing each other at least twice a month, despite the fact that we lived across the pond from one another. With work and romance keeping me busy, time was flying by, and the completion of my condo building was fast approaching. Elated to be moving into my new oasis overlooking the New York City skyline, I believed this was going to be my forever place.

My vision included having a significant other in the future to share my condo with as a second home.

After unpacking my things, I threw away every moving box, and the special packaging for my hand-blown wine glasses went into the trash, because I wouldn't be leaving this home anytime soon. Or so I thought. Luckily, John's schedule aligned with mine so that he was able to visit me in my new condo the day after all my furnishings were moved in. Watching the sunset over New York with a bottle of bubbles and a fun guy by my side was a wonderful way to bless my new space.

Meanwhile, we anticipated receiving an FDA approval for the product my team had worked so hard on preparing for launch. Unfortunately, we didn't receive the anticipated labeling from the FDA, which reduced our ability to be differentiated in a heavily saturated market. Without a unique indication, it would be impossible to launch the TV commercial, making it unlikely to achieve its anticipated sales goals.

Several months later, my boss, Karl, came to my office. I'd interacted with him regularly in group meetings, but it was unusual for him to come to my office and sit down for a chat. I was curious what this meeting was going to be about.

"Have you ever been to Singapore?" he asked as he sat down.

"No, why?"

He explained that the head of women's health in the Asia Pacific regional office had called and inquired if he thought I'd be interested in a position they were scouting to fill in the Singapore office. I was secretly embarrassed that I couldn't pinpoint its geographic location, except that I knew it was near Bali. Intrigued by this unexpected opportunity, I was taken aback: I felt that I'd only recently arrived back in the US, and I wasn't looking to move.

He said, "Think about it; it's a great opportunity."

Doing some quick research, I found that Singapore is located just south of Malaysia and north of Australia. As I further searched the internet to get a flavor of the city, I learned that the resident population was primarily a mix of Chinese, Malaysians, and Indians. I found this intriguing, as I had little familiarity or exposure to these cultures. I remembered that another colleague who'd lived there had said, "It's like Asia 101," referring to it being a great place to be based because it could be a springboard into all other Asian countries.

Seriously? I am thinking about the possibility of moving to Asia? I was feeling quite settled in my new condo. However, I liked the idea that I could fly to Bali on weekends to get away.

A few days later, my boss and I had some casual time to talk at a team-building event. He looked at me and said, "So, do you want to go?"

"I don't know anything about the job!" I replied. I hadn't talked with the hiring manager yet and hoped to obtain some insights about the position. I asked him several questions, all of which he answered with "I don't know; you'll have to find out." He continued, with great optimism and encouraged me to seriously consider it. I felt a little perturbed that he thought I could make such a quick decision about a life-changing event, then laughed at myself because I'd done precisely that in Australia after my session with the tarot card reader.

I wondered if Singapore had high-rise buildings similar to my condo. Would I make more money? Was it a promotion? What exactly were the job description, role, and responsibilities? There were a lot of unanswered questions and people to talk with before getting prematurely enthusiastic about the position.

The truth was undeniable: I loved my new condo and my baby blue Lexus convertible, and I didn't desire a dramatic life change.

> I quickly reminded myself that when the Universe
> provides me an unexpected opportunity, I must explore
> it—especially if I have initial resistance.

I had learned over the years that the more resistance I have to an idea, the more I need to pay attention to it. It often meant the emotional charge behind it needed to be uncovered. The only way to know what was behind it was to go directly into the resistance; I couldn't go around it and certainly couldn't shove it to the side or ignore it.

I made appointments to talk with the management team members in Asia, a German colleague working on the Asia Pacific team, and the gentleman I'd be replacing. All these discussions left me with undeniable intrigue. When I inquired about the living situation, they laughed at my question about high-rises, responding with "That's pretty much all there is!" As I reviewed the expat package, I found it enticing, and the perks were too good to pass up. Most importantly, the job itself would be an exciting and enjoyable challenge.

Everywhere I turned, there was a green light, green light, green light. One last place to check in with was my parents, specifically my mother, as she was so happy to finally have me back in the US. She'd mentioned several times that she feared I'd move to Europe, so I figured Asia would push her over the edge, and she'd be begging me not to go. When I delicately announced that I'd been approached for a position based in Singapore and that I'd soon be flying there to interview and do an area tour, there was complete silence. After what felt like minutes, my mom said, "You'll know what's right for you, and I'm sure you'll make the best of it." I was shocked. It appeared that she was open to the idea.

Everything happened quickly. The team in Asia scheduled a series of interviews so I could meet with senior management and partake in an area tour. The direct flight from Newark, New Jersey, was the longest in the world and would arrive in Singapore in thirteen hours. It was early morning in Singapore when I walked through the jetway and into the terminal. The energy was quite different from any other place I'd been. The powerful air conditioners roared, chilling me almost instantly, while a refreshing floral fragrance permeated the entire terminal. I quickly found my luggage, made it through customs, and found the taxi stand.

On my ride to the hotel, the magic began. Unique trees arched over the road leading away from the airport; it looked like a scene out of a Disney movie. A voice in my head said, "I am moving here." It felt strange to have such a sense of knowing when I hadn't yet seen anything, but I unequivocally knew it was my destiny. Of course, I went through all the motions of interviewing, asking lots of questions, and walking the city. Assuming all went well, the assignment would last two to three years.

Returning to my condo in New Jersey, I was surprised at how motivated I felt to move again. I discussed the opportunity with John, and he immediately encouraged me to take it. He'd been based in Asia many years prior and knew this type of expat position would provide incredible life experience and bolster my résumé. Suddenly the new home I'd waited to be complete for over two years was going to become a rental after I'd lived in it for less than a year. *And* I'd thrown away all my moving boxes.

Karl announced at a department lunch that I'd be taking an assignment in Singapore in the coming months. You could feel the buzz in the air as many people lit up with curiosity. Later that afternoon, while I was at the watercooler, a colleague approached me excitedly, suggesting that I'd be perfect for the show *House Hunters International*. Since I hadn't had a TV since 2005 (it was now 2011), I had no idea of the program she spoke about. I laughed as she jokingly narrated, "Which property will Beth Bell choose? The unit by the beach or the unit in the city?"

Jessica had planned to come over for a weekend getaway, which was perfect timing, as I wanted to update her on this new development. The thought of moving far away from her was one of the most significant downsides. We chatted up a storm about my new opportunity, and I mentioned my colleague's idea to be on *House Hunters International*. Jessica quickly said, "Yes! Of course you should be on that show!"

"What?" I was surprised by her conviction and that she even knew about it.

A moment later, she flipped open her laptop and said, "Let's see if they're casting."

They were.

She and I immediately filled out the casting form and made a video to send to the producers the next day. Reality shows weren't my thing, but I had an ulterior motive for applying: Jessica, Jane, and I were concepting a talk show, and we wanted to learn about back-end production. Soon after I'd applied, I was emailing Jessica and Jane to announce that the producers had accepted me.

On my very last day in America, the crew from *House Hunters International* came to shoot the Jersey City footage. The movers had packed everything, so my home was empty. I was catching a flight later that evening for a stopover in Venice, where I would celebrate my birthday with John before heading to Singapore.

A month after my arrival in Singapore, we were scheduled to shoot the back end of my episode. Jessica flew over and was thrilled to participate in the taping as a sounding board to create dialogue for my reactions to potential homes I'd be viewing. During the "get to know you" process with the producers, they asked me if I wanted to learn anything in particular about Asian culture. My answer came quickly: feng shui, which resulted in the producers scheduling Joey Yap, a famous feng shui consultant, to come to my apartment. This conversation was the most memorable aspect of taping the episode.

On the day of filming, Joey and I got right to it, and he asked me about my life goals. I told him that finding a life partner was at the top of my list, along with career success that would catapult me into my life's purpose. He gave me a brief overview of feng shui and talked about the earth's elements and how a home can leverage them to help achieve one's desired goals. Many aspects of the outside elements such as water, mountains, and surrounding buildings were evaluated when considering where the inside features of my home should be placed. This included making recommendations for the orientation of the front door, my bed and household furnishings that could make all the difference. Everyone knows how it feels to walk into a room and experience a good or bad feeling. Joey's goal was to help energize my flow, not drain or distract me from accomplishing my desires.

After assessing my home with a map and his compass, he made a few suggestions on how the layout could better reflect my life goals. One of the first recommendations was to acquire a water feature and place it in the right front corner of the living room. He said bringing in the water element would help create a peaceful, harmonious environment. He explained the profound aspects of water are connected to wisdom, insight, and intuition. In contrast, the more flowing side of water can represent our social connections and how we interact with the world around us. I'd always wanted an aquarium, so this felt like a perfect addition to implement Joey's water feature recommendation. Everything he said resonated with me, and I was grateful to have received these suggestions to optimize the feng shui in my new home.

While standing at the front door at the end of our session, Joey commented that the entrance was in the perfect orientation for my goals. Jokingly I asked, "What if the door hadn't been in the correct position? Would I have to move?" With a serious look on his face, he calmly informed me that most people hire him for consultation *before* buying a property or moving in. He offered that if people cannot move or make structural changes, it is best that they change their goals for the timeframe they plan to live in the property. Otherwise, the clashing forces of energy would hinder them from achieving their goals. This practice might still be an "ancient Chinese secret" for many Westerners.

My new apartment in Singapore was on the thirty-third floor of an impressive high-rise and had many similarities to my Jersey City condo. While I didn't have a view of a dazzling New York City skyline, my oasis in Singapore overlooked the marina, the historic Fullerton Hotel, and the Marina Bay Sands Hotel and Shoppes. Sitting in my living room was akin to having box seats that displayed the waterfront events below, including many breathtaking fireworks displays. A flagship Louis Vuitton store appeared to float in the water as a backdrop to the nightly laser light show that beamed into the sky in front of me.

Within the first thirty days, my company provided cultural sensitivity training to help me with my international move. Not only was I living in a country very foreign to me, but my job also entailed working with people from several Asian countries, all having different nuances. It was sensory overload learning about the Vietnamese, Chinese, Malaysians, Singaporeans, Australians, and New Zealanders, to name a few. My primary role was working with the country division heads and marketing directors to create strategic marketing plans for the contraceptive product portfolio.

When the culture coach shared a graph displaying a "honeymoon period" that is experienced after making an international move, I didn't think much of it. She pointed to the steep upswing in mood and excitement in the first few months. Then the graph dipped below the base-line, representing the culture shock that can set in. She warned that this stage often resulted in homesickness, loneliness, and even depression. I'd lived internationally before and saw life as an adventure. As a result of my resilience and extensive travel, I wasn't worried about the plummeting of the graph and was confident this was not going to affect me. Little did I know what the future held.

Work was instantly busy. I learned new things daily and incorporated my knowledge into the region. My calendar booked up, and I was on the road more than 70 percent of the time, as anticipated. As I traveled to several countries, I met many team members and heard about their struggles and wishes for resources and financial support. Affordability issues and myths about hormonal contraception provided unique challenges compared to those in Western countries and required drastically different strategies and tactics.

My experience working in Asia was a paradigm shift that changed my life and perspective forever. Living on the other side of the planet gave me the most extraordinary glimpse into the differences between the Westernized world and Eastern wisdom. You don't know what you don't know until you see it or experience it firsthand. It was as though the Universe had planted me internationally so I could intricately understand the diversity of humans. I viewed American culture with an altered lens, now I understood others' distaste of the sense of entitlement and the lack of sensitivity for the suffering in other countries.

A few months into my assignment, I was chatting on the phone with a world-renowned OB-GYN with whom I'd maintained a friendship over the years. Although based in the US, he'd traveled and spoken extensively throughout Asia as a thought leader in women's health. It seemed to be a good time to touch base to have a friendly catch-up and tap into his insights. At one point during our call, he asked how I was doing. The way he said it made me think there was concern behind the tone in his voice.

"I'm great," I said and inquired why he was asking.

"Because you've said to me three times during our discussions that you're not lonely, which makes me think you're lonely."

I was a little taken aback; I hadn't even realized I'd said this to him. In complete denial, I replied, "No, I'm good."

The truth was that being on the other side of the planet creates a separation from family, friends, and familiar people. While I had some acquaintances, I didn't have an inner circle of friends, and this created a sense of loneliness.

It wasn't long after this that I was introduced to a woman named Lei, who was relocating from the US to the regional office in Singapore. We quickly hit it off as we talked about the relocation and housing process, as well as the best places to live. We soon fell into a Saturday routine of attending a yoga session, going to spin class, then heading to the Marina Bay Sands Shoppes to eat our favorite Chinese food. To top it all off, we'd schedule ninety-minute foot reflexology sessions with our favorite therapists, Tan and Chan.

On the romantic front, I had broken up with John not too long after my move to Singapore because our life plans weren't aligning. Although my heart was sad, I decided to make the best of it and explore the international dating scene. I hoped Singapore would provide an exciting dating life, as the men here would have global perspectives and life experience. Unfortunately, I wasn't meeting anyone who was of remote interest to me romantically.

One weekend, Lei and I were on a chartered yacht with a group of expats for the day. I was primarily interested in relaxing from a busy week and wasn't jumping up to mingle. While sitting with a small group of people, I noticed a man, whom I didn't know, peering over from the other side of the boat. Although he seemed to be trying to make eye contact with me, he didn't approach me, which made me assume he wasn't interested.

An hour or so went by, and eventually the boat came to a planned stop in the ocean. Lei and I geared up to be among the first in the kayaks. After Lei jumped in, she realized she didn't have sunscreen on. While she went to get some, the gentleman taking notice earlier in the day jumped into my kayak in her place. I rolled my eyes and told her, "I'll be back in a few minutes." Turning around from the front of the kayak, he introduced himself as Klaus and began asking a barrage of questions. He said he was from Germany and lived in India. I wasn't interested, as he seemed a bit pushy, and as he talked, all I could think was, *This guy is full of shit*. After ten minutes, I switched him out for Lei.

Lei and I were treading water and chatting a little while later when he appeared again. Thinking this might be a potential romantic opportunity for me, Lei jumped back onto the yacht. Klaus carried on telling me of his thriving business in India and that he was looking for a business partner. When he inquired if I had any interest, I promptly told him I was not the right person for many reasons. He pressed on, wondering what my objections were, which was weird because I wasn't looking for a new job, nor was I expressing interest in his. I played along and shared that I was never moving to India, I had no interest in building international schools, and the role couldn't come close to my salary requirements. Quite frankly, I wasn't interested in him. Although I did find his tenacity and persistence intriguing.

He continued to stay close and found attention-grabbing ways to engage me in conversation. When he started to talk about the spiritual development of children and teachers, I thought perhaps I'd been too quick to judge him, and maybe there was something to this guy. Later in the day, when he suggested we skip out of the group and go to drinks and dinner by ourselves, I thought, *What could it hurt?* and agreed.

When we reconvened that evening, we were both cleaned up and changed out of our swimming attire from the yacht. As we walked toward one another, he was looking better than expected. He was tall and had a refined, sleek look about him, while his soft, curly hair brought a sense of merriment to his character. He appeared well put together, wearing high-end designer clothes, which wasn't important but made a statement. His style was European, which I liked, and his confidence made him even more attractive. As we sat at one of my favorite rooftop bars, his mannerisms came across as sophisticated, and his personality sparkled, enticing me to want to learn more—a drastic turnaround from my view of him on the yacht. He started again with a barrage of questions inquiring about me, to which I responded, "Tell me about you." I wasn't going to disclose anything more about myself until I understood more about him and what he was up to.

Klaus described how his business helped children by incorporating meditation, spirituality, and yoga into the learning process. He was eager to expand into a global franchise, using the foundation of the current business model along with some new twists he thought I could help him make. Listening to his big vision and contribution to the planet, I felt comfortable sharing my life's vision. Our conversation flowed along with the bubbles that seemed to pour endlessly into our glasses throughout the evening.

I shared with him my love for my corporate career and the clarity I had regarding my desired destiny to do something more than work in the pharmaceutical industry. My self-created sabbatical years prior had given me more focus on helping humanity and wanting to do this through products I'd created. The flower bouquet albums had blossomed, and I'd developed many other flower-themed products focused on empowerment. My website was basic and showcased only a handful of products I'd produced in Bali with the goal of "Pollinating the Planet with Love." I disclosed that I didn't know all the details of *how*, but I was certain that my life's purpose would eventually lead me to leave my corporate career to launch my product line in retail stores.

Klaus listened intently to me, and when I was done, he responded with one line that literally captured me. He said, "If you want to make a difference, why wouldn't you start with the children?"—encouraging me to consider becoming a partner in his business. It suddenly felt like a new epiphany. Why wouldn't I want to start with the children, their parents, and the teachers? If we could make a difference by changing how people start out in life, we'd make a difference for the future. Perhaps my focus didn't need to be solely on adults who were already so ingrained in their ways. It was like a light bulb came on, and I realized this guy was adamant about helping humanity.

Perhaps it was our cultural difference that initially turned me off or the enthusiasm with which he approached me that threw me. I wasn't sure. Suddenly I was certain that this guy had the same tenacity to make things happen as I did, and we were perfectly aligned to do it!

Well, other than the fact that I wasn't interested in moving to India. I'd been there for work many times and joked around, saying, "I would *never* live in India!" I still wasn't fully recognizing the power of saying "never" and that it often led me to doing the opposite.

The next few months were a magical whirlwind. We were in our early forties, and so it seemed we knew what we wanted in life. Sharing our desires seemed to streamline our relationship, allowing it to move quickly, romantically, and professionally; everything seemed to be aligning perfectly. On one of his visits, he saw that I had a vision board in my apartment and was eager to work on this together, stating, "We should make it *our* vision board." I'd never had a boyfriend interested in participating in this cut-and-paste activity and was keen to incorporate his desires and make it ours. Plus, he understood the power of manifestation, as I did, which added an adventurous aspect. It was invigorating that we both believed anything was possible.

Working on the vision board quickly led us into life plan discussions. Knowing that I had zero interest in living in India, Klaus insisted that we could live in any location of our choosing once the global franchise plan was launched. Hong Kong was at the top of his list, and it seemed enticing to me as well, so we added this to the board. At this stage of life, I wasn't interested in having children of my own and had shared this the first night we met. However, he was adamant that we should have a child and wanted to place baby stuff on the vision board. The next thing I knew, he'd found an image of a Mercedes G Wagon and added it. I wasn't familiar with the vehicle, but it looked interesting, and I was happy to have his earthly desires splashed amongst mine.

Klaus remained persistent that we should have an extension of "us" and that it would be easy with his business situation. Having decided that I desired a partner with grown kids, I began reconsidering having a child but felt a baby might be a distraction from my life's purpose. Not to mention he already had a nine-year-old son, and I was happy with just the three of us. Miraculously, he quickly warmed me up to the idea by making it seem so easy, reassuring me that I wouldn't have to sacrifice other important aspects of my life's dreams.

Klaus traveled back to Singapore several times and eventually brought his son Peter to visit. He shared that Peter's mother, an ex-girlfriend, could not care for him properly due to Peter's attention deficit disorder. Wanting to eliminate prescription medication, he'd convinced her that Peter should live with him indefinitely. When I met Peter, we instantly adored one another, and I was eager to have the three of us spend more time together.

On my first trip to India with Klaus, he introduced me to his business and took me to high-end hotel restaurants near his home. However, the hotel he booked for me to stay in was not very nice, although it was close to the school. The visit was surprising; I experienced India differently being in a community neighborhood rather than being sheltered by the grounds of a five-star property on a corporate trip. Although the beach was nearby, it was filled with trash, chickens, cows, people, and all sorts of health hazards. Klaus saw the look of dismay on my face and assured me we'd look for a new area to live in. There were many cultural aspects of India that I found fascinating. However, my resistance to living there was still lurking, as the living standards were quite different from Singapore or the Western world.

As I continued to express my concerns about living in India, Klaus made suggestions that he hoped would shift my apprehensions. We looked at several places on that visit and found the perfect home in a gated community reflecting a contemporary style we both liked. I focused my sights on this home, knowing it would make all the difference to have an oasis away from the chaos. He assured me that he'd secure this home we loved, and that India was temporary—we would live there one to two years at the most.

As I explored further, I discovered that the opportunity to join him in business was not as buttoned-up as he'd presented it to be and anticipated several hurdles ahead. However, being an optimist and trusting my robust skill set for business matters, I believed all challenges could be overcome.

After all, everything seems possible when you're in love.

At the same time that plans were developing with Klaus, the regional office in Singapore appeared to be heading toward some significant downsizing. The women's health division around the globe was being hit hard by new generic medications coming to market and legal issues. Perhaps the Universe was shifting so I could easily bounce out? Although there was still much work to be done, it seemed this might be the best jumping-off point. Other than moving to headquarters in Berlin, the options for different positions were not enticing, and I wasn't interested in moving back to the US quite yet.

On one of Klaus's trips to Singapore, he proposed marriage to me with a ring engraved with his family emblem. Months prior, while I was on a business trip, he'd had me visit his jeweler in Berlin to have the ring sized. So it wasn't a surprise that he was giving it to me, but it was still exciting. The evening he arrived, I was curious about how he would propose and thought maybe he'd do something special at dinner. Moments before we walked out the door, he handed me the box and said, "Here's your ring." I wasn't sure what to make of this but thought perhaps our cultural differences were at play again. Since we'd been talking about it, I could justify that there was no reason to make it a surprise. Of course, looking back this was only one of the many signs I chose to ignore that disclosed a lot about Klaus's character.

During my next visit to Berlin, he wanted me to meet a few other people, including his homeopathic doctor. She was lovely, but there was something strange about our interaction. Thrilled to be starting a life with Klaus, I gushed about all our plans. Her response seemed to lack emotion, and I wondered why. It was as though she wanted to say something but couldn't—or maybe it was an aspect of German culture, which can be a bit stoic, or perhaps it was a reflection of professionality. I knew she was friends with his ex-partner and thought maybe it was difficult for her to see him with someone new. I really didn't know.

As the year 2012 was wrapping up, I finalized negotiations for my departure and set a date in December as my last day. The timing seemed ideal to start the new year in India together. These were exciting times as I was ironically and unexpectedly checking off "nevers" number four and five: leaving my job for a man and moving to India.

When I told people the story of how we'd met and what we were up to, everyone thought we were a perfect match, although few had met him. When my mom and her friend came to visit me in Singapore, Klaus came to meet my mom so we could all spend time together. During my mom's visit, a few red flags were presented as he bailed out of our lunches and dinners just as the check came to the table. At the time, none of us were too fussed, as we were all accomplished women and didn't expect men to pay for or take care of us.

The reality was I didn't want to see that anything was wrong; I wanted to stay in the illusion and fantasy we were creating about our future. Certainty emanated, and I believed I was entering the most magical time of my life. My intuition felt like it was at an all-time high. It was probably fair to say I'd completely lost my mind, as many of us do when romantic love takes over.

Similarly to the last time I'd left my corporate life, I didn't tell anyone at work. The only people who knew were my boss and the head of Asia Pacific. The regional head was new to the position as the previous gentleman had been promoted to an opportunity abroad. This guy didn't know me very well, but he called me into his office when he heard the news coming from the US that I'd be leaving. It was the first time I'd sat with him, and I was surprised he was engaging me, as my final days were winding down. He expressed a sense of loss regarding my departure, stating that he'd heard "great things" from peers back in Berlin. He inquired, "Is there *anything* I could do for you to reconsider staying?"—suggesting that he might be able to facilitate a pay raise if it would help. I was flattered, and it was a great boost for my ego. It was nice to be appreciated and considered an asset by colleagues and upper management back at headquarters. But there was nothing anyone could have offered me in those days to convince me to stay. I was determined to leave and was clear about why I was doing it. Madly in love and thinking I was invincible, I looked forward to the endless possibilities that lay ahead.

PART II

Healing Journey
of the Soul

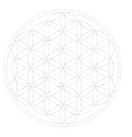

CHAPTER 10

Sleeping with the Devil

STANDING IN MY high-rise apartment overlooking the marina, I watched my household get packed up yet again. My company had done all the paperwork when I'd moved to Singapore, so I had trusted in the process. This time around, I wasn't sure if the movers knew all the details necessary to get the shipment through customs in India without any drama or fines. But I was in love, so what did it matter?

As I closed the door, my heart was beaming and my thoughts were on my next big life adventure and our anticipated trip to Vietnam. We'd spend two weeks there over Christmas and the New Year before touching down in India to start our life together. I was taking only two large suitcases filled with my bare essentials, so I hoped the sea freight wouldn't be delayed to India; it was notorious for taking months to arrive.

Once the last box was on the truck, we hopped into a taxi and were on our way to Changi Airport in Singapore. I was on cloud nine. Sitting on the plane next to my guy, I was happy not to be traveling alone, as I did 95 percent of the time. After a brief flight, we landed in Vietnam and headed to our hotel to dine in the hotel restaurant.

The next morning, we boarded a small boat for an overnight in Hanoi Bay. We sipped martinis, looking out over the majestic Ha Long Bay where the enormous, jagged edges of the rocks in front of us pierced up through the water and towered into the sky. I noticed a gentleman sitting near us, traveling alone. I felt the sadness of what this was like, as I had often done this over the years since my divorce. I thought to myself, *I'm so glad I'll never have to do that again.* Traveling either alone or with girlfriends can be fun, but I was ready to explore the world with a romantic partner and was elated to have Klaus by my side.

The following day we took a car to Hue, where we'd reserved a hotel on the beach to celebrate New Year's Eve. A few days after our arrival, I started to feel unwell. My body was experiencing severe inflammation as every lymph node was swollen and painful. I was immediately concerned about my immune system. Previously, I'd had one or two lymph nodes swell up during a cold, but I'd never experienced the intensity of *all* my lymph nodes swelling at the same time. I thought it best to see a doctor sooner rather than later, as serious disease is common in developing countries.

We asked the hotel to recommend a doctor, and they directed us to the local hospital. Venturing into the city center, we found ourselves entering an emergency room filled with very sick people experiencing grueling health issues, and no one who spoke English. Not wanting to contract whatever dreadful diseases patients were suffering from, Klaus and I were both eager to leave the hospital. We'd be arriving in India a few days later, and Klaus said he'd take me to one of the top medical facilities the day following our arrival.

Unexpectedly, the shipping company notified me that my household container would arrive on the shores of India before our arrival. To play it safe, we decided it was best to delay the shipment and put it in a storage unit in Singapore, not wanting to risk having Indian customs officials rummaging through it. Since Klaus was still negotiating the rental of the contemporary home I'd been dreaming of, it made sense to wait to ship until we were settled. Again, the Universe seemed to be aligning this better than we could have planned it.

I decided not to let this mysterious health issue ruin our trip and focused on the time we had alone before things would become busy in India. It felt a bit like a honeymoon, although some odd moments gave me pause. We had planned an all-day spa visit, but Klaus's mind seemed to be elsewhere. When I tried to open a conversation, he didn't want to talk. Deep inside, my intuition told me there was something more. But I quickly brushed it off; I knew men needed their cave time and didn't need to talk everything out like women do.

The trip was delightful. We dined at local restaurants, took in the sights, and partook in fun activities like supporting a local seamstress who made a few pieces of clothing for us. Flowers were prevalent, and I enjoyed leisurely photographing them near the beach and on the hotel property. This activity always made me feel connected and at peace. And, of course, we spent plenty of intimate time in our hotel suite overlooking the ocean. Although it was all relatively relaxing, I looked forward to our arrival in India to start our new life. In a few weeks, Klaus's son would be arriving from Germany, and I was elated to be building a home for the three of us to be together.

After we arrived in India, I wanted to take photos along the way home, but I couldn't quite capture anything with the chaos in the streets. Animals, people, random crowds, and funeral processions were everywhere. Cars, buses, and motorbikes swerved to avoid the hazards on the roads, and dark clouds of exhaust created an ominous layer of muck between vehicles. Klaus reassured me I'd get used to it, and my sensitivity to the scenes of poverty would diminish over time. Being a compassionate person, I wasn't sure these scenes were forgettable or ignorable.

That evening Klaus broke the news that the owner of the house we both loved would not rent it to him. Although we'd planned to stay at the school property upon arrival, this was meant to be temporary. Now it seemed we'd be there a bit longer, and I tried not to allow my disappointment to overcome me. His home was modest, not decorated very well, and not my style. He said we could buy a few things in the meantime to make it feel like ours. For India, it was clean and seemed to be safe, as it was gated with a full-time guard. However, I didn't like that we had to use padlocks on the front door.

I was still feeling ill and was concerned about my medical condition. First thing the next morning, I asked him to ring the doctor he'd spoken so highly of while in Vietnam. Klaus nodded in acknowledgment but didn't seem to give this much attention, as we were walking out the door. He was focused on introducing me to everyone, yet my number one priority was my health. Maintaining an optimal immune system is crucial in countries struggling with serious communicable viruses and diseases, and I was worried.

By afternoon, I asked if he'd made the call to the physician. He replied no and still didn't seem to be paying the matter much interest. While in Vietnam, we'd agreed that seeing a doctor would be first on our agenda. Now he looked at me and said, "Why don't you just go?" I was astounded by his lack of caring and outright dismissal of the seriousness of my condition. Taking a taxi was not possible, as they weren't easy to schedule where we lived. They weren't trustworthy, and he knew I had no idea where the hospital was or who to call to find this medical facility on my own. I sat there stunned and found myself pleading for him to help make the call so we could go as soon as possible. He eventually got around to it and informed me we could go the next day.

Upon our arrival at the hospital, we were ushered into a private waiting room to see the head doctor of the hospital facility. He was a jolly Indian man who seemed very happy to see us. He knew Klaus, and they made small talk before turning their attention to me. The doctor asked me to lie on the table so he could examine my lymph nodes. Within a minute, he said, "Yep, it's lymphadenitis," meaning my lymph nodes were swollen. Well, duh! That was obvious. I was looking for him to identify the root cause. He quickly admitted that he had no idea but would help me find out.

Since the lymph nodes in my groin were especially swollen and sensitive, he suggested I have a gynecological exam. He rang the gynecologist's office and said they could take me right away. Before we left for the other building, Klaus insisted that we stop by another physician's office, as he was recruiting the hospital to support his business endeavors. He wanted to see if he could attain sponsorship funds for his educational program.

I hesitated upon entering the gynecologist's office. I had observed these types of clinics in my corporate career, but now I was a patient in an office with dirt and grime on the walls. Feeling distressed, I hoped not to be exposed to anything more, fearing additional strain on my health. She performed the pap smear and said the test results would be available in about a week. In the meantime, I would have to watch and wait, hoping the issue with my lymph nodes resolved itself. Even if it did, I wanted to know what had caused all these red lights to go off. My body was trying to tell me something, but I couldn't figure out what.

On the way home, we passed a cow standing in the street, licking a poster that was peeling off the concrete divider that separated us from oncoming traffic. It was "normal" for India, but there was nothing natural about cows being part of heavy street traffic, nor did it seem plausible a cow would like the taste of the glue. This added to my feeling of being in the "twilight zone," as I was so out of my element.

A few days later, we had a formal introductory meeting with the entire school team. After this, I scheduled one-on-one meetings with each team member to hear about their experience. Almost every team member entering the office burst into tears, telling me how awful the work environment was and pleading for me to help. They were all Europeans who'd moved to India to join the school. I listened with dismay, getting my first glimpse that perhaps the dream I'd come for might not be what Klaus had described it to be.

When I approached Klaus about the team members' distress, he seemed emotionless, calling them complainers. He stated that they were all acting ridiculous and didn't know how good they had it. He flat out didn't care about them, and he didn't seem to care what I thought either. This was the exact opposite of what we'd discussed as we'd aligned on each team member feeling valued was imperative. The goal was to develop the team, offer them growth opportunities, and fine-tune an optimal template to implement around the globe.

Knowing things were off with Klaus and his management skills, I continued to give the situation the benefit of the doubt. I was determined to get to the bottom of the toxicity and turn things around. I went so far as to speak with a friend in the US about the possibility of them coming to work for the school. I thought bringing in some fresh thinking and positive perspectives could make all the difference for a quick turnaround. I wasn't one to throw in the towel early, and there was no turning back. I'd agreed to build this foundation and was on the hunt for solutions.

The energy shifted dramatically as Klaus's son Peter was returning from the holidays with his mother in Germany. I was looking forward to his arrival because we'd bonded on previous visits and had gotten to know one another. Thinking it might be the closest opportunity to being a mom that I might have, I wanted to make the best of it. Sadly, the day we picked him up at the airport, he cried all afternoon and evening. I sat with him in his bedroom, hoping to comfort him, figuring it was natural to be upset after leaving his mom. It would likely be six months or more before they could reconnect.

Each day brought new challenges to the business. During our courtship in Singapore, Klaus had wanted me to be a business partner and invest US $180,000. I had been willing to invest my time but wasn't so sure about investing money, as I questioned the company's worth. We'd had a few calls with our respective accountants on the phone while still in Singapore. This resulted in me being completely transparent about not seeing the investment potential based on the current financials. Because I desired to build a partnership with Klaus, I was willing to be a part of the working vision. A few weeks after arriving in India, the rubber hit the road on this discrepancy.

Klaus insisted we meet with his accountant to discuss the numbers. The three of us sat in the accountant's boardroom, where he presented the company's value, and it still made absolutely no sense to me. When I questioned the accountant, he often didn't have an answer, and most of the time, Klaus interjected with a response. I couldn't see how the story fit together. As we left the accountant's office, Klaus grew increasingly angry because I did not agree with his demands. Appalled that he thought there was anything reasonable about what he was asking me to do, I was shocked and disturbed that the man I loved would be talking to me like this. I was willing to put in the sweat equity and build, but I was not willing to dump my nest egg of hard-earned savings.

Later that day, Klaus took me to a dark, dingy bar near our home. He ordered us drinks and went on to say I was a "greedy bitch," which shook me at my core; I had no idea where all of this was coming from. I wasn't in this relationship because of money, but it became apparent that he was. I was devastated and felt vulnerable. The floor was falling out from underneath me. My inner dialogue was loud; I questioned myself and wondered what I'd missed, as I sat there feeling my body start to go numb. Had I misled him in any way about my skepticism in investing? I didn't think so, and now his behavior seemed bizarre.

That night I started to come out of the love fog. But as soon as I did, Klaus turned around and became intimate with me, pulling me back into the magic of how we became connected in the first place. He grabbed me, made me laugh about something, and affectionately started kissing me and holding me close. This shifted the mood, making me think I was taking this all too seriously. One minute I was sexually and intimately connected, and the next, my fear was rising regarding the situation. I was usually full of ideas and solutions, but now I felt scrambled. Nothing was clear or logical, and it felt odd not to be able to see a way out. It sounds crazy, but I was in love with this man, had left my life behind, and wanted to see if the relationship could be fixed. Maybe we needed to work through things? Perhaps I had misunderstood, although I knew I hadn't. The writing was on the wall. I just didn't want to see it.

A few nights later, we were out to dinner with Peter at a nice hotel on the beach. After dinner was served, Klaus became vulgar and condescending to me in front of his son. The only way I could see stopping it was to walk away as the conversation wasn't appropriate for any child, and I was about to burst into tears. As I left the table, Peter came crying after me, saying, "Please don't leave me with him!" The plea coming from this young boy was full of terror and fear, making it obvious there was a history behind it. I was sufficiently scared; too much was wrong with this situation.

I felt as though I couldn't leave, having nowhere to go or any way to get there if I did. As we walked back to the table hand in hand, it became obvious that I had to do something, but I had no idea what or how. I was at Klaus's mercy. I'd left my job and home and was in India without another soul to help me. What was I to do? Whom could I call? I couldn't possibly abandon Peter; I adored him and felt an obligation to him. Bewildered about how Klaus had a grip on me that made me incapable of getting out, I struggled to think clearly. It wasn't a "love goggles" issue; something much stronger was at play that I'd never experienced before.

By now, two months had gone by, and I felt increasingly disoriented and helpless, as my life was crumbling more each day, despite my optimistic delusion that the situation could shift. After devastating incidents or erratic behavior, there'd be lovely moments when the three of us would have fun together. Sunday brunch at one of our favorite hotels was something we all looked forward to. The array of fantastic food was superb, and we'd have fun trying new Indian dishes as well as traditional Western foods. One day, a lovely Indian couple and their daughter, who attended the school, dined with us. I enjoyed getting to know local parents and learning more about their culture. We had so much fun and great conversations, facilitating the fairy-tale aspect of our life.

On our drive home, the incident with the motorbike and tuk-tuk took place. Peter was sitting in the back seat, and we were all quietly riding along through the bustling streets containing hundreds of people and cars, along with chickens, cows, and dogs randomly crossing the road. There were several lanes of traffic, and we were in the high-speed lane on the far right. (In India, they drive on the left side.) I was looking straight ahead when I noticed that Klaus had an intensity about him that was concerning. He was skilled with this kind of traffic, and I was always impressed with his ability to navigate calmly through the streets. However, something about this situation felt different.

I noticed him glancing back and forth at the rearview mirror with some level of concentration. Moments later, he made a quick movement with the steering wheel, swerving us to the left and then back into our lane. In that instant, I glanced to the left, seeing a motorcyclist smash into a tuk-tuk in the lane next to us. It all happened so instantaneously, and I heard the eerie sound of metal on metal. The rider quickly disappeared from view, and Klaus stepped on the gas and sped away. Going from being a happy family to witnessing death and destruction minutes later shook me up.

My body went numb, and my attention returned to Klaus's swift swerve to the left. Although I wanted to give him the benefit of the doubt, my mind focused on his body language and emotionless face. A sinking feeling emerged: Klaus appeared to have intentionally cut off the motorbike. I immediately questioned myself, wondering if I was making this all up, when Peter screamed from the back seat, "Dad! Did you do that on purpose?" The car fell silent. The fact that Peter had just stated my thoughts out loud spoke volumes and confirmed that we'd both witnessed the same horror. I'm sure Peter had seen his dad do many things over the years, and this was one more to add to the list. Stunned and in shock, I contemplated the danger Peter and I might be in, with a madman at the wheel.

I began shaking as Klaus quickly pulled off the main road and onto a side street, navigating back to the house. As he continued to check whether anyone was following us, he yelled at me, "What's your problem?" Petrified, I didn't respond for fear of any retaliation. Was he really capable of intentionally killing another human? Or was my perception of this situation all wrong? I didn't think so, and I needed to find an exit plan from this nightmare. I started investigating the basics of getting to the airport. It wasn't easy to find trustworthy car service companies that were guaranteed to be safe, and I wasn't sure Klaus would let me go if I tried. I needed to get clarity and remain grounded so I could think straight and devise a plan as to how I would leave.

Coincidentally, the next day the head guard outside of the school called out of work, saying his brother had died in a motorcycle accident the day prior. I wondered what the chances were that his brother was the person who'd smashed into the tuk-tuk next to us. Granted, there are millions of people within a mile radius, so it was unlikely. But I wondered if, when Klaus heard this, he felt anything or questioned his actions of the previous day.

Needing privacy, I went to Peter's room one afternoon, thinking no one would look for me there. I locked the door and called Axel. If anyone could talk me out of the craziness of this situation, I thought he could. Or maybe he could help me get my wits about myself.

"BB! How are you?" His familiar voice of sanity instantly warmed my heart and calmed me down.

I hadn't talked to Axel much while living in Singapore, so he had no idea I'd left my job, fallen in love, and moved to India. Looking back, it seems strange that we weren't in touch. But with time zone differences, my busy travel schedule, and me dating Klaus, we'd dropped out of communication during this time.

Remaining as composed as possible, I said, "AA, something's happening here that doesn't feel good, and I need your help."

I'd barely begun to explain the back story when Klaus came pounding at the door. My heart raced as I said, "I'm on a call to the US; I'll be out in a little while." It fell silent in the house, so I turned myself away from the door and proceeded to speak softly as I tried to briefly explain my complicated situation.

Axel shared his typical profound teachings to help diffuse my anxiety. He repeated the message he'd first delivered as he walked the streets of New York City near Ground Zero, days after 9/11. At the time, Spirit's voice had come through him, saying, "I'm only in your dream for a moment, to remind you that you're safe, asleep in heaven. None of this is real. God is love. And this is not love's will." I'd heard him state this many times over the years, which brought me a familiar sense of peace as I reconnected to a higher state of consciousness. Life was but a dream, and I needed to remember that I was the dreamer and creator of my life.

> I was not a victim; I needed to take action to move through the fear and shame that was debilitating me.

As our conversation ended, he exclaimed, as he always did, "I love you, BB!" and I replied, "I love you too, AA!" While I had no tangible solutions from my conversation, as I couldn't possibly tell all the details, it temporarily stabilized me from the spin I'd been experiencing. As I unlocked and opened the door, I believed the best thing to do was cooperate, lay low, and trust that solutions would soon surface.

The next day, Klaus was in an incredibly loving mood, which led to us having sex in the hammock on the private porch outside. Somehow intimacy was still working between us, or perhaps it was the only thing that brought me illusionary hope that this story would end on an amicable note. Maybe I was doing this under the guise of cooperation or avoidance of profound heartbreak. I really didn't know, as my life was so shattered at the time.

As we were about to get up to get dressed, I happened to look down at his naked body and noticed that he had five open wounds on his penis. They were perfectly round and raw. Shocked, I asked, "Do you have herpes?" He paused and replied with some vague answer, suggesting that it was from childhood and he didn't know it was sexually transmitted. I immediately fled to the other room and began to sob in complete disbelief. He knowingly had open sores, had sex with me, and exposed me to the virus. As if everything else wasn't bad enough. I couldn't stop crying. Eventually, he came into the room and firmly questioned, "Now this is going to be a problem too?" My heart raced, and I prayed there would be a way out without more drama.

I couldn't understand how an educated woman with life experience had gotten herself into this situation. My only focus now was escaping quickly and safely. Living with a man who I couldn't deny was inflicting emotional abuse, had no regard for others, and was exhibiting traits of violence made me more concerned than ever for my safety. I should have been angry, but at this moment I was terrified that lashing out or showing more emotion could have potentially put me at greater risk. I realized this was a life-changing moment that might haunt me forever.

I gathered myself, quietly got on the computer, and booked a ticket to Singapore. I emailed Lei, kept it simple, and asked if she'd be okay if I came for a long weekend. She was planning to be home and said she'd be happy to have me. The next morning, I informed Klaus that I'd scheduled an appointment with my chiropractor in Singapore and had booked a flight for the next day.

He quickly responded, "You can't leave."

I said, "I can, and I've already asked one of the staff to drive me to the airport."

He was losing control, and he didn't like it. I proceeded to tell his son I would be going to Singapore to take care of my back pain. Peter asked with excitement, "Are we all going?" Sadly, I stated I'd be going alone. On one of their trips to visit me, he'd inquired numerous times why they couldn't come to live with me in Singapore. I was heartbroken at the thought of leaving him.

While I waited to leave for the airport and board my flight, time moved in slow motion. Klaus insisted he'd take me and informed the staff they would not be needed. This was most likely because he didn't want me to disclose anything or alert his team. I'd built rapport with them, something he'd never done, and this would be a blow to his business. He wanted to control the narrative around my departure, although I wasn't about to share anything, as I desperately wanted to catch my flight.

As we were about to leave, Klaus pulled Peter and me into our bedroom. He proceeded to give his son a family emblem ring, which was the same as my engagement ring. Peter was thrilled. His eyes lit up, and a big smile crossed his face. Then a moment later, he said, inquisitively, "It looks used." Klaus told Peter it was an old ring he'd taken back from an ex-partner. As Peter looked on, Klaus quickly put mine back on my finger, stating that we were a family, and we'd never break apart.

His son was the only thing he knew I'd most likely stay or come back for, so he used our connection. My heart shattered into a million more pieces knowing I wasn't coming back. I could hardly bear that I was leaving this little guy behind. I'd packed virtually everything I had into one suitcase and left behind the other one, along with a few clothes, so I wouldn't sound off too many alarm bells. I had so few things anyway, as the contents of my household were still in storage in Singapore. Thank God.

As Klaus arrived curbside at the departure terminal, my heart raced. I felt numb getting out of the car, as though I was having an out-of-body experience. Cordially hugging Klaus, I quickly squeezed Peter tightly as car horns blared behind us to keep traffic moving. Navigating through the crowds of people with all my luggage was difficult but distracted me just enough to keep tears from bursting from my eyes. I'd escaped the most horrendous mistake, and I was ashamed I'd been so stupid. I was now lost, having no idea where I was going to go. Lei's Singapore apartment would be a great temporary place to stay, but not long-term.

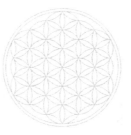

CHAPTER 11

Escaping India

I APPEARED ON LEI'S doorstep with my luggage, and her smile was exactly what I needed, as she welcomed me in with open arms. She was anxious to catch up because I hadn't talked to her much since leaving Singapore. We'd planned to have dinner that evening with our mutual friend Claire. So I decided to wait and share the details until we were all together. I was in a fragile state and didn't think I'd make it to dinner if I got into the story with her upon arrival. I found myself still in denial, shock, and awe about everything. I felt betrayed by my intuition and couldn't begin to process any of the details of how I'd gotten myself into this situation.

At dinner, I gently began to reveal some of what was happening but left a lot of the details undisclosed. I shared that being with Klaus in India wasn't what I had expected. Before sharing much more, Claire said she was coming with news from a friend in Berlin who knew a previous girlfriend of Klaus's. What a small world it suddenly felt like.

The message was, in a nutshell, a warning that Klaus was bad news. She went on to say that a friend of one of my colleagues was trying to alert me about his past and his pattern of pulling in women who had money, impregnating them, taking their money, and kicking them to the curb if they didn't comply with his wishes. He had it down to a system. And I fell for it. I wasn't the first one, as she knew of three other women who had been under his spell; he had fathered children with them but was not involved.

This was more embarrassing than I could have ever thought. Clearly, love is blind. While this was all bad news, it was mildly comforting to know I had not been the only fool tricked by Klaus. He was calling, but I couldn't bring myself to answer. I only sent a few responses via text that I wasn't coming back. He was kind in his responses, requesting several times to talk but not being overly aggressive. My heart was bleeding. As ridiculous as it was, a part of me still wanted to find a way to talk this through and find closure.

Lei offered to let me stay at her place, wanting to allow me the space I needed to process my situation. I stared at the walls in her guest room, intermittently crying my eyes out for two days in between my self-inflicted judgments of what I could have or should have done differently. I'd need to come up with a vision for my life, but I felt shattered. Making a plan wasn't something I felt capable of, although I was clear that I didn't want to go back to America. Unfortunately staying in Singapore wasn't an option, as obtaining a resident visa was nearly impossible without corporate sponsorship. I spent that first week focused on finding ways to feel through it, move forward, and not flounder in a pity party.

I needed to make the dreaded call to my parents to let them know I'd left India and Klaus for good. I didn't want them to be alarmed; I provided some short, generic story about how it didn't work out. They were both concerned, and I could tell their hearts were heavy and sad, but they did their best to reassure me that everything would be okay. I believed it would, but there was a lot to process, and the grief had only begun. They were both good at knowing when not to ask many questions and knew I'd talk in due time. I'm sure they would have preferred

I come back to America, but they knew by now that I'd find my way and would do what was right for me. I reassured them that I'd keep them informed of my movements and when I'd be moving on from Lei's apartment.

From *A Course in Miracles*, I knew all about special relationships and the slippery slope of the fantasies and illusions we build around romantic love. But why did I have to go to such an extreme? How could I have so much "knowing" and yet be so stupid? I tried to fall back on the spiritual wisdom I had as my foundation.

> It was clear that relationships are simply experiences to help us learn more about ourselves, to heal our wounds and break open our hearts so more light can shine through.

While this spiritual contract felt so much more painful than others, I knew I'd called this in for the evolution of my soul and expansion of my consciousness. Although having this knowledge didn't take away the devastation I was feeling.

Knowing I had been exposed to the herpes virus, I decided to make an appointment with my OB-GYN in Singapore to have a blood test and find out if I'd contracted it. A few days after my test, the results were emailed to me, and while I had no physical signs of having herpes, I was positive. This prompted me to think back to Vietnam, when my immune system went haywire and all my lymph nodes swelled. Was this why? The results from my pap smear hadn't detected anything, but I didn't think to ask about testing for herpes at that point. I trusted Klaus would have told me if he carried any sexually transmitted diseases.

I had a sinking feeling that I was now damaged goods. Finding a new partner and having to share this would take away numerous freedoms I'd taken for granted in the past. I knew it would take a lot for me to trust another man, but I was determined to work through this and not give up on love. Being angry would only close my heart, and I believed forgiveness was the only way through.

Over the years, I'd had a few partners in my life who'd shared that they carried the herpes virus before becoming intimately involved with me. So I knew what it felt like to be on the other side. I hadn't rejected them and actually respected them more for telling me. But it did make me think, *Is this person worth it?* as no one wants to contract an incurable virus that painfully impacts the genitals. Would I ever find someone who would want me now that I was infected with this virus? I wasn't sure how I would face this in the future.

I made an appointment with my homeopathic doctor and was petrified and sweating in the waiting room as I contemplated whether to share my diagnosis with her. This was the first time I would disclose this information to anyone since the initial discussions with my OB-GYN. When the doctor asked me if I was having any emotional struggles, I began to cry on the spot. Through the tears, I shared how Klaus had intentionally infected me with the herpes virus. I was mortified and emotionally raw. I needed guidance, although I wasn't sure what she could do for me since there's no cure for herpes. If sharing this with a doctor who might help me was so difficult, I wondered if it would even be possible to tell future love interests.

To my surprise, my homeopath said she had a remedy to prevent outbreaks. She asked me to promise not to send anyone to her for this, as she would not typically help with sexually transmitted diseases, especially outside of marriage. She softly explained, "Due to your circumstances and the trauma you've experienced, I want to help you." I faithfully took the remedy and didn't experience outbreaks.

I figured traveling might help me work through my devastation since this had opened my heart and mind before. So I booked a trip to the Andaman Islands, in the Indian Ocean. The photos online displayed bright white sand and teal ocean coastlines; and the islands appeared to be a heavenly oasis that would provide a perfect refuge to process all I was experiencing.

A week or so before my departure, I received another call from Klaus. My emotions had settled a bit, and I still hoped for some peaceful resolution between us. I remained adamant that I wouldn't be returning to India and planned to travel for a while. Then I made the mistake of mentioning I'd booked a trip to the Andaman Islands the following week.

The next thing I knew, Klaus sent me an email displaying air tickets for him and Peter to join me on the trip. He had called the best hotels on the island (there weren't many of them) and inquired whether I had a reservation at their property. The staff was incredibly friendly and happy to help; without any regard for confidentiality. All he said was that he was my fiancé and was planning to surprise me on the trip. Based on this, they gave him every detail about my arrival and departure information. Baffled by this, I realized how easy it was for privacy to be breached in these islands governed by India. He went on to tell me that he'd added his name to my reservation and upgraded the room to a suite.

In my broken state, I thought that maybe this was an opportunity for resolution and closure. I'd already contracted the virus and didn't feel I was in physical danger meeting with him. Since everything had happened so abruptly, I still wanted to work through the lessons I'd called in with this relationship. My heart was hurting, and I had a desire to talk it through with the only person I thought could stop the pain. I made it clear this wasn't an effort to rekindle and hoped it would reduce the trauma from the dramatic departure.

I'd regained some strength as the fear I'd experienced in India had dissipated. Desperately wanting to spend time with Peter, I was not going to cancel the trip. I still felt responsible for him and hoped he'd somehow understand I wasn't abandoning him, although I knew it wasn't rational to expect a child to understand any aspect of this situation.

But when the heart bleeds, it does irrational things.

The beaches and hotels in the Andaman Islands were beyond my expectations. They were not five-star properties—quite the contrary—but our hotel's landscape was magical with island huts tucked away among its natural beauty. Upon reconnecting with Klaus and

Peter, sadness enveloped my heart and I longed for the feelings of the fantasy family I desired to experience. We participated in daily adventures like hiking, swimming in the crystal blue water, sunbathing, and even washing an elephant in the ocean. The three of us enjoyed our time together as we pretended everything was okay, for the most part. But then the mental torture would surface when Klaus would try to manipulate and guilt me back into the relationship. When I didn't agree, he would become nasty, confirming yet again that he did not have good intentions for me or our relationship. Mother Nature seemed to hold me in her healing sanctuary, helping me to experience moments of peace and enjoy the beautiful scenery despite the volatile situation.

One afternoon I slipped away to find an internet café so I could book a small yacht in Thailand, although I didn't have time to research all the details or connect all the dots on how it would align. Hoping the boat would carry me and my tears away, I desired to keep traveling and wanted to have a scheduled place to go next. It was important that I not be followed, as I needed to find a safe place to continue to heal and get stronger. What a crazy situation to be in: only months prior, I had been at the top of my game in my corporate life, madly in love, and totally clear that I was on *my* path to live my purpose of helping humanity. Knowing how wrong I had been didn't help me as I continued to question myself and the Universe.

In addition to playing the romance card, Klaus did everything he could to make me feel guilty about giving up and not returning to India. My rational mind was clear, but my emotions were still wrapped up in the connection we experienced together, and it felt mysteriously difficult to break free. As the time came for us to go our separate ways, I again felt relieved to be escaping the twisted drama. But the deep sadness felt unbearable. Nothing had been resolved, and no healing had taken place; there was only a wound that was gaping open.

We took a powerboat out to an ocean pad to board a seaplane that would transport us to the main airport. Climbing into the small aircraft, Klaus ignored me, and we all fell silent on the brief flight. Soon, they'd be departing for India, and I would go to Thailand. Once in the terminal, Klaus said goodbye and walked away from me with his son in tow. It was crushing for me not to be able to hug Peter goodbye. On the other hand, I was eager to start over with the healing process and feel better.

I walked through the airport alone and in a daze, trying to find the departure gate for my flight to Koh Samui in Thailand. I planned to stay there one night before taking a ferry to a small island named Ko Tao. When I was completing the booking at the internet café in the Andamans, I didn't have time to make all the logistical plans and trusted that everything would continue to come together. Somehow, I knew that in those moments a force much bigger than I was watching over me, keeping me alive and moving me forward.

Upon arrival in Koh Samui, I took a taxi to an area I knew was safe and booked a budget hotel for my brief overnight stay. Since my hotel was incredibly underwhelming, I went to explore the W Hotel nearby. The entrance led directly to the upper pool bar, which provided expansive views over the Gulf of Thailand. Sipping on a glass of red, I gazed at the seamless line of the infinity-edge pool as it blended with the blue ocean water on the horizon. It felt so romantic with the setting sun, and it was hard to stop myself from thinking, *Why am I here alone?* I didn't stay late since I was scheduled to catch the first ferry out to the island of Koh Tao to meet the captain and board the chartered yacht.

The instructions I'd received from the captain via email were relatively vague, stating I should look for the name of the boat in the marina. Coincidentally, the name of the ship was *Fargo*, the same as my college town. A small reminder of home in a foreign land goes a long way! As the ferry docked, I looked around and spotted the German captain and his Thai girlfriend. He'd mentioned she would be the chef and cleaning lady, and having another woman on the boat made me feel more comfortable. It was easy to spot them since they were both vigorously waving at me. I waved back, and the captain's girlfriend proceeded to bring the dinghy ashore. Without delay, she scooped up my luggage and extended her hand, motioning for me to jump in. I took off my shoes and waded through a few feet of water as it splashed up onto my shorts. The adventure at sea had begun.

The views, the food, and the captain's nightly guitar playing at sunset turned out to be perfect. The captain knew all the great snorkeling spots and guided me into caves no typical tourist could find. If we docked in areas that had commercial sightseeing boats, we were always first into the caves because we'd wake up early, sip some coffee, and then plunge into the ocean's magic. This allowed us to spend the rest of the day at sea, taking in the many gorgeous sights.

I felt so fortunate to have time to sit, reflect, journal, and read. Experiencing this quiet time took me straight back to my first breakaway in Costa Rica. Although this was a very different experience, I knew it was all about soul time yet again. My goal was to get grounded and reconnect with my inner guidance, along with learning the lessons being presented so that I could heal and move beyond the trauma.

After only four nights at sea, I wasn't eager to end my time aboard *Fargo*, but being in such close quarters with a couple who were strangers to me made it easy to depart when we docked. I hired a taxi on the shore and asked him to drive me to a hotel nearby. I found myself at a breathtaking eco-friendly property a few minutes up the hill. The only room available was the honeymoon suite, which felt like a stab in the heart. But the spectacular views of the ocean and the reasonable last-minute price helped me get over the fact that I was there alone.

As the sun rose and the wilderness started to awaken, I was ready for the dawn of the new day. I only had time for breakfast before making my way down to catch the first ferry back to the main island. As I sat with an incredible array of food in front of me, I couldn't have been more blessed, but my sadness was palatable as I asked myself the question, *Where is my life going?* I knew I'd need to be patient and discover the answers as my life unfolded.

> From the heartbreak of my divorce, I knew that the only way through these life situations was to stay centered and allow the stillness within to guide me.

But this time, I was on the other side of the world, and the entire foundation of who I was had disintegrated before me. How was I going to maneuver this next phase of my life? It was clear that I was being asked to practice this trust thing once again, but with a deeply broken heart and no life plan, I felt bewildered and broken.

I knew that most people would say moving too fast with Klaus had been a mistake. Of course, in so many ways, this was true. But another part of me also felt this was all Divinely guided, even though it had become my biggest nightmare. Maybe my stubbornness held me back from admitting that I'd made some wrong turns or ignored the illusions I'd built. Or perhaps my tenacity helped me to keep following my heart and pursuing life's adventures.

> I loved like I'd never been hurt, and I miraculously knew
> that I wasn't going to let this crush my heart forever.

Moving through the emotions and allowing myself to experience the devastation seemed to be the most healing thing I could do. I was still disillusioning myself about forgiveness and resolution that I desperately desired, but I didn't quite grasp this yet.

Traveling back to Singapore, I felt grateful to stay with Lei again. During our heartfelt discussions and exploration of "what's next," Lei threw out the idea of going back to Bali for a few months. She knew the month I'd lived there years prior had provided a wonderful energy that inspired my creativity, and we'd both recently experienced its magic on a trip celebrating her birthday. This seemed like a perfect option, as Bali is world-renowned for being a powerful healing sanctuary. I soaked up some love with my Singapore friends through conversation, great hugs, and incredible meals at some of my favorite spots before heading to Bali for an indefinite amount of time.

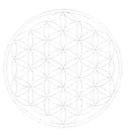

CHAPTER 12

Bali Bliss Calling

I ARRIVED IN BALI under very different circumstances than I had on all my previous trips. I wasn't coming for a holiday, and once again, I was building a life alone. As I stood in the long lines at customs, the aroma of incense heightened my senses and filled me with a feeling of serenity. I wanted nothing more than to drop into the Bali bliss quickly, heal my wounds, and move on. Most importantly, I desired a place to call home where I could unpack my bags and let the chaos settle. Customs would only secure a sixty-day visitor's visa, so I planned to either fly back to Singapore to renew or, more likely, take a much-needed trip back to the US. My parents were anxious to see me and needed to see that I was okay. I trusted this clarity would come in due time.

A friend from Singapore introduced me to Sarah, who rented me her villa in the heart of Seminyak. It was nestled into a bustling area but was cozy, decorated in a shabby chic style with Balinese culture infused throughout. It was in the perfect location, near all the fun restaurants, bars, and shopping, with the bonus of only being a seven-minute walk to the ocean. Because I didn't have a motorbike or car, this was a key attribute. The kitchen and living room were wide open spaces seamlessly merged with nature, and the villa had a small dipping pool that you could almost fall into by taking a few steps out of the living room. With a roof over my head and a pillow to lay my head on, I was grateful to have so quickly manifested this magnificent space.

I quickly settled in and was soon out and about to find some expat friends to connect and have some fun with. Lightening the stress of the last several months seemed a necessity. Hearing that I was in Bali, a friend in Cambodia introduced me to Heidi, who'd been living on the island for several years. She was a clothing designer who managed a boutique in the tourist shopping area. We hit it off quickly, spending several nights sipping the best marginal red wine we could find. We laughed hard and talked about all the love we'd gained and lost, highlighting the hidden blessings learned along the way. It was exactly what I needed to stop taking everything so seriously and stay in the gratitude of the gorgeous Bali life that I was now living. We quickly became fast friends.

I was still moving through the motions of my life partially in shock while moving more into the awe of so many beautiful alignments that were happening. In a matter of months, I'd spun out of my corporate career, dodged an emotionally destructive relationship, and was now living on this idyllic island. I felt grateful and blessed to have had a lucrative corporate career that helped me shore up some savings.

> Now I was faced with waffling between the freedom to do whatever I wanted and working through the anxiety of having nothing to do.

I looked back at my time in Costa Rica and realized it had prepared me for this dramatic lifestyle change.

Inevitably, one thing I knew for sure was that creating something new always helped shift my mood. I loved building brands and creating products from scratch. My professional background was in marketing, so why not leverage this and start working on more of my products? Before I met Klaus, that was what I thought I'd be leaving my corporate job to do. I was optimistic that *now* was the perfect time to begin conceptualizing all I'd dreamed of creating and a most serendipitous time to pick up where I'd left off with the products I'd been designing. I had also finished my book on the wisdom I'd learned from flowers and was interested in getting it published and devising a launch plan.

In some ways, I was starting to soften, realizing that leaving for love might have been the only way I could have made the big jump out of corporate life. It was a traumatic way to do so, but perhaps everything was in Divine order. Now I had an opportunity unfolding in front of me to become an entrepreneur and run my own business. I'd dreamt of this for years, and it was finally coming true.

As a side hobby to my corporate job, I continued to work with the manufacturer of the flower bouquet photo albums. Since my original trip to Bali, I'd designed and produced several paper products, including flower affirmation cards, blessing tabs, and greeting cards, that included my flower photography. Upon moving to Singapore, I'd had production quantities shipped to my apartment, intending to sell them online in my spare time, although this never came to fruition because I traveled so often and my job was too demanding. Now the products were trapped in my shipping containers in Singapore.

Since I didn't have easy access to these products to sell them, I decided to pursue my passion for designing and creating jewelry. Within days, I'd finished my first draft of sketches and was looking for a silversmith to bring my designs to life. With the magic of Bali at my fingertips, things swirled quickly, and it was no surprise when a few silversmiths appeared out of nowhere.

My plan started to unfold as I was working diligently on my jewelry designs until my visa expired. Then I would head back to the US for some family time as the jewelry samples could be made while I was away. Upon my return to Bali, production quantities could start and the business could officially launch shortly after. I was in flow creating the jewelry collection names for my designs, and my memories from India were slowly fading. I'd had no communication with Klaus and was excited about my new business.

A month or so had gone by, and I was dog sitting Heidi's fur baby in her home while she was away for a few days. I had a printed copy of my *Flower Power 4 Pure Love* book sitting on her coffee table in the living room. I'd had two prototypes produced while I was living in India, and one still remained on Klaus's coffee table. I felt compelled to look through the copy in front of me and review the sentiments the flowers had given me. The beauty of Mother Nature always brought me happiness and swiftly shifted me into a blissful state.

This day, something unexpected happened. As I read through to the end of the book, I read the flap containing my photo and profile description. My author's biography said that I lived in India with my soul mate. This triggered a slew of memories, and I recalled that Klaus's birthday had taken place only a few days prior. Weirdly, I was inspired to write him a belated birthday greeting via email. It felt like a good opportunity to reach out with something positive to bring more closure to our turbulent relationship. Rather than being angry with him, I believed healing this wound would be helpful, especially since some time had passed. Being *A Course in Miracles* student, I knew the importance and power of forgiveness and desired to achieve a level of emotional neutrality with this relationship. Wouldn't it be a miraculous gift to be able to forgive myself and him for what felt like such betrayal and treason? Yes, of course this was a silly idea, and I knew this somewhere deep within my rational mind, but my emotions were still involved.

Upon sending my belated birthday greeting, a response popped up in my inbox almost instantly. Klaus was happy to hear from me and I could feel an intense energetic connection come through. He said that he'd been thinking of me moments earlier as he was looking at my flower book. The communication lines were open again, and I was once again naive to how he was manipulating our connection and what would happen in the days to follow.

We reconnected on the phone, and upon hearing his voice, my heart somehow opened. At the same time, I felt my thoughts become a little scattered and scrambled again. Why was I even talking to him? The magnetism between us came rushing back, although, oddly, it was not a feeling coming from a thought in my head. It was an experience taking place in my physical body. I was flooded with the same chemistry that connected us on our first night in Singapore, which quickly grew stronger and felt unstoppable. I couldn't think logically, almost like I was being hijacked somehow, yet knowingly walking in front of a bus. The next thing I knew, he had invited himself to see me in Bali. Yes, I knew this wasn't a good idea, but he said all the right things and wanted to talk it through. Perhaps he'd done the spiritual work necessary and was open to new perspectives and healings that could take place between us.

Time was ticking: my departure date to return to the US for a few months was fast approaching. So joining me in Bali, as he'd proposed, needed to happen imminently.

> I remember the "trance feeling" saying yes but knowing that no was the only answer that should be coming out of my mouth.

Why would I bring him to my sacred place, the island where I came to rebuild my life and remove myself from any memories that could trigger me? Leaving as abruptly as we did from the Andaman Islands and not speaking my truth left me empty. Somehow our connection was clouding my logic, yet again, as I stepped right back into his energy field. I kept holding the illusion that there were still lessons to be learned, and I hoped healing could occur.

Klaus arrived a few days later, and the moment I saw him at the airport, I knew, once again, exactly who he was by his devilish demeanor, the words he spoke, and the web he weaved, yet I could not seem to break free from the spell he had over me. My clarity quickly dissipated when he swept me off my feet, as he always did. He harnessed our sexual chemistry, and taking our connection to another level suddenly made his arrival magical. We had the most incredible time, as though we were on a honeymoon, going nowhere. The first few days made me feel like nothing bad had happened between us; I was ignoring the writing on the wall.

In the days before he departed from Bali, he suggested I stop in India on my way back to the US. Again, I knew the correct answer was no but heard myself say yes and booked my airline ticket to the US through India. Klaus insisted that we go on a holiday with his son and booked a backcountry tour for the three of us. Yes, this was insanity, but I was looking forward to spending some time with Peter.

Why didn't I want to accept the reality of who he was and keep him away? Perhaps my desire to hang on to the romantic love illusion? Or not wanting to admit I'd been so wrong because I thought I was so clear? I kept convincing myself that I could help the devil in disguise instead of moving on for my health and well-being. Plus, the hope of stopping the pain of intense heartbreak and shattered dreams appeared to weaken my logical mind. Although I wanted to step through the heartbreak, beyond the illusions, and into my power, Klaus would continue to over-power and overshadow my innate wisdom until I broke through the illusion of his spell. My innocence was due to a naivete of how darker energies worked, and I continued to allow him to swoop in like a hawk on my desire for sharing love and companionship. The profound lesson I kept missing was staying in my true power and not allowing someone else to take it.

Upon reflection, I began to understand that people really do tell you the truth of their character within the first five minutes. My intuition hadn't failed me; I'd pegged him perfectly when he first jumped off the yacht and into the kayak the day we met. Instead of trusting this, I allowed my lens of perception to be clouded by what Klaus wanted me to see, which overshadowed my inner knowing. The issue was that I didn't listen to my intuition; instead I fell quickly for the illusion of a life partner I so desired.

Once I'd fallen for all his lines the first night, my mind kicked in mag- ically, making him into what I wanted in a partner, and I believed he was capable of filling this role. I was keen to call it a spiritual alignment of souls, thinking our relationship was Divinely guided. Now it was clear that what had happened between us had nothing to do with love. I needed to finally let this dream go and see reality. Just when I thought I'd gotten all the lessons, I found there were still significant insights yet to be learned.

Before heading to India, I had a few days on a stopover in Singapore and scheduled a lunch with my friend Sarah, who owned the villa I'd been renting. We chatted away, updating each other about our lives, and I shared how I felt emotionally scrambled by Klaus. Sarah was known as a talented intuitive, and I hoped she might have some insights for me.

"What do you think is going on?" I asked.

With a concerned look, she said, "You're being psychically attacked by Klaus."

At that moment, the hustle and bustle of everyone dining around us started to move in slow motion for me. "What? What does that mean?" I had never heard of such a thing, and it sounded scary. At the same time, the statement resonated within me and I was curious if some of the eeriness I'd been experiencing was about to be explained.

Sarah proceeded to share that when someone psychically attacks you, they are attaching to your ethereal life cord. She further explained that those attacks can feel like someone is scrambling your energy field and violating your thoughts and emotions. She said it could also be described in the realms of black magic, but either way, your energy system is hacked by someone with bad intentions to manipulate a situation. Our connecting through my book at Heidi's now seemed intentional on Klaus's part. Pondering with Sarah whether this was possible, she quickly exclaimed, "Of course!"

I'd thought I was at a place in my spiritual journey where I had a grasp on the realms of light and dark, but this was getting bizarre. Was the Universe offering me an opportunity to understand darkness more profoundly? It was starting to make sense as we don't know the light without the contrast of darkness, similar to the balance of yin and yang.

The concept of being psychically attacked rocked me. It felt like something had taken me over or possessed me when I was in contact with Klaus. This new revelation gave me tremendous insights into how others can impact my energy systems and perform magical spells without me even knowing. I didn't want to put too much energy into these ideas, but my friend continued to warn me of the dangers I could be in while under his energetic attacks. She shared that most people aren't consciously aware of others hacking into or attaching to them. This was all new to me and sounded a little like playing with voodoo dolls, which freaked me out further.

Knowing I wasn't his first victim, I should have recognized that Klaus was very conscious of what he was doing all along. Up until that day, I did not want to believe he was nefarious with bad intentions.

> In many cases, I defended him, as most enablers do in
> relationships, and saw him as a wounded person I could
> help heal.

The problem was that he had no desire to heal anything. All the while, I continued to fall back into his trap. He knew how naive I was and enjoyed the game he played. I finally understood that the fear rising within me needed to be tackled head-on, or there would be serious consequences to my life.

I felt numb as Sarah told me about what I needed to do to protect myself. She advised me to delete his contact information and all photographs of him, change all my passwords, and light a candle through the night for protection. The list went on as I feverishly took notes. Everything seemed extreme, but she was adamant that I should be smart about this and not blow it off. The sooner I did these rituals, the faster I'd disconnect, release myself, and start the deeper healing process. This resonated, as I couldn't quite pinpoint how or why I kept letting him back into my life when I had the clarity of his character. I kept chalking it up to a broken heart, but she pressed on about the urgency of me taking this situation seriously.

After our lunch, I read more about Etheric cords and realized it's a natural occurrence to attach cords with people we're close to. Children and parents are always entwined on one another's cords unknowingly. I could see how a child comes in as an innocent bundle of love, only to learn thought constructs and beliefs through their family system and external world reflections. This helps them fit into the collective conscious and societal programming. Seeing the world through love, they do what they can to help reduce a parent's emotional suffering, intending to assist on a soul level. Unknowingly, they often take on the wounds of their parents. This made me wonder what I might be carrying on behalf of my parents' wounds and programming. How was this impacting my life? Interested in finding out, my focus remained on protecting my Etheric life cord from Klaus and learning how to prevent this from happening again. I took Sarah's guidance to heart that day: I bought a candle and was ready to do whatever was necessary to stop the insanity and break away from Klaus.

Upon leaving Sarah, I notified Klaus that I would not be seeing him nor doing the backcountry tour with him. I still had to fly through India, as I couldn't eliminate the stopover without losing my entire ticket back to the US. Luckily, I was able to reduce my layover to two nights and didn't share any information with Klaus.

It felt odd and creepy to be landing back in India. I'd left in trauma and was now returning with more trauma. Could this situation get any worse? I arrived at the hotel and checked into a lovely room that provided a safe cocoon to await my departure in a few days. As I settled in, the phone in my room rang. It was Klaus. "I see you've arrived," he said. My entire body went numb, and then adrenaline shot through my system.

Klaus was in the lobby with his son and requested that I come down, saying, "I'm excited to see you." Then he put Peter on the phone, who said in a sweet voice, "I want to see you too." I started shaking slightly, wondering what to do. He'd tracked me down again, just like in the Andaman Islands. Did he know my room number too? Knowing how forward the Indian staff can be when pressed for information, I shouldn't have been surprised that he found me. I decided to go downstairs and face him head-on. My heart was also breaking knowing that Peter was waiting for me, and I didn't want to disappoint him.

As I walked up to them in the lobby, my heart was beating out of my chest. I would no longer believe the stories he'd weave, knowing that anything he said would be to manipulate me. I immediately hugged Peter and smiled cordially at Klaus, trying to remain calm and act as though everything was okay. As we made small talk, my focus remained on Peter, as I hoped for updates about his life. An hour or so went by before I announced I'd need to rest. I waited in my room for a little while and then requested that the front desk switch me to a different room. I also demanded that my personal information not be shared with anyone. I couldn't bear to think that Klaus might come knocking in the night.

Once I was in my new room, a hot bath was calling my name. I also lit a candle, as Sarah had insisted. Another technique she shared to energetically protect oneself was to imagine being surrounded in a purple bubble filled with bright white light. I'd learned from the Balinese a belief in ceremonies, as they performed them daily to protect against lower energies. It was time to protect myself, and this ritual made me feel better, even if it might only be a placebo.

The next morning, I headed to the amenities floor to swim in the pool, exercise, read, and write to keep myself distracted and calm. Afterward, I popped into the hotel restaurant, and as I peered across the room, my legs went weak. There Klaus was, with a group of people from the school having a meeting. Of all the places he could have gone, he came back to *my* hotel. He looked my way and smirked as I glanced away. Swiftly filling my plate from the buffet, I found a table tucked away on the other side of the restaurant. Upset, I quickly ate my food and went back to my room. Later that day, I asked to change my room again.

My ride to the airport couldn't come fast enough. Crushed by life's circumstances, I eagerly boarded the plane. I was more than ready to return to the safety and security of my parents' home in the prairies of North Dakota. It seemed imperative to get back to my roots, to a place where I would be taken in, loved unconditionally, and protected in all ways. All the crazy energy and untrustworthy people in the world would soon be a distant memory, or so I hoped.

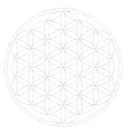

CHAPTER 13

Healing in the USA

I couldn't wait to see the US flag again as I crossed through the customs area. It jolted my memory back to my return from Costa Rica. At that time, I was relieved to be out of the drug and crime threats that plagued the peninsula. I never dreamt I'd encounter situations more dangerous. But here I was, escaping the darkest energies that only lurk in the underbellies of places I never thought I'd be. Although different circumstances, I was experiencing a similar joy of being on the soil of America.

My parents were thrilled to see me. They didn't know everything I'd been through, as I felt it was better to spare them the details. What good would it do to freak them out by telling them all I was learning? I was barely ready to receive such information regarding my own experiences and didn't expect them to make sense of all this craziness. It also seemed unfathomable that they would be receptive to the concept of psychic attacks, which I couldn't explain at the time since I was just learning it myself. I certainly didn't want them to think I was going off the deep end. But was I?

Keeping in mind the protection modalities that Sarah had recommended, I asked both of my parents to delete all the photos they had of Klaus. It should have been easy for me to wipe this character out of my life, but the wounds were still fresh and the emotions raw, and it felt impossible to stop feeling the connection to Klaus, which was crazy. Our unhealthy bond, connection, and spell needed to be broken.

I was ready to move on from it all, but I felt that there was so much left to process to be able to successfully disconnect. There were times when I felt numb and hopeless, wishing the memories and emotions of Klaus would miraculously go away. But that would mean I'd missed the lesson and would most likely have to repeat it.

> My soul was calling me to dig deep into why I'd called
> Klaus into my life, along with how to eliminate him.

I continued to practice the mental exercises intended to delete his energetic imprint from my field. My parents complied by erasing the photos they had and not asking many questions. I think they understood that their only job was to love me and let me heal, and they trusted they'd learn all they needed to know in time.

My college friend Jane had since moved from the East Coast back to North Dakota, upon the encouragement of her New Yorker husband, and was living an hour away from my parents. We were both excited to have a sleepover and spend some sacred girlfriend time together. As we sat on her sofa, I shared my stories and quickly fell to tears describing all I'd been through. Hearing myself tell these tales brought the details alive, and the trauma continued as I sat shaking my head in shame of my naivete.

Being a gifted psychic medium, Jane wasn't going to step into my pity party without first diving into reading Klaus's energy field. At that moment, we realized that we'd not been in touch during my courtship with Klaus. It seemed odd that I hadn't reached out to her at any point to inquire about her read on this new love interest I'd professed to marry. I reflected on how Klaus had a way of distracting me from communicating with my inner circle of support. He was always with me, and I didn't have much free time, or me time, to talk with others. He had kept everything at a fast pace and in a whirlwind, moving everything forward to solidify my investment in his business.

It didn't take long for Jane to adamantly confirm that Klaus's character was "super dark." She elaborated, saying, "Klaus is the darkest character I've ever encountered on the earth plane." While I trusted her experience with spirits on the other side, I wasn't anticipating her ability to see things so clearly with humans here on the earth. This made my head spin, as it seemed like my worst nightmare.

Not knowing the implications of what this could mean, I pressed for more information. Jane said that in her experience, she would at least see a crack of light when encountering dark souls. In viewing Klaus, she saw nothing but darkness. She added, "He's not working alone." Now, this kind of language terrified me. My tears dried up fast, as the intensity of what she'd said startled me. I inquired further: "Who is he working with? What does this mean?" I'd never liked the unknowns on the other side, and this "darkness" discussion was making me very uncomfortable. I had no clue what to do about it except light a candle and imagine a purple bubble with bright light. What the f—k?

As I lay in bed that night, it seemed impossible to fall asleep, and I doubted whether my mind went offline at all that night. The haunting fear keeping me awake at night was never about who would come through the door; it was always about what might appear in my room. Now my dearest friend has told me that I'm in some type of spiritual warfare? All of this was so much more than I was ready to handle; I still felt emotionally fragile. Healing a broken heart seemed to pale in comparison to the dark spiritual lessons being presented.

Luckily, Jane had some additional techniques and said she'd ask my guides on the other side to assist. Since I'd seen the five people in my living room years prior, I believed this was possible and was happy to have any "light beings" by my side. It became painfully clear that I was a novice at all of this and needed some help.

I returned home to my parents and rejuvenated myself as best I could while soaking up love and support. I'd soon be off to visit my brother's family, Axel, and dear friends in California. Then I'd have a stopover of a few days in New York to see Jessica's family (including her little boy, who's my godson), Katarina in New Jersey, and a few other friends before exiting the US.

Upon my arrival in Southern California, Axel's place was my first stop. Almost as though no time had passed, I continued the storylines from where I'd left off in India, the day I locked myself in Peter's room. The only difference was that I wasn't trying to sugarcoat the stories as I had then, when coping with the fear and dismay I was enduring. I hoped that Axel could help further disintegrate the entanglement bond that allowed Klaus's magic to scramble me.

Although I trusted Axel explicitly, I found it impossible to share with him that I'd contracted herpes from Klaus. I knew this information would have been helpful for Axel to assist me release the trauma, but I couldn't talk about it. I decided early on that it was the card I was dealt in life, and there were only a few friends I'd ever tell. When it came to potential love interests, I'd hold back any intimacy until I could trust them with such sensitive information. I dumped every other detail about Klaus onto Axel.

I was taken aback when Axel said, "He's a sociopathic narcissist."

"What?" I couldn't grasp the actual meaning of the titles, and I asked for more explanation.

> "For a sociopath, people are toys. For a narcissist, people are trash. You were both to him."

Then Axel continued to describe Klaus's character perfectly as he overlaid the definitions precisely on his behavior.

I often forgot about Axel's background as a social worker, and this wasn't his first time dealing with these types of characters. I couldn't help but ask why I would create these dramatic storylines in my own movie. Axel ever so gently reminded me, "Life is but a dream," a concept that I knew in my mind but wondered if I'd ever really grasp. *A Course in Miracles*, along with my quantum physics books, provided my first glimpses of the idea that this is all an illusion and the scientific community describes it as a Holographic Universe. Even when I didn't completely understand these teachings, I could feel Axel's unconditional love and encouragement for me to one day fully embody them. I was all ears, as my perspective was reframed and intense lessons of self-love, boundaries, and discernment began to sink in, humbling me to a whole new level.

I had no problem surrendering on the massage table as Axel worked his magic and performed his perfected angel wing massage on me. The miracles took place one right after the other as we worked through the trauma, deleting "files" that were no longer serving me, and relieving me from these storylines. It was amazing to experience how two hours with one of the most talented *Course in Miracles* masters could help dissolve the spell of the energies consuming me over the last year. I wished everything could be gone from my ego-mind forever, but there was still more work for me to do. Unfortunately, the external environment often assists the mind in bringing back memories, thoughts, and ideas with persistence. Being diligent about keeping these storylines of the mind unraveled requires dedication. My time in California was complete, and it was time to visit my brother's family. Seeing my nephews was always one of the highlights of every trip back to the states. I loved spending time with my three nephews in these precious pre-teen years.

While in transit to the East Coast, I scheduled an appointment with my trusted hypnotherapist, Deb. She'd assisted me in several sessions years prior while I was living in New Jersey, and I needed her help now more than ever. I'd had profound encounters in previous sessions accessing information from the depths of my subconscious mind along with experiencing Angelic realms. Feeling intrigued to see my situation from a higher perspective of consciousness, I couldn't wait to arrive.

When I walked through Deb's door, I felt like I was seeing a long-lost sister. Her loving energy pulled me in, and she wanted to hear all about what was going on in my life. I didn't want to spend the entire session talking about the details of my story, as I'd been sharing ad nauseam with so many others. I did my best to summarize my situation and then stated what I hoped to gain from the session. It came down to a few crucial factors: safety and serenity.

Although Klaus's "spell" seemed to have been lifted by the many modalities and healers that had helped me, my mind appeared to be back online stronger than ever. My thoughts were running in circuitous loops and draining me. I still didn't understand exactly what I needed to do or shift to protect myself from experiencing the drain from my mind and the active psychic attacks still looming.

As I lay on Deb's table, relaxing into the hypnotherapy session, I felt the presence of several beings in the room. This was happening more frequently as I became comfortable letting go of what I thought was normal. After they'd appear in sessions or situations, I'd often ask if it was my imagination or if I was making stuff up. But then circumstances would take place in the physical plane, seemingly connecting the energies of paranormal experiences to something relevant here in my body on the earth. I didn't want to discount or ignore these entities and welcomed them, wanting their guidance.

Deb asked me to close my eyes and visualize a door, which quickly appeared. She softly requested that I open it and walk through. Immediately, images were vividly emerging as I could see everything in the room. It was a huge, bright white space set up for a banquet. I could see every detail, down to the napkins, water glasses, and sun rays that were beaming through the paned windows up high, near the ceiling. My senses were activated, and the scene felt graphic and real, although I had no idea what I was doing there. Then Deb asked, "What are you wearing?" Looking down, I saw a red dress, Betty Boop–style, with a ballooned bottom. This seemed odd, as I'm not a fan, nor had I seen anything recently that reminded me of this character.

When Deb asked, "What are you in this room for?" enthusiastically I stated, "I'm here to speak to a group of people." I sensed that the information I was about to deliver was in the sweet spot of my calling or purpose here on earth. While I was still in hypnosis, she asked me, "Do you see Klaus in the room?" I looked around with wonderment and said, "No, I don't see him anywhere." It was such a lovely banquet hall with an enchanting buzz in the air, until Deb said, "He's there. Wait a moment." I felt an innocence about myself and thought perhaps I'd see him show up in a suit and tie, wanting to be by my side. Suddenly, I felt his energy come into the room. It startled me as dark smoke appeared, swirling in an ominous stream toward me. Fear ran through my body as though a poltergeist was coming for me. Because he wasn't in the form of a body, I had no idea and couldn't imagine what would happen next.

Moments later, I softly screamed with trepidation, "He's behind me!" He was now in human form, wearing a dark cape, and my heart raced. I viewed the scene from above but at the same time felt myself standing in my body in front of him. It was like watching a movie, fully awake and aware that I was lying on Deb's table, while at the same time seeing this entire scene play out from two different perspectives, as though I was asleep and dreaming. The characters felt real, and the fear was palpable. Klaus's right arm came up around the front side of my neck. There was a knife in his hand, which prompted me to say out loud in desperation, "He's going to slit my throat!" as if to silence me. Deb then softly said, "Okay, thank you; you don't need to experience the rest of the scene." She then guided me out of the room and explained that we don't need to relive any traumatic experiences—thankfully, as this was a relief to say the least. Fortunately, I was still able to understand the dynamics and began reflecting on the lessons from the scene.

The messages being relayed were bringing great clarity.

> I'd called in this relationship as an opportunity for me to see how others try to take us off our paths to living our purpose.

This lesson was incredibly valuable, as it provided a catalyst for me to know and experience the many characters and archetypes we ask others to play for us. Seeing this scene brought me insights regarding the internal blocks we build when we hold on to traumatic memories. Deb re-emphasized the importance of clearing memories through healing, not stuffing them into the subconscious. Uncovering and letting go of the story entirely blossomed the freedom that allowed me to see things differently, stop the suffering, make new choices, and move on.

Sharing this experience didn't seem necessary, as it was irrelevant whether others would believe anything that happened in this session. Strength began to build within me, moving me out of the fear and trauma of the relationship. But our session wasn't done yet; we shifted into another scene.

Deb shared that she felt the presence of Archangel Michael in the room. I believed in angels, had read a lot about them, and had an archangel card deck that I used almost daily to receive messages. But I'd never considered that one of them might show up in a session, at my service. I could feel his presence as Deb described him placing a mosaic of tiny little mirrors all over my back. It was as though I was floating off the bed to give him access to different parts of my body. I could visualize the pieces coming together, almost like a shield. As I wondered why he was doing this, Deb began to explain that he was helping me protect my light, which is sought after by darker spirits.

The work Archangel Michael did was fascinating as it appeared meticulously detailed. Or was the power of suggestion leading me to believe there was an entity coming to help me? Did it matter what was perceived as "real" and what was not? I decided to accept the journey and receive any blessings or healings necessary to keep me moving forward.

I was learning the hard way that all relationships provide us with a mirror to see ourselves in a different light. Klaus was knowingly and eloquently blinding me with my own loving light by reflecting it back to me. Meanwhile, behind the mirror, he maneuvered around me to get exactly what he wanted. He knew all along how vulnerable I was to his manipulation. This is how sociopaths and narcissists work. They have no problem extracting your energy to bolster theirs or breaking you down and scrambling your sanity so they can remain strong and in control. The key to remember was that I'd allowed Klaus to do this. As the entanglement dissipated, I could see he'd played an essential role in my awakening journey and soul evolution.

Turning onto my side and preparing to sit up after the session, I felt incredible. A rush of energy cleansed through me. I'd allowed myself to receive blessings from another dimension and sat relishing it. The dynamics of the victim and perpetrator archetypes I'd been studying about were also becoming apparent. Now I had the knowledge and insights to move forward, knowing how to navigate this dynamic to protect and preserve myself. I was grateful to have learned the lesson now instead of later in life, when a destructive relationship could have taken down me or my business, dramatically derailing my life.

I spent the remaining days in New York City with Jessica. I needed the love of a childhood friend who knew everything about me and loved all aspects of me. As we sat at a coffee shop, I happened to glance at my emails and saw that Peter's mother was reaching out to me. This prompted me to share with Jessica that she'd called me right after my departure from India, concerned and inquiring about her son's safety. With great empathy, Jessica requested that we pause our conversation and that I read it immediately. Her email was filled with questions she hoped I could answer regarding Peter.

I felt petrified to share anything with Peter's mother. Plus, I didn't know her very well and wasn't sure how she would use any information shared. Recognizing how destructive Klaus was, I was determined not to give him any reason to come after me. I knew she remained desperate to learn more, as I'd kept her in close contact with Peter while I lived with him, which Klaus was unwilling to do. In her email, she more urgently wanted to know if I thought her son was in trouble being alone with Klaus. I desperately wanted to be disconnected and not get in the middle of any of this for fear it could backfire on me, especially after all the work I'd been doing to disconnect from Klaus's energy field.

As I shared the story with Jessica, she looked at me with the eyes of a mother and said, "She needs to know; please share with her." So I wrote to her and conveyed all that I'd witnessed—the name-calling and the verbal abuse—and acknowledged I didn't think Peter was safe. I asked her to keep our conversations private and prayed that what I told her was helpful and would remain confidential. Suspecting he'd been emotionally traumatized for years, I hoped Peter would make it through.

After being back in the States, sharing love in friendship, telling tales, and feeling supported, I was keen to head back to Bali. I felt more balanced, more alert, and ready to face the challenges and opportunities of the unknowns building my business in Bali. As I boarded the plane out of New York City, my heart was full, and I was excited to create a new, more permanent home upon my return.

CHAPTER 14

Creativity Unleashed

BEFORE MY DEPARTURE to the US, I'd given detailed instructions to the manager overseeing the silversmiths crafting my jewelry and was optimistic they would hit the mark. This would mean we'd be off and running to production upon my return to Bali. Soon after the collections could be launched, but it all depended on the samples, which I was excited to see.

I was back in my friend's villa for a few weeks before I'd have to find something more permanent. I excitedly cleared off my large dining room table so the manager of the silversmith had room to lay out all the jewelry for review. He set each piece down, and my heart sank as I saw the jewelry being revealed. The pieces were nothing like the sketches and drawings I had provided. They were the ugliest items I'd ever seen! I was stunned and asked why they made everything drastically different from the sketches I'd provided. He responded, "The artist wanted to make it better, so they made changes." Better? All I could think was that my time away in the US was wasted, and I'd need to start over.

When one door closes, another one opens, and my new silversmith, Kadek, walked right in. She spoke good English, had worked with a Canadian silver designer, understood Western quality standards, and seemed to have a passion for business. I felt we would work well together and looked forward to her being a key member of the team. To further enhance our relationship, I took Kadek on a tour of the manufacturing facility of John Hardy, an internationally famous jewelry brand. I wanted to provide an inspiring vision for my dreams to build a successful jewelry company and wanted her to share in the experience.

What I wasn't accounting for was how completely different our perspectives were. I was coming off an executive-level corporate job in big pharma, and she was a Balinese woman who'd never been off the island. The disparity was massive, although I believed I could provide her an excellent opportunity to oversee production and help establish a manufacturing facility on the island. First, we needed to recreate the collection pieces and find more silversmiths who wanted to work on fine detail. Kadek and I worked for months finding a select team of people with the right skill sets and techniques to make the designs uniquely handcrafted.

I was sensitive to wanting to build a strong foundation for our relationship, as she'd mentioned that the Canadian designer had previously burned her. She never shared much detail, but I understood that she felt ripped off in the business relationship. Not for a moment did I think she had bad intentions or saw our relationship to be only about money.

When Kadek offered to introduce me to her family and take me to the priestess in her village, I thought this would provide the perfect opportunity to learn more about her and build trust between us. She picked me up on her motorbike, and we arrived at her parents' home in the afternoon. We appeared to mutually enjoy each other's company as we sipped tea and ate some fruit. I anticipated a brief stopover, and I was under the impression that we were going to see the priestess in the afternoon. However, Kadek kept delaying our departure, and it wasn't until nightfall that we made our way over to the temple. Having never met a high priestess, I was intrigued to meet her and learn about the Balinese Hindu culture.

Upon entering the priestess's family compound, another five or six Balinese from her village were sitting on a raised platform they used for small gatherings. The priestess was actively creating energy sketches of people as we took a seat next to the others. Drawing stick bodies, comparable to hangman figures, she'd begin moving the pencil quickly from left to right, starting from the top of the head. Each sketch had different areas of the body displaying higher concentrations of lines. Kadek explained that this was how she identified areas of trapped energy needing to be released.

Interestingly, on mine, the energy lines were thick on the head and across my abdomen. Both areas made sense to me. Being in my head, thinking a lot was one of my primary character traits. I'd also suffered intestinal issues since having parasites from my first trip to Bali in 2009. Although I didn't realize it at the time, this technique gave the priestess permission to access my energetic template.

After we left the communal area and entered the temple—which is always at the northeast corner of the compound—an eeriness came through as I stepped through the gates. I wasn't sure what it was, but probably the darkness along with the Balinese statues made it look a bit spooky in the moonlight. I tried to not worry about it, and my thoughts were interrupted by the priestess motioning me to kneel on the ground below her, as Kadek had done prior. The priestess sprinkled and poured sacred coconut water over me as she chanted. Even though I wondered what was going on, I didn't ask any questions, thinking it might be culturally inappropriate. A frightening feeling came through me in the next few minutes, which made me feel uneasy. Unexpectedly I began to chant phrases from *A Course in Miracles* in my head, which wasn't typical of me. Something was happening, and it didn't feel good.

As I got up, I could barely move and felt completely drained of my energy. It was still early evening when I discreetly requested that Kadek take me directly home instead of visiting her sister. It had been a long day, not to mention unsettling. The idea of black magic didn't cross my mind, although maybe it should have. I viewed the Balinese as having loving intentions and thought the lessons of the dark energies were behind me.

I had a good night's sleep despite my uneasy feelings the night before. My focus quickly shifted to finding a place to call home, as I'd need to move out of Sarah's villa soon. When I started my search, Spirit whispered in my ear, saying, "Go to Ubud." I thought, *Ubud? Why would I go there?* It wasn't near the ocean, and I'd only been there one other time, but it didn't seem like my kind of place. It had a super laid-back hippie vibe, which didn't resonate with me; I was on a spiritual journey with my soul quickening. However, removing myself from the memories of Klaus in my beach town would be good.

While planning this move, my relationship with Kadek unexpectedly deteriorated before my eyes. Our feelings around building the jewelry business were mutual, but something incredibly odd was happening between us. She took some nasty turns, refusing to give me some completed jewelry pieces I'd paid for. Then she refused to do any work unless I gave her advance payment in full for high production quantities, even though we didn't have our samples finalized. As her demands for money became increasingly unreasonable, it became apparent we'd need to part ways.

The situation was disappointing and upsetting, and I was confused about how this falling out had happened. It seemed unbelievable that there was no chance of recovering our relationship. Our cultural differences and her wounds from the previous Canadian designer seemed to be driving a huge wedge between us. I still wasn't connecting any of the dots about black magic, the high priestess funny business, and Kadek's financial demands, which would all come to light later.

I realized that I was missing something, and it appeared to be the result of a communication breakdown. My natural default is to see the good in people, which was now a detriment, as I was missing Kadek's true character. I was being naive, not realizing she saw me as an American bank account. Losing Kadek also meant starting over with my collections yet again. I wanted to find the silver lining—yes, pun intended—and I hoped the Universe would soon connect me with a more sophisticated and trustworthy jeweler.

Hearing about my frustration, a Balinese friend introduced me to a silversmith he trusted. His name was Putu, and I'll never forget the day we met. He was so overjoyed to have me in his family compound that his eyes twinkled as I showed him the samples of my jewelry line. He'd recently come back to Bali after working as crew on an international cruise ship for the last six months. He had two young boys and wanted to be home with his family. His English was proficient, and his energy and attitude were very different from Kadek's. Miraculously, it was only days before he got started, and he quickly produced samples. We were on our way to production for the jewelry line in no time. I couldn't have been more grateful.

It seemed that now more than ever, Ubud was calling, as I would be close to my new silversmith and could work with him without a long commute. I packed all my things, hired a driver, and headed to the middle of the jungle and rice fields near Ubud to find a place to live. I found an economical hotel to stay at for a week while I looked for a long-term villa to rent. The following day, the owner of the hotel I stayed at was eager to drive me around to look for rental properties. Within a week, the perfect villa appeared in the middle of the rice fields. It was encapsulated by Mother Nature's magic on all sides, was nearly new, and had a small swimming pool with a spectacular view of the nearby volcanoes.

The challenge was that you could only arrive by motorbike since the trail leading in was about two feet wide. This required drivers to drop me at the road, and then I had to walk in about a quarter of a mile. Carrying luggage, groceries, or boxes along the dirt path wasn't always an easy task. Luckily my new friend, Wayan, who worked in the rice field next to me, would often come to the rescue by transporting items on his motorbike.

The villa was sparsely furnished, which was ideal, as I've always enjoyed finding all the perfect accessories and furniture for new spaces. The owner was adamant that I needed to sign a one-year lease and required the total amount to be paid up front. Yes, all twelve months before I moved in. I'd come to find out that this is the standard in Bali, as the full payment replaced a paper lease agreement. Wanting the villa, I made the one-year commitment and within a week was able to personalize the décor and make it my own home sweet home. It was the first time in my life that I'd had my very own private pool, and the views were to live for.

Remaining focused on my jewelry designs, I didn't become involved in the community or meet many people. Building the foundation for a sustainable business was my priority; I desired to replace my abundant income from my pharmaceutical career by thriving as an entrepreneur. My goal was to develop my jewelry line and sell it back in the US. Working on my designs, creating products, and living in flip-flops brought me immense joy and gratitude. I'd fallen into a slice of heaven.

Each jewelry collection had a different empowerment focus intended to help people achieve their desires and assist in "Pollinating the Planet with Love," and this guided my mission. Having Balinese artisans with good intentions was important, as each piece of jewelry was to be blessed and infused with the intention of love. I woke up each day with enthusiasm and passion for my new endeavor.

One day at a restaurant in town, I met an American woman named Chloe. She'd recently moved to Ubud with her nine-year-old daughter, Celia. We enjoyed each other's company, so we found ourselves getting together frequently. One day I shared with her the Flower Bouquet Photo Albums and other products I'd previously made in Bali. She was ecstatic about them and suggested I consider opening a retail shop in Ubud. I immediately responded no, as all the products were stuck in my storage unit in Singapore. The idea of opening a shop was intriguing, but this wasn't where I wanted to focus my time and energy. However, I reflected on my strong emotional response, which often meant there was more to investigate, and decided to keep an open mind about it.

Driving a motorbike or car in Bali, along with driving on the other side of the road, seemed too chaotic for me. Getting random rides from drivers wasn't of great interest either, so I decided to hire a full-time driver. This was something many expats do because it's not that expensive. Sometimes we'd go by motorbike and sometimes in a car. One day Celia came with me to Ubud Fitness, where I did my daily workout. Afterward, she requested that we take the scenic route home down Monkey Forest Road.

Celia had overheard her mother's suggestion a few days earlier that I should open a retail store, so when she spotted an empty storefront, she asked my driver, Jimmy, to stop the car. She was a savvy little girl, but this surprised me. Jimmy was quick to respond and pulled over to the side of the road. As he motioned for me to go, I asked him to inquire about rent, as I thought he'd get the best price, and it would give me a gauge for prices in the future. Happy to do so, he walked across the street and quickly returned, saying, "You'll have to negotiate the price; it's perfect for you." I didn't know what was perfect for me, so how did he? Hand in hand with my young friend, I went to tour the inside.

As we walked in I thought, *This is perfect,* and felt goosebumps all over. It needed some serious renovation work, but it was an incredible space with floor-to-ceiling windows, white floor tiles, and a high ceiling. I spoke to the owners as I sat sipping a coffee out of courtesy and was instantly intrigued about this opportunity. How funny was this? I wasn't planning to open a shop, but upon contemplating the idea, the perfect location showed up days later. Having a child by my side made the experience more fascinating, as she cheered me on while negotiating the lease price. Both Jimmy and Celia were telling me, "Just do it!" I laughed, saying, "I have to go home, take a cold shower, and think about it." The flow of my life felt incredible.

I knew in my bones that there wasn't anything to think about.

> Contemplating would only conjure up fears, taking me
> out of my flow state.

They wanted a five-year commitment, which I wasn't ready for, although I was confident we could come to some agreement. Compared to retail rents in the Western world, the prices were very reasonable, and the numbers to make a profit seemed achievable.

The next day, I paid a deposit and began to do a deeper dive into all the logistics of opening a shop. I soon learned that it wasn't easy: it required designing the layout and storefront, creating a proper Indonesian company, obtaining a sales permit, and applying for a work visa so I could work in the store. I knew momentum was with me in those moments, as I became unexpectedly ready for this adventure.

The reasons why Spirit had nudged me to move to Ubud seemed to be multifaceted. Many things were happening off the grid of *my* plan: opening a shop, living in the rice fields, and of course, the anticipation of partaking in many healing modalities. The word *Ubud* originates from the Balinese word for medicine and the town has been known as a mystical epicenter on the planet. All the Western expats were modernized hippies on spiritual steroids, and tourists who were coming to Ubud for three days or more were almost guaranteed to have some type of out-of-the-norm spiritual experience. It wasn't uncommon to walk down the street and receive an invitation to a ceremony, healing modality, or yoga class. All were elements of the magical mix that aligned perfectly for my products to have a storefront on Monkey Forest Road.

I spent the next three months preparing the shop, as my lease would start promptly upon the government issuing the sales permit. Jimmy and I drove around the island to search for manufacturers to build display cases, create more products, and completely renovate the store. In 2013, there were no options to buy off-the-shelf fixtures, so designing my own required a lot of time and effort in order to reach the level of quality necessary to achieve my vision for the store.

Another "not part of my plan" moment was when Heidi called, informing me she'd rescued a dog near the beach. Heidi already had a dog and couldn't have another one in her house. I can still hear her voice saying, "She's an old soul, and you need to be her mommy." Mommy? I didn't have a desire at this point to be anyone's mommy. It was the farthest thing from my mind, as I was gone most days, and the timing wasn't right with my store and products in development mode.

I also didn't know how long I'd be living on the island of Bali and if adopting a dog was the right thing to do. Heidi persisted and explained that the tiny puppy had been hit by a car or motorbike. Fortunately, she'd been checked out at the vet and didn't have any broken bones. My response was, "Are you serious?!" while rolling my eyes. She ignored my resistance and said, "Just come have a look," and I agreed.

My friend Tara's daughter, from Australia, was visiting me in Bali at the time and had brought one of her friends. Both in their early twenties and animal lovers, they were eager to go along. Celia was also keen to go check out this puppy with me. As the four of us ventured down to Heidi's house, about an hour's drive, I overheard the girls whisper amongst themselves, "She doesn't realize she's bringing home a dog today." And I didn't; I was in denial that this was actually happening.

The tiny puppy was sitting on a round bohemian-style pillow trembling as she saw us all walk in. We stared at her, and the oohs and aahs of love came pouring out of us uncontrollably. Jimmy thought we were all crazy, as he saw these abandoned puppies by the side of the road all the time. I walked closer, took one look in her eyes, and instantly fell in love. Heidi was right; she was destined to be mine. Her old soul came shining through her big, sad eyes as she gazed at me in surrender with a dash of apprehension. You could tell she was done running and wanted to be found. Celia knelt next to her and said, "You should name her Lily," and I replied, "You're right!" Being a flower whisperer, this name immediately resonated and felt perfect for her personality, which we barely even knew yet.

Her ear was bloody, and one of her paws was split open. She had several scabs on her side where her fur had been sliced off in the accident. Her light caramel-color coat was infested with mange, a skin disease caused by parasites, making her undercoat feel bumpy. Urgh! I'd already dealt with parasites of my own. I didn't need another exotic creature living in my skin or intestinal system, wreaking havoc. But there was no way I was leaving without her. I wrapped her in a towel to protect myself from the mange and carried her to the car.

All the girls were giggly, including me. I was slightly shocked, wondering how it was possible that I now owned a dog. As if someone had handed me a baby on the street, I hadn't had any time to prepare. We went directly to the pet store and bought all the supplies: the kennel, the bowls, the food, the harness, and the leash, to name a few. Jimmy was beside himself, shaking his head, when he saw all the pink things coming out of the store and into the van. He could see that this dog would live a great life and couldn't help breaking into a smile watching us all chatter away with excitement. The next day we paid a visit to the clinic to learn about vaccinations, treatments for her skin condition, and when to have her spayed. The last thing I needed was a litter of Lily's in my villa.

The distractions Lily provided kept me from getting some things done, but the overwhelming love she exuded made all the delays worth it.

> Then again, love catapults us, and she inspired me every
> day to keep going to prepare the store for opening.

She didn't like riding in the car, but she was small enough that she could fit comfortably on my lap with her legs all spread out, sleeping through most of the ride.

Eventually it became stressful to take her everywhere, and I needed to leave her home. Jimmy complained about having to dog sit during my appointments and didn't like her hair in his car. Leaving Lily in my bedroom wasn't an option; I was concerned she might scratch the wood or the walls if left home for long hours at a time. Jimmy advised me to let her stay out in the garden, but I was concerned that she would run away. He reassured me that Bali dogs don't run away. If you feed them, they know their only job is to protect the villa and its owner. After doing a lot of work trying to fence in my garden, I hesitantly let her stay outside on her own. Days later, I learned that there was no way to contain a wild Bali dog; she could easily jump the six-foot wall. It was as though she had springs in her feet. With the barriers around the garden useless, I had to let go and trust that she wouldn't run away.

Surprisingly, it took me a long time to allow myself to truly express my love for Lily. My fear that she might leave me pushed me to reflect on my fears of losing love. She had no intention of doing anything other than love me unconditionally every day. She created her own boundaries in the rice fields and didn't stray far from the villa, as she was serious about her job protecting our home. By day, she frolicked in the fields with other wild dogs, and by night, she snuggled in my room with me. One of the worst things she ever did was kill a farmer's chicken, which I had to pay for. A close second was when she ran through a rice field with a pack of dogs and ruined a portion of the crop. Neither expense set me back too far, and for the most part, there were no problems in our little house of heaven. She made every day brighter, and in record time the store was ready, despite the needs of my new fur baby.

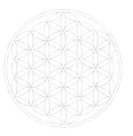

CHAPTER 15

Monkey Forest Road Brick and Mortar

MY SHOP WAS close to opening when Chloe told me about her unique healing experience with a "water purification" performed by a high priestess. I had no idea what this entailed and was intrigued when she invited me to join her and Celia. Wondering if it would evoke darker energies and possibly drain me like my previous experience with Kadek's village priestess, I had many questions. Chloe described being soaked by buckets of water poured over her head by the high priestess. Many questions circled in my mind, like *Could I drown?* I couldn't imagine how it was going to work.

Chloe reassured me that the high priestess had good intentions and I shouldn't worry. She was making a return visit with her daughter, which made me feel that it couldn't be too concerning. Chloe guided me on the proper costume to wear. This included a kebaya on the top, which consisted of an ornate long-sleeved cotton blouse that hangs down over your bottom. Underneath, a sarong is wrapped to cover you from the waist down to the ankles. This is tied off with a fabric sash worn tightly around the midsection and symbolically intended to cut off the energies of the lower chakras.

Upon arrival, we sat down near the high priestess's temple in time to see two Balinese priests step up, bowing with their hands in Namaste position. The priestess sat high on a platform, towering over them, and proceeded to dump buckets of water that had been blessed in the temple as she chanted continuously. It was a unique combination of singing and yodeling that sounded foreign yet magical at the same time. The high priestess was intense and appeared to have a clear focus as the two men began stomping their feet and yelling out with deep visceral outbursts. It scared me a little because I didn't know what was happening. It didn't seem pleasant, but neither malevolent.

Two Western women stepped up next. As the water poured down on them, one woman began sobbing uncontrollably. I didn't know her but felt her emotional pain in my chest. Tears welled up in me as I wondered what was happening for her. My curiosity and anxiety rose as I witnessed these emotional releases from people and wondered what might happen to me.

When it was my turn, I was uncomfortable yet eager to let go of anything coming up for purification. The high priestess prayed and then started splashing water and flowers on me. Then the waterfall began. She repeatedly said in a firm voice, "stomp your feet" and "let it out." I kept pushing the water back from my face as I stomped my bare feet on the small, pebbled ground below me. My arms started to go numb from my hands up to my elbows. This felt bizarre as I continued pushing my hair and the water back but couldn't feel them anymore. Then the fat on my inner thighs went numb. How was this possible? I'd never felt this area of my body singled out before. Now I was experiencing keen awareness of this specific part of my legs. I stomped harder, and she kept encouraging me to release with greater intensity. The bottoms of my feet hurt from pounding my feet on what felt like a hole in the ground. I wondered if I was going to break the bottom of my feet open and expected to see blood on the ground once I finished.

As the water slowed down, I had an out-of-body experience, and many areas of my body were numb, but I didn't cry or scream like the others. When I looked down, there was no hole in the ground, nor were my feet bleeding. I saw only small, smooth, rounded pebbles embedded in the paved area; they weren't jagged, as they'd felt during the stomping. The priestess asked me to step away, stretch, and reach for the sky.

As I backed away, tears involuntarily burst out of my eyes and rolled down my face. There were no thoughts attached, only emotions flowing out of my body like a well burst open. I felt incredible as I sat back and found myself feeling lighter and happier. I didn't know exactly what had happened, but a significant energetic shift had taken place. I wanted to intellectualize this experience but resigned myself to being okay not knowing. It became evident that many others were having miraculous experiences as well.

A few months passed, and the date for the store's grand opening was set. Conducting a ceremony to honor the spirits and the Gods before doing business was a Balinese tradition and requirement. I thought, *Who better than the high priestess to purify the shop?* At this point, I'd been to her several times and felt I'd built a relationship with her. Knowing that she rarely left her village and many people from her community relied on her, I wondered if she would be able to break away to do this for me. Would she want to? I figured it wouldn't hurt to ask. These ceremonies can be expensive, as they require donations to the high priestess and money to be given to the local *banjar*, something like a city council. A few weeks later, I inquired if she would be willing to do my ceremony, and she happily said yes!

On the ceremony day, the high priestess walked around chanting in the store, clearing energies, and adding blessings. I was thrilled to have her as a part of my grand opening, and she made me feel that her blessings would bode well for the business and all the customers who'd be walking through the doors. Moments after she left, we had our first sale.

Jimmy, my Balinese director, Budi, and the sales staff all made a big deal out of this, saying it symbolized good luck for future success!

In these early days, the inside of the store looked more like an art gallery than a retail shop, but I was super pleased to have it opened in record time. The only decorations on the walls were large flower photographs printed on canvas, which brightened the space. It would be several weeks before the custom cabinets arrived and the whole retail shopping experience was complete.

Having a storefront in Ubud brought people from all around the world.

> It seemed my mission of "Pollinating the Planet with Love" was finally coming to fruition through my high-vibe, Bali-blessed products.

It all felt so Divinely guided. I enjoyed creating new items and I was adamant that each product be blessed with the intention of love to empower others to manifest their desires. The name of the store was Blossom BLISS, and that's precisely what customers were intended to experience.

My Mini Mantra Word Bar necklaces—with several mantra options to choose from, based on the desires customers wanted to blossom—became one of the top-selling products. One of my favorite mantras was "I am pure love" and thought it would be a bestseller. Ironically, I found that many people said, "Oh, I'm not that," which surprised me. It showed me that people were seeing themselves as their faults, not the Divine nature that they really are. I also created Life Journey bracelets that contained charms serving as symbolic reminders to enhance peace, joy, and love. Two of my favorites were the airplane and angel wings, which were created to remind people of memories such as the joy of traveling, living happily on life's journey, and knowing angels are always with us to guide and protect.

Eager to train the Balinese staff on all the products, I bumped up against my first challenge. I quickly learned the Balinese didn't want to strike up a conversation with customers. They preferred to sit and wait for a customer to ask, "How much?" or say, "I'll buy this." I needed to be tenacious to overcome this challenge, and eventually the staff started having fun getting to know customers as they practiced.

After I got over this training hump, implementing sales incentives and contests for the staff seemed a logical next step. I created a fun poster to hang in the back room to track everyone's progress selling the product on the weekly promotion. While explaining the contest to one of the staff, she looked at me like I had two heads. She simply said to me, "It's all karma." Now it was clear to me that there would be no "selling" taking place; they believed it was up to the Gods. From that point on, I shared with the team that we had only one goal: customers should leave the store happier than they came in. If they were inspired to buy something, great. If not, there was no pressure.

One of my areas of strength and opportunity when embarking on my own business was seeing employee's potential. I enjoyed helping people grow and accelerate. The key was maneuvering through the cultural differences and finding what gave them joy. I was reminded that achieving one's potential needs to be an intrinsic desire from deep within. Over time, it became apparent that the staff had little interest in growing or developing new skills no matter what opportunities I provided. They lived in the now, and I needed to find a way to meet them where they were, not try to change them into Westernized staff—a massive challenge for me.

My friend Heidi warned me, based on her experience, that the staff would steal from me. She said the only thing I needed to do was to get comfortable with how much I was comfortable losing. I was adamant that this would not happen to me; I believed that if you treat people well and like family, they wouldn't steal. It didn't take long for me to learn that I was wrong.

Several months after opening, my visa agent requested that I not be in the store during the final stages of my visa approval. If the immigration officials caught me "working" without my paperwork, it was a severe offense, and I could be heavily fined and/or deported. I took her advice seriously and didn't go into the shop, trusting that the staff could carry on without me. A friend of mine was visiting from Europe, which allowed me to devote my time to sightseeing instead of being in the store.

One day my guest and I decided to tour the Monkey Forest Sanctuary. Knowing that the monkeys could be very naughty, it was best not to have bags, hats, water bottles, or any loose items. Since the store was a block away from the sanctuary, we went to drop our bags in the back room. Upon our return around 5:30 p.m., several customers were in the store. The only staff member working quickly said she needed to leave, as her shift was over. Since it was evening, I let her go home and thought I'd promptly finish with the customers, lock up, and exit the store. I suggested that my friend have a drink next door, implying I'd be over soon to join him. As I walked to lock the front door, a motorbike pulled up, and a Balinese man walked in briskly before I could close the door. I knew he wasn't a customer and had a sinking feeling in my gut. My legs went numb as he pulled out his immigration badge and asked for my passport.

Someone must have alerted him that I was in the shop in those fifteen minutes. I remembered Heidi saying, "Don't ever give them your passport, if possible." But he threatened to take me to jail for immigration violations if I didn't produce it. Under pressure, I coordinated a motorbike driver to take my friend back to my villa to grab my passport out of the safe. It was a very stressful night and, unfortunately, only the beginning of the debacle. This unfortunate event certainly made my friend's trip unforgettable, as they watched me go through this ordeal.

Going into the immigration office the following week was one of my worst and scariest experiences. Because I was alone on the island, I felt incredibly vulnerable, especially as a single woman who didn't speak the language. Let's just say it's not something you want to experience. After paying a hefty fine, I was given my passport back but still needed to wait a few weeks until the paperwork was finalized before I could enter the store.

As I reflected further, this caused great concern for me, as it was clear someone close had reported me to the authorities that evening. I didn't want to consider that it could have been my staff member, so I figured the security guard next door had called me in. As I waited for my visa to be finalized, I often sat in the restaurant across the street to work in the event that an issue arose for the staff and they needed my assistance.

One day, I had a hunch that one of the staff was not recording all the sales and possibly pocketing the money. To investigate, I sent in a friend to be a secret shopper. After her experience in the store, she headed across the street to me with fire in her eyes, stating, "She's stealing from you big-time!" These were the exact words I did not want to hear. When she'd asked the staff about buying some glass candles, the staff member offered to sell them directly to her in quantity and much cheaper. My friend had also purchased several items and gave me the receipt so I could cross-reference it with the invoice book from the store. I asked my staff to bring it over. Keep in mind that nothing was done electronically, so I needed to examine whether she'd documented all the items on my friend's handwritten receipt. The two invoices didn't match up; the employee was faking the amount and keeping the money. But that wasn't the worst of it.

A few weeks earlier, that same staff member had offered to have her family make the next production run of the glass candles I'd designed. I was hesitant about mixing my business with employees but thought, if I wanted to support Balinese families, why wouldn't I hire her family and help them out? Now she was trying to sell this inventory on the side before it was even delivered to me. When I confronted her, she blatantly lied to me as she sat directly across the table from me. I found it to be the oddest thing: she was busted, yet she wasn't confessing or offering any apologies. I called my friend, the secret shopper, over to our table as I thought this would prompt her to confess. Granted, we were all looking at the documents and actual purchases in my friend's bag. I waffled between the welling sadness that I was being blatantly lied to and the anger within as I didn't know what to do next.

Since I still wasn't allowed to be in the store, I asked my friend if she would walk my sales staff back to the shop to gather her personal items, escort her out, and bring me the keys. As the two of them walked across the street to the shop, the employee once again offered my friend the candles at a discounted price. Even after being caught, she was still trying to strike a deal on the side.

Baffled by this, I asked my Balinese director to address the situation. He responded, "It's her first time; we can't report her." Well, it was the last time for me because I fired her that day. I couldn't believe he wasn't going to assist me in holding her accountable for lying and stealing.

I called Heidi. Recognizing that she'd warned me about this, I could tell she wanted to laugh. Instead, she consoled me, knowing all too well what it felt like. She guided me with some tips, like having each invoice numbered so they could be tracked to reduce stealing. Even with invoice numbers, she warned that I should only have one book on hand and should check the sheets toward the back. This bummed me out as it wasn't the bliss I'd signed up for!

This stealing incident hit me hard; it felt like a significant betrayal. I cried for three days and couldn't figure out why I wasn't recovering faster from this situation. I was crushed that of all the beautiful, good-hearted Balinese people, I was attracting ones who wanted to take advantage of me. The betrayal I felt was like a dagger through my heart, causing me to ponder why I was calling in these devastating situations.

My staff member didn't care about me or the ramifications of being caught stealing, even though she had been treated like family. I thought she'd be grateful for all the perks and bonuses she received, only to learn that the more I gave, the more she took. Little did I know that I'd have many others who would steal from me too. Luckily there was a balance of trustworthy souls who demonstrated the empowered hearts of the Balinese culture. As I discussed my situation with other Western shop owners, they confirmed that this was normal, and I learned that some people's idea of karma was a little different than mine. They believed that if you have more money than they do, it's no problem to take some of it.

My shop had to remain closed until another staff member came back from having her menstrual cycle. I didn't know that women received time off for this, so I thought she'd quit, as she didn't show up for work until her return on day seven. The timing was problematic since I was still waiting for the final paperwork for my work visa. Distressed, I decided to visit the high priestess for another water purification and hoped to talk with her afterward. I hoped she might provide some words of wisdom that would help me feel better. She gently explained that it happens to everyone and I should not take it personally. Finding trustworthy staff was easier said than done, but I'd have to find a way to do it and achieve a better balance of trust and healthy skepticism.

One day while walking into my villa in the middle of the rice fields, I stopped to chat with a lovely couple going into their home. They'd recently moved to Bali from Hong Kong. She was Indonesian, and he was from the Netherlands. As I walked away, I couldn't help but think she'd be perfect for managing the store. She understood Western ways and spoke the local language which would make a world of difference to have the staff report to her. Maybe it would also reduce stealing? If she came on board, I could withdraw from the day-to-day and focus more on increasing sales online.

I offered her the position, and she was thrilled to accept. She was very outgoing and more than happy to share information about the products with customers when they came in. Training the Balinese staff to be more outgoing and to talk with customers when they came in was a breeze for her and having her was a dream come true for me. I hoped my luck was finally turning around, though it was hard not to keep my earlier lesson close at heart.

Life in Bali was buzzing along, and the shop was doing well enough, but it became clear that many sales opportunities were being missed. The storefront was on Monkey Forest Road, one of the busiest streets leading up through town to the popular Yoga Barn at the top of the hill. This segment of the street was still "up and coming" as many of the shops were run down and not well merchandised. This should have showcased the uniqueness of the storefront, as the front was all glass, white, bright, and visually impossible to miss. However, the exact opposite seemed to be true; hundreds of people walked by my store each day as though it were invisible. It was the strangest thing to see tourists not even turn their heads, completely missing the store. Wondering what I was missing, I asked many Western friends and energy experts to come and see if they could help break this barrier. I installed a brightly colored awning, created a garden sitting space out front, hung inspirational pull tabs for people to take, handed out fliers—you name it, I tried it.

Once customers came into the store, they were inspired to purchase. But getting them inside the shop was hard to do, and I couldn't figure out why. I still wasn't ready to believe in black magic wholeheartedly, but I was starting to wonder if there were any spirits or forces at play or, dare I say, monkey business going on!

An acquaintance from New York City came to visit, and I told her about people not being able to find the store. Even my friends who knew where it was and had been to it many times would drive right on by.

> I mentioned to her that there was some type of energetic bubble outside, maybe even some sort of black magic.

She immediately said, "I don't think that's possible; I don't believe in that stuff." Shortly after our conversation, she decided to meander down the street, saying she'd be back in a little while.

About fifteen minutes had gone by when I saw her standing outside, in front of the shop. Another friend was talking with me inside, and we both saw her glance at my Vespa, peer down the driveway next to the store, and then look the other way. She didn't come in, so we figured that she'd seen me still talking and must have decided to keep walking. About thirty minutes later, she came into the store and exclaimed, "You're right. I've been trying to find the store and couldn't see it!"

At that moment, it was clear that professional spiritual help was needed, as I didn't understand the energies at play. This is where Tunjung, my Balinese healer, comes in. The way we met was serendipitous. Within a few months of the store's opening, she came in with some

Westerners, mentioning that she did healings. She gave me her business card, and I briefly looked at her website while she shopped. I didn't need a healer at the time and had forgotten all about her. Now I was sure she could address the energy repelling customers from coming inside. I'd searched for her contact details but couldn't remember her name. So I threw out a request to the Universe to help me find her. The next day a customer walked in and mentioned that a Balinese healer had sent her to my shop, recommending my candles. I asked the healer's name, and when she said "Tunjung," I knew it was her and immediately dialed her to book an appointment.

My session with Tunjung couldn't come soon enough—I was desperate for solutions. Was Klaus somehow energetically impacting me from afar? Did he even know I had a store? Or was there some residual energy from Kadek, whom I'd parted ways with six months prior?

When I arrived for my session with Tunjung, the front desk staff took me to her healing room, which was in one of the local spas. There were crystals, feathers, a massage table, and a small desk that she sat behind. She had a peaceful smile and motioned for me to sit across from her at the desk. I smiled back and took a deep breath, not knowing where to start. Getting into the details of what had been happening with the shop, I finally got to the point, nervously inquiring, "Is this black magic?" She responded by firmly stating, "Don't believe in that!" I was perplexed and couldn't imagine why she was discounting this so quickly. She went on to say that the owner of my building had some bad karma and a spirit following him. The owner was often in the small hotel behind the shop, which was accessed via a driveway to the left of the shop. She did not believe this spirit meant to cause me harm but validated that it was creating an energetic bubble around the store, making it invisible to others.

While this was all new to me, I was slightly relieved that there might be a solution and began to reflect more deeply on Balinese beliefs and energies. Although, I did ponder whether to believe in these ideas. She provided a remedy to clear the energy field, guiding me to sprinkle salt in front of the store while making a specific statement to clear the energy and protect the space. I felt strange doing this, but I desired to shift the energy because the business needed to bring more customers inside to make ends meet. Over the next week, I sprinkled salt, lit the incense, and stated the mantra repeatedly. Admittedly, after a week, I didn't see much of a difference but tried to stay in trust and gratitude that my actions had done something.

I had another great idea to partner with Alchemy, a popular restaurant selling cold-pressed juice and added an outdoor refrigerator to the garden café area. To cover all the senses, I crafted a unique brand of tea along with a local tea artisan and brought in gluten-free cookies from a bakery nearby. Having drinks and food outside would make it impossible for people to miss the store and would draw people in.

Unfortunately, none of these broke the barrier. I made just enough money to cover my expenses in Bali, but not enough to cover my US expenses or contribute anything to my savings account. Determined to get beyond this energetic barrier, I was tenacious and kept trying more business strategies and tactics. Then a brilliant idea came to me in meditation.

Many customers would ask for recommendations, which inspired me to create the *Savvy Insider's Guide to Ubud*. I listed all my favorite places in the categories I'd received the most requests about, including restaurants, shopping, healing, spas, and nightlife. Creating this also allowed me to network with many other business owners in Ubud, which I enjoyed doing. I hit the pavement, building relationships, and I received sponsorships from most of my favorite places to cover the printing costs of the guide. The brochure contained a map with all the incredible spots that many tourists wouldn't know about. And, of course, it featured the Blossom BLISS store, amongst many other great places to shop.

Despite the challenges of driving business into the store, my Bali lifestyle felt in flow, as I had so many incredible encounters. Every day I met new people from all over the world and exchanged incredible stories about love and life with them. Living this enchanting lifestyle, I hoped for a wonderful man to come along to share it all with.

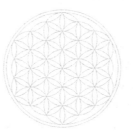

CHAPTER 16

Ceremonies, Spiritual Lessons & Sessions

B EING ON A spiritual quest is often referred to as "finding oneself," but the deeper I went, the clearer it became that

> I was stripping away my old self to unveil the truth of who I really am.

Although I hadn't fully embodied the concept yet and was still reflecting on myself as the Beth Bell character. The Universal Truth of who we all are had yet to be revealed. Bali was eloquently assisting and accelerating my awakening to greater levels of awareness and expanded states of consciousness.

The high priestess had taught me a lot about energy blocks and opening the flow in my body. At the same time, the retail store gave me a deep dive into lessons about karma and external energies at play. Yet there was so much more about to unfold for me, and I was innocently up for the journey. My experiences were beginning to break down my "American mentality" regarding power and money, helping me to shift into the power of my heart.

Making Ubud my home felt Divinely guided as its loving energy enveloped me. Every day seemed to reveal new aspects about myself, the meaning of life, and insights into how humanity can heal by connecting back to Source energy. The community was filled with high-vibrational people focused on spirituality and love. I witnessed people coming from far and wide to this part of the island to partake in the healing energy of the Campuhan River. A beautiful temple resides at a sacred spot on the water's edge and is acknowledged as one of the most potent vortexes on the island.

I began dipping into my healing journey upon leaving my corporate life in 2008. Now, almost five years later, I'd moved from dabbling in it to immersing myself. I was inspired, now more than ever, to participate in numerous unique healing modalities. Inevitably, health issues I'd been struggling with for years were brought up for deep healing.

Before leaving for Costa Rica, I'd followed the guidelines for international travel and received the flu shot along with a hepatitis B vaccination. At the time, I didn't blink an eye. Unfortunately, within thirty minutes, I was disorientated and had brain fog and skyrocketing high blood pressure. This was especially concerning because I was in optimal health otherwise. Little did I know at the time that my gut health had been severely compromised and would take a toll on my body for years to come.

After my first visit to Bali in 2009, my intestinal health continued to decline, and I unknowingly contracted parasites. After appointments with several specialists, I had a lot of opinions but nothing that eliminated the struggle I endured as a result of parasites wreaking havoc in my GI tract. Unless I ate squeaky clean, which was challenging, brain fog and fatigue issues continued to haunt me years later. Now that I was living in Bali, parasites were becoming a serious challenge again, and I needed help.

I was eager to find solutions but wasn't sure where to turn, and then an effortless alignment pointed me in the right direction. One morning two lovely ladies, who were glowing, walked into my store. I spoke to them about their time in Bali, as I did with all customers walking through the door. Happily, they told me they'd recently finished a twenty-one-day Panchakarma cleanse at an Ayurvedic clinic only five minutes away. They couldn't say enough about this ancient cleanse that Indians used to purify their bodies.

Interested in learning more, I found myself at the clinic having a healing consultation within the next few days. The head doctor started the exam with some questions and then asked me to lie on the table. This wasn't a typical exam; she scanned my body energetically, and this was followed by a method called Theta Healing. She asked me to place the tips of my thumb and my middle finger together. Then she asked me to repeat statements while muscle testing how well I could hold my fingers together. If they easily separated and there was a large gap, the statement was a clear no. If they remained tightly together, it was a clear yes. If they were partially open, she would rephrase the question to clarify. She started with something basic, like "My name is pineapple," and my fingers easily fell apart. Then she said, "My name is Beth," and they remained tightly together. The questions and responses took place quickly, which didn't provide an opportunity for me to think about a response. She continued on by making more significant statements that got to the core of my issues.

I was a little skeptical, wondering if my mind was telling my fingers how to respond. However, I remembered back to my psychology class in college when the instructor showed the muscle testing technique with a subject's arm strength after repeating statements. It had been used in clinical trials, so there was something scientific to it, and magically, it seemed highly accurate. This method of getting the body to provide guidance became incredibly useful, providing a convenient way to get around my mind and gain insights from my inner wisdom.

One of the last statements she asked me to repeat was, "It's easy for me to ask for help." Upon repeating these words, without any conscious thought, tears immediately ran down my cheeks as my fingers sprung far apart, symbolizing a definite *no*. My brain had no time to process, and I was shocked that I could have a tearful response so quickly. I could feel the emotion emerging from deep within; she was onto something. I was born and raised to be self-sustaining and not burden anyone else. The last thing I ever wanted to do was ask someone to help me because I saw this as a sign of weakness.

The doctor suggested that the cleanse would help me release some of these hidden beliefs that were creating blocks and causing discord in my body. My energy system was holding vibrations at a cellular level that needed to be cleared. If I opted to do the Panchakarma cleanse, I had to commit to fourteen or twenty-one days, which required me not to work, not to use my computer or phone, and to sit quietly in my home. What? I didn't think this was possible for me. But then she looked at me with her warm eyes and said, "The more you disconnect and go inward, the more you'll get out of it." Spirit seemed to be calling me to do this, as I was determined to feel healthier on a whole new level.

In order to do the cleanse, I'd need to trust the newly trained staff to run the store in my absence. I'd also have to push through the fear that they'd steal from me again. Signing up for the fourteen-day cleanse, I was expected to arrive at the clinic around 7:00 a.m. each day to drink the special ghee specifically formulated for me. During the three mealtimes, I could eat as much food as I wanted, but only food prepared in the clinic's kitchen. The first seven days consisted of only kitchari and soup, both very basic foods that didn't contain additives such as salt or butter. They were completely organic, squeaky-clean foods with a few soup variations, including cauliflower, beetroot, or squash. This particular diet would allow the ghee to pull toxins from my body and prepare me for the final release, fondly known as D-day, standing for Detox Day.

I was never starving at any point, but I felt hungry most of the day, which was atypical for me. Oddly, this led me to obsessively ponder about what I would eat when I finished at the clinic. Apparently, in Ayurveda, it's essential to eat when you're hungry to keep the fire going. It's not about fasting, as many might think. Almost all other people doing the cleanse were rarely hungry, especially after ingesting the ghee. But I could suddenly eat more than ever before, and I was losing weight!

The ghee was a bit of a mystery; it pulled toxins at a cellular level, bound to them, and assisted them in exiting the body. It also significantly slowed down my brain, giving me a reprieve from my fast-moving thoughts. Everyone's ghee is medicated with different Ayurvedic herbs specific to their identified issues. The doctor emphasized that being still was the most important thing. Being quiet was challenging, but it provided a lovely opportunity to sit in my villa and appreciate the surrounding rice fields. It was fascinating to listen to myself think, allowing a true form of mind monitoring to take place and help me go inward.

D-day was different. The clinic staff explained that I'd be taking the first dose of medicine early in the morning. Then I'd be placed in a steam bath for thirty minutes. After that, I'd consume another alchemistic drink containing a mix of medicinal herbs. Within twenty minutes, I'd be expected to be in the toilet for most of the day and quietly resting in my villa otherwise. Getting home quickly would be important.

During my journaling over the previous days, I realized the Universe had been telling me to have fun and work less. I struggled with this idea but decided to make it easy by looking through my photographs and reliving pleasurable memories I'd already accumulated on life's adventures. This didn't require me to go anywhere and allowed me to feel into the playfulness of life. I remained focused on the fun factor of all these great endeavors, including holidays, boyfriends, and work events. Surprisingly, I didn't miss any of it. I was okay not being in the corporate world, even though financial freedom was a nice benefit. I didn't have any regrets regarding previous romantic relationships. I didn't long for Singapore as I had in the first few months after I'd left. And I didn't miss my Jersey City condo, although I loved it and was looking forward to going back to it one day. Happily, I didn't feel any qualms or doubts about any of the jumps I'd made in life, no matter how crazy they were or how they turned out.

Then another revelation hit. There was an area I felt called to heal in order for anything else to shift. My ancestral programming needed to be identified and cleaned up to release thought patterns and ideas that no longer served my higher good. My parents had only loving intentions with the values they instilled in me to achieve a successful and fruitful life. My consciousness had expanded to knowing that I'd chosen my parents before coming into this lifetime. So whatever they may have done or not done was part of the Divine plan for me to experience in this lifetime.

My awareness heightened that their programming would be an integral part of the unraveling process to unveil the truth of who I really am. I admired them the most for being incredibly kind, loving, compassionate people who provided a steady stake in the ground for the stability, love, and trust that my brother and I experienced growing up. I cherished these core elements about my parents even more after seeing all the wounds many others had to heal due to broken and destructive family relationships.

The evening of day six, I heard the Divine presence visit me in the most unexpected way. While sitting at my bedroom desk journaling, I felt a loving presence envelop me, almost like a warm hug of air coming up around my shoulders. I had six days of ghee accumulated in my system, and I strangely felt more grounded than ever sitting in my chair. Being very still but not meditating, I experienced a rush of love flow through me when wisdom came telepathically from my higher self. I felt grounded on the earth and had a strong connection in my heart to what most people would likely describe as God. I like to refer to it as Source energy as it's a connection to white, bright light that brings a great sense of peace, belonging, and remembrance. I'd been longing to tap into this field and desired to strengthen this connection I'd only read about, until now. I had worked for years to quiet my mind and hear guidance from my higher self. Now I hoped that my ability to connect so effortlessly would remain long after the cleanse was over.

D-day had arrived, and I felt irritated and annoyed as I entered the clinic. I'd need to sit encapsulated in a steam container for thirty minutes, with only my head sticking out of the top. Before stepping into the wooden steam container, I stated my intention, "To expand to greater levels of consciousness," and drank the medicine. I was quietly ruminating about the steam not being hot enough, questioning why the clinic didn't have a better system, and contemplating why they couldn't speak good English for the high prices I was paying. I projected such frustration to the staff, and all she did was look back at me with a loving face, answering each of my questions with another question. In the final ten minutes I got *the message*. I needed to stop critiquing and let whatever's meant to happen, happen.

> Frustrated with myself, I questioned why I couldn't simply
> go with the flow of life all the time. Accept things and
> people as they are. Stop thinking so much. Relax more.
> Have more fun. Laugh more.

Achieving this would require setting the monkey mind aside and listening to my soul speak. Little did I know that it would take me several more years of practice to figure out how to do this.

As I moved out of the steamer, emotions began to bubble up, and I was given the final alchemistic drink containing a secret blend of herbs. I never thought to ask exactly what it contained and drank it, trusting what the doctor felt was right for me. With everything kicking in, purging would be imminent, and it was imperative that I get home quickly so I'd make it to the bathroom in time. All the while on the motorbike ride home, I held back tears, as intense emotions were surfacing. Fortunately, I made it home before the seven-day buildup of ghee began evacuating my body—I was literally full of shit!

As the movements on the toilet began, downloads of information came to me effortlessly as my higher self was speaking to me directly again. This time the messages were about ideas and beliefs held by my ancestral lineage. Revelations streamed in about areas that needed to be healed for all of us:

1. **The desire to be heard**. Both of my parents struggle with this, and so had I in my relationships. I didn't feel "heard" in my relationship with my husband. I could see this created resentment that became deep wounds. It also brought forward my awareness regarding my ability to listen. I realized that when I didn't help my partners feel validated, it was nearly impossible for either of us to be present for one another.

2. **Critique**. In my experience, this was disguised as "I'm only telling you this because I love you and want you to be better." Our relationships are only mirrors to see what we don't like in ourselves, and critiquing others reflected my lack of self-love.

3. **Acceptance**. I wasn't loving others enough for their uniqueness. I began recognizing that I was seeing a slice of the world through my lens and wanted to cherish our differences more. We get programmed through our family dynamics, believing that things are supposed to be or function in a certain way and wanting others to fit into our molds.

I wasn't sure how to release the programming and issues I was carrying from childhood, but it seemed important to start addressing this as part of my spiritual work. Little did I know that the Universe would soon introduce me to one of the most powerful healing modalities for ancestral wounds.

One day a friend of mine introduced me to a woman named Angelique who'd arrived from San Diego with her partner. She felt like a familiar friend from back home, and we immediately hit it off. She was a biofield energy worker and had a healing sanctuary in a popular clinic in Ubud. I wasn't familiar with her type of work but was always interested to learn and partake in new experiences. She explained that she didn't do massage or reiki; rather, she would be holding space for me in another dimension.

The day I arrived for my session, she'd put the finishing touches on her beautiful space, which felt light, bright, and airy. Relaxing music played in the background while she placed a soft lavender-scented mask over my eyes, causing my body to melt onto the table. She began by saying an invocation to get my body and mind to a restful state. After this, Angelique remained quiet in the background. Several minutes into the session, a surprising paranormal experience began.

With my eyes covered, I sensed an energy come into the room. He appeared as a man in a white robe with a distinctive large nose with a rounded tip. I could see it clearly as he leaned over the bed, examining me. The energy felt warm and caring, as though he'd come to heal something in me. As I lay there, he began guiding me off the table and into the light. It was as though we were ascending through space and time, out beyond the earth's atmosphere and into the cosmos. When we approached an indescribably bright light in the distance, it was like a space of nothingness filled with a comforting, blissful feeling.

I felt Divinely held, analogous to what people describe heaven to look like when experiencing a near-death experience. I felt embraced and supported, and at the same time expansive in a weightless body.

> I had never felt as safe and secure at any other point in
> my life as I did while I was held by this bright light.

I was in another dimension, experiencing myself in an Angelic way. Soon it became clear that I would need to go back to earth, and immense sadness came over me. Tears started to stream down my face because I knew I couldn't stay in this familiar place. Upon opening my eyes, I lay on the table staring at the ceiling in awe of this mind-blowing experience.

Receiving numerous insights during this session made me pause and reflect on the power of connecting into our higher selves, God, and other realms. I couldn't conceptually explain how the experience had occurred, but it opened my mind to new possibilities. The fact that I was not being touched, hadn't taken any herbs, pills, or medicine, and yet could transcend the realities of this earth plane so easily led me to want to learn more. I'd had a glimpse on the cleanse of what it felt like to be surrounded by, and tap into, Source energy. But other than my hypnosis sessions and water purification, I hadn't had an out-of-body experience like this before. Now I was traveling to different dimensions, which gave me greater confidence in tapping into my relationships with guardian angels, spirits, and entities in other realms.

Even though Ubud was like a Disney World of wellness, I didn't have much free time to investigate healing modalities. I was busy with my retail store. I knew whatever was needed the most would come to me naturally if I remained open to it. That's exactly what happened as my dear friend, Katinka, came to stay with me for a month and ended up inviting me to join her for a Family Constellation session. Although I had little understanding of this technique, I'd heard several other people talk about it. I was curious to see how it worked and happy to participate.

Arriving at the private villa where sessions took place, we were greeted by a lovely woman from the Netherlands. She was friendly, as were the other ten to fifteen people participating. We were asked to sit on the floor in a circle as she described what she called "the knowing field." She also spoke about her background and training with Bert Hellinger, the founder of Family Constellation work in Austria.

The session started with us introducing ourselves by providing our name, the country we were born in, and the countries our parents were from. A short meditation followed to bring our presence into the room and quiet our minds in preparation for the session. Afterward, the person having the constellation session would state their wish or problem they wanted to solve.

My friend wanted to uncover blocks holding her back from attracting her romantic soul mate. The facilitator guided her to look around the circle and identify someone to play her mother, her father, and finally, someone to represent herself, which were all referred to as "representatives." We began the constellation with these three people standing in the middle of the room, anticipating that more representatives would be called in as insights unfolded.

The facilitator encouraged everyone to follow their movements, explaining that it was essential to allow the body to reposition in whatever way the energy moved them. Then she said, "When emotions surface, communicate them, but don't try to assign meaning to them," emphasizing that it was her job to put together all the pieces from each participant's body movements. This allows Spirit to come through instead of what the mind wants to project onto the experience.

People started playing their roles, effortlessly moving and using body language to convey emotions and insights. I wasn't familiar with Katinka's family dynamics or either of her parents' background. Naively watching, I had no idea if what was being displayed by the participants was true or not. Everything was unfolding like a movie, when out of the blue, I started to feel really, really angry. This surprised me; I rarely get angry. In this circumstance, I had no reason to be angry, and it didn't seem to be directly related to what I was watching. I just felt angry.

About that time, the facilitator looked over at me and said, "Are you in?"

"I don't know. But I am so angry right now. I just feel so angry!"

"You're in! Come over here."

Not knowing what was going on, I was placed next to the person playing my friend's grandmother on her mother's side. Upon the facilitator's suggestion, I suddenly and keenly knew I was the grandfather. How I knew that, I wasn't sure. However, it was clear that the woman standing next to me was my wife. It seemed like the spirit of her grandfather took over my body, guiding me to play out his role in the family dynamics. All the while, I knew that I was Beth but was embodying his character through body language and displays of emotion.

Watching the woman playing "my wife" brought up deep hatred toward her. I could feel it in my bones; it was bizarre because I, Beth, didn't hate the actual person standing there. But the grandfather I was playing certainly hated the character she was representing. Then things got incredibly interesting. All the grandfather's emotions must have taken me over, and I started expressing his feelings involuntarily. The storylines of our history poured through me as I received downloads of the early years experienced with his wife.

It was revealed that we'd had premarital sex, and she'd become pregnant. Out of embarrassment and fear that she'd be in trouble, she told everyone I'd raped her. She was playing the victim, and I (the grandfather) became the victim, as people believed I'd forced her to have sex against her will. It was far from the truth, but I was guilted into doing the right thing and married her. I hated every minute of it because we lived a lie. Because of this, I resented her and treated her very poorly over the years.

It was clear to me, standing there as the husband to my friend's grandmother, that I was a mean person who yelled and beat her. The baby born out of this premarital affair was my friend's mother. As a small child, my friend's mother experienced the hatred and the physical, emotional, and verbal abuse her father directed toward her mother. This energy came through the lineage, and my friend received a belief system identifying abuse as a way men show love. This also resulted in learning how to sacrifice her feelings to help make someone else feel okay about their actions and assuage them to avoid anger. These belief systems came down the ancestral lineage, creating difficulties attracting unconditional love.

My friend uncovered some deep-rooted ideas, beliefs, and thoughts that she didn't know existed because they were hidden within the depths of her genetic ancestral DNA lineage. Once these were highlighted, she saw that some of her behavior was not even of her own doing. That did not mean she was a victim. It demonstrated a learned behavior that attracted unappreciative and abusive people into her life and romantic relationships. This was one of the lessons she set herself up to uncover in her subconscious programming.

I learned a tremendous amount in Family Constellation work that changed my life, and I saw firsthand the impact ancestral programming can have on how we view life. This made me incredibly curious, which led me to desire more experiences with this work. I was excited to learn more about channeling people whom I did not know and who may or may not be alive. If I hadn't experienced it for myself, I wouldn't have believed it.

People had come to these sessions from all over the world, which allowed me to play a variety of roles, experience numerous cultures, and channel many different types of people. Shockingly to me, I wasn't channeling only dead people; I channeled people who were alive, small children, objects, and the energy of angels, God, and the devil.

> As a result, I learned that the energy lines being carried from our ancestors and collective consciousness could be blown up, releasing limiting patterns and beliefs from our energy fields.

It's kind of like "the buck stops here" with ancestral lineage crap, preventing it from going any further down the ancestral line by healing it now.

Whatever was happening always seemed to be spot on for what the individual needed to hear, see, or feel. Many family secrets were revealed, and people were stunned to find the truth within their family's lineage. The benefits went beyond the person requesting the healing, as all participants felt shifts when the truth was unlocked. Freeing the emotional baggage of others facilitated profound healings for all of us by releasing the trauma held in the collective subconscious. Often people didn't know why they were attending, but upon leaving they felt healed, whole, and connected to Spirit in a way they didn't expect.

One of the most remarkable aspects of participating in these constellations was that I could experience emotions in my body like never before. Most likely because they weren't my own, and I wasn't trying to protect myself from feeling something painful. These sessions also helped me be less in my thinking mind as I channeled the energies through feelings in my body. Wanting to practice this led me to volunteer every week as a representative in Family Constellation sessions.

It became clear that ancestral work in these sessions was only the first step. While issues seemed to vanish as we gave limiting beliefs back to the ancestors, it was important to be aware of not reformulating old storylines. Knowing that our external world reflects what our inner world is thinking, expanding awareness to the thoughts and ideas one contemplates is imperative. This further solidified the importance of changing my internal perception to influence my external world.

While many things were transforming through my healing work, I also worked hard. I was busy designing new products, managing ongoing staffing issues, and attending to all the details of running a brick-and-mortar store. The most frustrating aspect was feeling that my business capacity was being highly underutilized. Going from having a significant corporate job to owning a retail store sounds glamorous, but it was starting to become evident that I needed a lot more stimulation from my business. I deeply desired to contribute to humanity. Running the shop didn't seem to fit into my larger mission. It was clear that exercising the option to extend my three-year lease an additional two years wasn't my calling. Not knowing what was next, I had a premonition that new opportunities would soon be presenting. And I was right.

During one of my visits to the States visiting family and friends, I was asked to be a guest on a radio show. This inspired me to create a radio show of my own interviewing conscious entrepreneurs, a twist I wasn't expecting! But I was living in creative and spiritual flow, so it seemed perfect, as I loved highlighting other people's stories and businesses. My show would allow others to learn how to break through the fears holding them back and provide pearls of wisdom to catapult them forward. And from a business strategy perspective, it would allow me some additional exposure for my products.

Within a month, I was accepted onto the VoiceAmerica network in the United States. I began interviewing interesting and popular guests from my villa in Bali. This was a sweet spot for me, as I enjoyed harvesting pearls of wisdom to share with listeners. After much success, I made another big move to build my own channel, which allowed me to archive my episodes on my website, BethBell.me/show. In my early episodes, you can hear the ducks, monkeys, and bugs buzzing, accentuating the blissful Bali background.

Shortly after my return from a trip to the US, a friend came to visit me at the store. He'd lived on the island for over twenty years and owned a large, beautiful spa and healing center. I'd often called him to talk about business situations or get friendly advice to help me understand the ways of the Balinese culture, as he seemed to have encountered it all. Walking into the store that day, he expressed how impressed he was with the design, the cabinetry, and the details. In the next breath, he said almost the exact words I'd been reflecting on: "You need to be out of this shop and doing something so much bigger to utilize your talents!"

Unexpectedly, he went on to offer me a mini store in his new galleria, which he planned to open in the coming months. This would be a fantastic alignment, and I was grateful for his offer. It made my decision to close the store much easier, knowing that the products would have a "mini" Blossom BLISS store. An additional bonus was not having to manage or hire staff to run the store, which gave me the liberty to move back to the US when the timing was right.

As the last month the store would be open approached, I felt relieved, sad, and eager to be moving in a new direction. I'd had the store for three years, and while I hadn't achieved all the lofty goals and dreams for my business quite yet, it was clear that closing was the right thing to do. If I wasn't spending so much time on the little things, I could focus on my website, online sales, and my show interviewing entrepreneurs.

Locking the doors for the last time, I thanked the beautifully painted sky ceiling, all the incredible memories, and the customers I'd met in my time there. Undeniably, the people I encountered from all over the world had enriched my life tremendously, as the deep soulful conversations with strangers were priceless. Many of these customers became my friends, whom I stayed in contact with over the miles, helping me feel connected to the planet on a global scale.

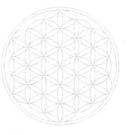

CHAPTER 17

Shaking Ashram and Paranormal Encounters

ALREADY ON A steep learning curve, I thought I'd seen and experienced pretty much everything in Ubud when it came to spirituality. However, the Universe was planning to take me further than I imagined. While I was immersed in doing my inner work, I was not like the droves of seekers who followed anything and everything that came through town.

Years earlier, I'd become friends with an Australian woman named Ivanna, whom I'd met during my Ayurvedic cleanse. We'd often find ourselves dining together, and one evening she spoke about her experiences at a shaking ashram she'd just come from days prior. I'd never heard of such a thing and was fascinated to learn what she had to share about the ashram and its guru leader, Ratu Bagus. Those of us sitting around the table were flabbergasted by her stories and couldn't fathom shaking for eight to nine hours a day as she described. On the surface, I thought it was one of the craziest things I'd heard of. But she was passionate about the healing effects and professed the extensive hours of shaking each day were healing the wounds she had as the result of being an orphan throughout childhood.

We remained in touch, and she'd call me upon her many returns to Bali. Because of the profound nature of this technique, she was inspired to stay at the ashram twice a year for seven to ten days to participate in the healing shake therapy. When we would connect for dinner in Ubud afterward, she'd share increasingly intense and emotional stories of her mind-bending, intriguing experiences. She always encouraged me to try it, but I didn't desire to do such a thing.

Over time, I started to hear others talk about the ashram, which piqued my curiosity, making me wonder if I should add it to my eclectic repertoire of healing modalities. Around this time, my friend Rica from New York City happened to reach out to me as I was contemplating going. She'd been staying with her family in Japan and hoped to visit me in Bali before heading back to the States. I mentioned possibly going to the shaking ashram and was surprised when she immediately said, "I want to go!" I had no desire to go alone, so her excitement helped finalize my decision. The only challenge was that it required a five-day commitment at the ashram, requiring participation in the three shaking sessions each day. We both decided to commit and booked our spots. I upgraded us to a double room with a private bathroom, thinking this might make the experience more pleasant.

Upon arrival, we found the accommodations shocking; they were minimal at best. The grounds were cluttered, the rooms marginal, and the bathroom primitive—a partial garden hose hung as the showerhead. Since Rica and I were both there for the experience, we quickly set our judgments aside, as we needed to get ready to attend our first evening shake.

We arrived at the shaking hall and found at least twenty to thirty people already gathered in the room. As we entered, a temple attendant encouraged us to take some of the special tobacco blessed by Ratu. They told us to place a pinch in our bottom lip like you would with chewing tobacco. Then we were guided to place more tobacco into a small needleless syringe and add hot water. Once the tobacco was steeped, we used the syringe to squirt it up into our noses while snorting it in. Snorting tobacco? Really? I thought shaking was enough of a leap. My friend had mentioned the tobacco, but it wasn't until I saw what we were being asked to do that it sunk in. *Oh wow, am I really going to do this? And why?* We didn't have time to let it sink in, as we were invited to join in a mantra that everyone was chanting. For us newbies, they had laminated copies we could carry to make it easy to learn as we began the shake.

It seemed like a dream—or maybe an episode of *Candid Camera*! I continued to shift my focus to the stories my Australian friend had shared and all the good things she had experienced in her twenty-plus visits to the ashram. I decided, *What the hell? I'm here, and I should give it a whirl.* Rica and I went from looks of terror to laughter as we snorted this tobacco up our nose and watched some of it run down our faces. Thank God I didn't come alone!

There wasn't anyone instructing us on how to shake. Whatever movement created the most motion was accepted, and the chant of the mantra was intended to evoke a wave of energy. Many people had some kind of rhythm going on, but I'm sure I looked worse than Elaine dancing on *Seinfeld*. Doing our best to shake, Rica and I would occasionally glance at each other. When we made eye contact, we'd inevitably break into a smile and would try not to laugh. Honestly, it felt super weird and dumb. Many others had spectacular releases, and a few looked like they were in euphoric bliss. I wondered about the states they were in and whether I'd be able to experience something more than the aches in my knees from forcing myself to shake so profusely. I hoped this wasn't merely a bunch of lost, crazy people wrapped up in a spiritual awakening blanket about to be filmed for a Netflix documentary of silly things people do to heal themselves!

About twenty minutes into the shake, Ratu Bagus came into the room and created an energetic whirlwind. People bowed to him on their hands and knees with adoration as he passed by them. Their actions seemed somewhat involuntary; I thought for sure it was a cult and we would somehow not be able to leave! A few moments later, he walked right up to me, looked me in the eyes, and touched my back with the tips of his fingers. I immediately felt a zing of energy, then realized I was not chanting the mantra correctly, and I felt a bit embarrassed. I smiled and shook it off; no pun intended.

That night, Rica and I lay in bed pondering why we'd come to this ashram. There was something powerful going on, but did we really want to be part of this? Was it a cult? What was in the "tobacco"? Would Ratu or the spirit realms he worked with be doing some strange programming of our minds? Why did Ratu come up and address me so specifically? Was this creepy, or should we stay the course? Our curiosity and commitment to the five days overshadowed the weirdness of our first shake.

In general, I love mornings, but jumping out of bed at 5:00 a.m. for the next shake wasn't the easiest thing to do. This time we were all outside in the fresh air with rays of morning sun shining down, snorting the tobacco up our nose again. I was hoping for a cup of coffee or green tea but learned that wouldn't be available until after we were done. Ratu talked before the shake officially started, and everyone gathered around him like bees to a honey jar.

Bizarrely, people seemed to be mesmerized by him as he had a way of controlling them through a mysterious energy. He could look at someone and make them do crazy movements or bow at his feet. I've never been a fan of gurus, especially ones who manipulate people, so I wasn't impressed. Observing from the edges of the crowd, I found it fascinating how powerfully he used his energy. It was almost like watching a superhero in a movie who uses their forces to move people without touching them physically. He could make people laugh uncontrollably with one look into their eyes. Freaky.

If Rica hadn't been with me, I would have called my driver to come for me. Because we were together, we felt a sense of camaraderie and were confident that we wouldn't fall prey to his mysterious power, whatever it was. I had no idea what he was technically doing with it or how he was performing these bizarre acts. The shakes themselves seemed to move a lot of energy around in my body. However, I became increasingly disappointed, not achieving the state of euphoria others exuded.

Rica and I witnessed many unthinkable things, like people taking Ratu's used tobacco chew and sniffing it. When they did, they would laugh uncontrollably. These strange reactions became amusing, as neither Rica nor I was drawn in by whatever was happening to them. By the fifth day, we were both feeling lighter and happier, and were laughing a lot, which was a great outcome. Who couldn't stand to lighten up a bit more? At the same time, we were ready to leave. We realized we'd shaken for about thirty hours in total. Needless to say, we were all shook up when we left! As we said goodbye to the interesting people we'd met, we believed we'd never go back again. But we know what happens when we say never; little did I know that I would end up back at the ashram three more times!

We loaded our bags into the car and were on our way down the winding volcano road, headed back to Ubud. Along the way, we asked our driver to stop so we could photograph the beautiful scenery from the side of the road. The plush green palm trees glowed from the setting sun, which highlighted the rice fields cascading down the hill. As I stood there witnessing the beauty of Mother Nature, I felt a warm radiance throughout my body as my heart expanded. Turning back toward the car, I noticed an older Balinese man by the side of the road and felt a great, flowing love for him, although he was a stranger. It wasn't romantic love, but a genuine love for humanity and appreciation for all the beauty before my eyes. Maybe something *had happened* back at the ashram. I felt different now that we were out of there: I had a unique, euphoric, unexplainable feeling of unconditional love and connection.

From my quantum physics books, I knew that

> everything in the Universe is made up of energy vibrating
> at different frequencies.

This also means our thoughts carry a vibration and can impact our state of mind. Masaru Emoto, a well-known Japanese businessman, studied how human consciousness can affect the molecular structure of water. His findings demonstrated how words, images, and phrases that carry varying levels of vibration can impact the shapes of water crystals. When Ratu spoke, there had to have been a vibrational transmission, as he communicated telepathically with people. But how was Ratu manipulating this energy to influence others? Rica and I spent the next few days in my villa laughing and trying to figure out all the peculiar experiences we had and had witnessed. While no answers surfaced for us, we agreed it was a unique bonding experience that neither of us would ever forget.

My questioning continued. *Was there a link to the ancestral energy being played in the Family Constellation process? Was the shaking technique tapping into another dimension of consciousness? Could I unlock this same power within me? How are psychic attacks linked to the manipulation of energy? Was black magic at play? Did I even believe in this?* I started to have more questions than answers, and my curiosity for learning was heightened. This made me want to pay another visit to Tunjung. She knew quite a lot about Western thinking and yet deeply understood the cultural beliefs of the Balinese. Maybe she could shed some light on Ratu and his mysterious manipulation of energy.

I was heading to my appointment with Tunjung in hopes of receiving some clarity on all these questions. I had a few extra minutes, so I stopped at my mini shop in the galleria. I greeted one of my favorite sales associates, and she smiled back and appeared to be perfectly fine. As I turned to greet another sales associate, I heard a collective gasp from the ladies behind me. They quickly began speaking in Balinese with urgency in their voices. As I turned around, the associate I'd spoken to had fallen backward, and her eyes were rolling to the back of her head. Her hands were being manipulated in a strange way, and she didn't appear to be fully present.

The ladies rubbed some medicinal oil on her forehead, as they all seemed to understand what was happening. The head of HR arrived, and I asked, "Is this energy coming into her?" You were never supposed to bring up black magic, so the code word was *energy*. She nodded her head and said, "Yes, she'll be fine," almost as though she didn't want me to be involved. I had to leave anyway, as I was now running late for my appointment.

I shared with Tunjung all the energetic manipulation I'd just witnessed and inquired whether she knew Ratu and his work. Tunjung always seemed to laugh at me when I'd come in with deep philosophical questions or quandaries around the mysterious energy that seemed to circle me.

The first time I went to her regarding the energy impacting my store, she told me not to believe in black magic. This time she warned me again that the more I entertained the topic, the more I would attract it. Perplexed as to why I was calling in these experiences, I pressed on to understand the meaning of the lessons. I was concerned now more than ever about spiritual hijacking and anything having to do with mischief from the darker realms. Finally, Tunjung acknowledged that there were energies at play. She wasn't familiar with Ratu and couldn't speak about him specifically but reminded me that

> the most important thing was knowing my power and staying connected to the light.

In my time in Bali, I'd heard accounts from trusted friends about spirits coming into people's bodies and possessing them. Now I'd seen it for myself, which shouldn't have been a surprise since I'd had many experiences with channeling and working with others from "the other side" during Family Constellation work and, more recently, at a small group healing. But this was different, as they appeared to be hostile or involuntary takeovers.

Two American friends invited me to see a well-known Balinese healer whom I hadn't heard of before. This sparked my curiosity to meet him, and I was keen to have another healer to recommend to visitors. My friends invited a couple, who rode with us. They were in the front, while I was in deep conversation in the last row, which didn't allow me to get to know them.

I was surprised when the healer invited us to come in as a group; I thought we'd be seeing the healer one by one. He asked us to close our eyes while he chanted, and this was followed by a candle lighting for each other. During the meditation, I felt peaceful until, suddenly, the presence of a spirit entered the room, similar to how George's spirit showed up while I was on the Hay House cruise. He told me his name was David and he wanted them to know he was okay. I thought, *Who's them?* and *Who are you?* He went on to say that he was called to leave his eight-year-old daughter, as it was part of their plan coming into this life-time. As the chant ended and we started lighting the candles, I couldn't stop the tears from rolling down my cheeks. I felt obliged to share what had come through and told them exactly what I'd heard.

The couple stared at me with dismay as they began to disclose that their adult son, David, had committed suicide several months earlier, and they were coming to this Balinese healer for answers. I was shocked and felt blessed to be able to share such important information. I wondered, *Why me? Why did David choose me to speak to?* I wasn't a psychic medium, and the healer seemed the most likely person to have been selected to receive the message. As I continued with my day, I couldn't overlook how profound those moments delivering David's message felt.

My life in Bali was transforming me in ways I couldn't have imagined. The multitude of modalities expanded my consciousness beyond the visible aspects of everyday life. I was more consistently living in the moment and shifting away from the intensity that Westernized living and corporate life had ingrained in me. Were these fundamental shifts helping me to be more intuitive? More clairvoyant and clairaudient? How many more layers of myself did I need to uncover? How much more is there to learn about other dimensions? It seemed that the more I knew, the deeper the questioning became.

Through all these miraculous life experiences I acquired more wisdom than any university could teach. Being in Ubud, one of the most magical vortexes on the planet, I didn't want to stop continuing to explore the mysteries of the Universe. At the same time, I couldn't ignore the fact that I was still a bit lonely and sad because I didn't have a romantic partner to share my life experiences with.

PART III

Transcending to Unveil Illusions

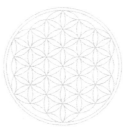

CHAPTER 18

Old Souls Reunited

I'M ALWAYS UP for meeting others, especially when the introduction comes through a friend. So when my friend, Laura, whom I recently met in Bali mentioned that she wanted to connect me with her high school friend Shawn, I was happy to make the connection. She went so far as to suggest he may be someone I'd be interested in dating. But if nothing else, she said he was a good guy and someone worth getting to know.

Shawn was living in Vietnam when we first spoke on the phone. He was friendly, and we quickly dove into sharing some interesting life stories. Our excitement to connect in person seemed mutual, and he was planning to move to Bali in a few weeks. Excited to meet up, we scheduled to meet for lunch in Ubud the day after his arrival.

We instantly jumped into our life stories, and I couldn't deny that I found him attractive and intriguing. He was a retired fireman and paramedic who was all muscle, with a big smile and twinkling blue eyes. To top it off, he had a unique voice that made me want to learn more about him. The chemistry between us was strong, and we immediately hit it off.

As we parted after lunch, he inquired if I was interested in meeting over the weekend. I was but had plans to attend a two-day program called Behind the Mask. It had been highly recommended to me, and after speaking with the facilitator a few times over the last year, I was keen to keep my commitment. Hunky, muscular men didn't pass through Ubud often, though, and I didn't want to miss the opportunity to see Shawn. So I invited him to join the program with me. I didn't know exactly what the workshop would entail, so I provided a vague description. I anticipated that it would reveal some deep emotions and vulnerability for anyone attending, which could provide a fast track for us to learn more about one another. I was thrilled when he said yes to attending and coming to Ubud for the weekend.

Of course, had Shawn known what he was getting himself into, he might have declined. We were asked to wear a leather mask that covered our entire face, similar to the ones used in theater or acting class. It's hard to explain, but something unique and mysterious happens when the mask goes on and you're given a specific task. You become more open and vulnerable, leading you to do and say things you normally wouldn't. Maybe this is a spiritual version of how your behavior changes when you wear a mask for Halloween—but instead of misbehaving, you become vulnerable and express your feelings. On the first day, we all cried at some point, even my new firefighter friend. That evening we had some intense discussions that we wouldn't have had without the all-day sessions that seemed to open our hearts and make expressing our emotions easier.

By the second day, I was pinching myself. It felt like a dream come true to have found a man who was willing to do spiritual work with me! Sharing our deepest vulnerabilities in the workshop instantly glued us to one another. I was aware by now that we attract others by our own wounds to help heal each other. Sometimes they were brief, and sometimes longer-term love affairs. Once the lessons in spiritual contracts were learned, it often meant it was time to close the relationship and move on.

> Romantic relationships are especially powerful, as they
> often lure us with the intention of bringing deep wounds
> to the surface and provide opportunities to heal.

I wanted a partner who also desired to work through wounds, release them, and support each other for a lifetime. Feeling a strong soul connection to Shawn, I was eager to explore our relationship and see what might happen between us. He made me feel safe and at ease in his presence, which was refreshing.

Everything seemed glowingly perfect, and we quickly swirled into romance through our open-heart conversations. At the same time, I knew this would inevitably lead to the dreaded feeling I'd have to tell him about carrying the herpes virus. I was never sure what type of response a partner would have, but disclosing this was always petrifying and embarrassing, because I anticipated rejection. Of course, having to share this type of humiliating information forced me to know someone on a deeper level before diving into a sexual relationship. Ours was moving fast, and it seemed the topic would be coming up sooner rather than later.

There Shawn and I were, in the heat of the moment, both wanting more, and I knew I had to stop the magic and have "the herpes talk." It was like reliving the trauma all over again. The tears rolled and my jaw felt locked. I softened when I saw the deep desire in his eyes to know what was so heavy on my heart. I finally got it out, and while he was taken back, he didn't overreact and was incredibly loving. He asked me some questions about breakouts and the risks of contracting the virus. I did my best to share the facts and didn't sugarcoat it, as there's *always* a risk. The way he handled it was so heartwarming, and he concluded on his own that it was a risk he was willing to take. The intensity and honesty we shared bonded us in this early phase of our relationship.

A few months went by, and we were entwined, wanting to spend more time together. Shawn commuted from Seminyak, over an hour away, and we desired to spend more than just the weekends together. This prompted us to start talking about the possibility of finding a villa we could share. I know. Moving in with a man, again? At least this time I wasn't leaving anything for him or being asked to financially invest in any of his endeavors!

We wanted to get to know each other more, so we decided to plan a trip to North America to visit family and friends. We were both ready for some time back home and thought it would be an excellent opportunity to travel and understand more about each other's backgrounds. We booked the airline tickets a few months out and continued to enjoy our time in Bali.

In anticipation of our goal to cohabitate after our trip, we decided to do a manifestation exercise describing and visualizing the aspects of the villa we both wanted. He was great at describing details of his desires, and we quickly learned we were envisioning the same type of villa. It appeared that there were no significant compromises we'd need to make. How wonderful!

The following Sunday, we decided to take a drive among the rice fields of Ubud to explore new areas and see if any properties existed like what we were envisioning, although the official house hunting wasn't going to start until we were back from our trip.

We were about fifteen minutes out of Ubud when we saw the most stunning villa that had beautiful views of the famous volcano Mount Agung. It looked brand new, was incredibly modern, and appeared to meet all our criteria. The previous renters had moved out earlier in the day, and the owner was having it cleaned and had just put the rental sign out. We tapped on the door, and the maid let us inside to tour the property. It was a manifestation come true: it contained exactly what we wanted, inside and out. This unique, modern villa would go quickly, but it was a few months too early for our plan. That night we couldn't stop thinking about it and came up with the idea of renting it now and then subleasing it until we returned from our trip.

Willing to split the rental expense, we'd be required to pay the customary one-year lump sum up front. It was a significant investment, but we were both okay to jump in on it. Then Shawn came up with a brilliant idea to request a one-night stay in the villa before committing. This would allow us to discover anything unexpected that we couldn't live with, like noise from the running river next to the house or mosquito attacks coming from the surrounding rice fields. The owner agreed, and we prepared our finances by transferring money into our Bali bank accounts to pay the owner the day after our stay.

It was so exciting as we prepared to spend the night in what we anticipated would be our new home. As the sun began to set, we opened a bottle of wine while enjoying our cheese platter and gorgeous views. We had fun discussing small decorating ideas that would make the villa feel like ours. Night fell, and we found ourselves by the pool as we took our last few sips of wine. Shawn started talking about maintaining the pool, which triggered him to reflect on his past relationship with a woman in Australia. The breakup had been abrupt and heartbreaking, which prompted his move to Vietnam a few years ago. He began to bring up specific memories, like how she wouldn't add the pool chemicals when he was traveling. These memories were triggering a myriad of emotions for him as the wine appeared to be kicking in. I didn't take it personally and felt that we could be more successful talking it out in the morning. I went to bed, figuring that sleeping it off would shift the spiraling dynamics of the storylines.

He didn't come to bed that night until quite late, and when he did, our normal snuggling and affection didn't occur. Feeling disconnected and sad that the romantic trial of our new place had imploded unexpectedly, I hoped we could talk through this. We packed our bags and headed to a breakfast place nearby. As we sat down, he did something my ex-husband used to do. He completely shut down, dismissed my feelings, and refused to discuss the situation. This triggered *me*, and I thought, *I'm not going down this road again.* Our interaction heightened my sensitivity to the fact that his recent breakup was still a bit raw and he might benefit from more healing time.

I wanted a partner I could count on to talk it out. The last thing I wanted was to shove down feelings at this early stage, knowing it would only pull us apart in the end. Red flags went off as I tried to learn from my past while still being in the moment. Maybe his wounds were too big. It became clear that I didn't know enough about Shawn, nor did he know enough about me. A sinking feeling came as I realized we'd moved too far, too fast.

As soon as we arrived back at Shawn's place, I told him that moving in together wasn't a good idea, at least for now. Upset, he canceled his ticket back to the States, and all our engagements were off, as he quickly detached and closed his heart. It felt as though he'd died; we were entirely out of contact almost immediately. I was heartbroken, as I didn't think this would end the relationship, but I trusted that everything happens for a reason.

Experiencing another relationship crumbling, I knew moving forward without him was for my higher good, although this didn't stop the love and deep connection we shared. My dreams for a partner I could build a life plan with were shattered, yet again. Now my focus needed to be on releasing the emotions that tethered us together.

My upcoming solo trip felt like a blessing to help shift me by refueling with friends and family back home. My ticket routed me through San Francisco; this was the segment of the trip during which we'd planned to meet Shawn's family and friends before heading to meet mine. Hearing of the breakup, Laura, who'd introduced us, encouraged me to keep my original ticket and come to their hometown and hang out at her house. I agreed and thought talking through it with her would help heal the wounds.

A few days after my arrival, Laura planned a trip to the nearby wine country for us. It wasn't until we were at her dining room table reviewing the route that I realized we might be passing by Robert's winery, which prompted me to mention him and ask if his estate was on our way. She replied, "Absolutely, and we should stop there." I pondered the idea of reaching out to Robert and hesitantly asked, "Should I email him and see if he's there?" She exclaimed, "Yes! Why wouldn't you?" I thought there really was no point. It might be awkward to connect since he was married now, and we hadn't stayed in touch. But encouraged by Laura's enthusiasm, I decided to send the email.

Within a few hours, a reply dinged back into my inbox. Robert was happy to hear from me, and said he was rarely at the winery but was planning to be there for those exact dates to attend a board meeting. His schedule was jam-packed, but he had a window of thirty minutes when we could meet, and he graciously offered to arrange a tour and lunch for Laura and me upon our arrival.

On our long drive through the wilderness heading toward wine country, Laura and I spoke nonstop about life, love, my breakup with Shawn, my admiration of Robert, and her married life. Before we knew it, we'd arrived at our hotel. It was a beautiful historic property that happened to have live music and a concert that evening. As evening approached, Laura said she wasn't feeling well and encouraged me to still go and not miss the concert.

Since I primarily traveled and lived alone, I was disappointed not to have her join me. As I sat listening to the concert, I wondered what Robert and I would talk about. I hadn't seen him in over a decade. *How would I feel? Why was I meeting him anyway?* I tried to blow it off, but I was speculating what the point of it all would be. Would I open a wound and feel bad? That's the last thing I needed, already having a broken heart from my unexpected breakup with Shawn.

As the music played, I suddenly felt so thankful that Robert had come into my life, albeit years earlier. As though Spirit was answering my question of "What's the point?" the answer came: "Share how grateful you are that he changed the trajectory of your life." My eyes welled up with tears. "What? What was I grateful for? He broke my heart!" I thought we'd had such a profound connection, only to find out that he was in love with someone else. But the recognition came from deep within me. If he hadn't kissed me that night on the plane flying across the US, I would have most likely moved to Oklahoma City and remained with a husband I wasn't soulfully connected to and was misaligned in values with. What could be worse?

Over all the years, I'd hung on to the fact that Robert and I could never fully explore our romantic connection. Now I felt that the Universe was aligning this opportunity so I could share my sentiments regarding the positive impact he'd had on my life. Excited about this shift, I couldn't wait to get on the road and share my revelations with Laura.

Unexpectedly, the next morning, Laura moved slowly and didn't seem to care about our agreed upon departure time. I was eager to make the lunch appointment Robert had arranged for us, so I was disappointed. It became especially difficult because she wasn't interested in sharing what was on her mind. I decided to head to breakfast and give her some alone time, as it was clear that she was processing something. When she arrived to join me, she was upset and informed me that she would drop me at a hotel near Robert's winery and go directly home. This meant I'd spend the next two nights alone before flying out to see my family. She was vague and curt, and I wasn't sure what was happening. I was sad that our beautiful time together was ending on such a bizarre note. Not to mention, how the heck was I to get around wine country without a car? I wasn't looking forward to doing this without her.

We were barely out of town when we came across a sheriff's barricade. There'd been a fatal accident on the highway, and the road wasn't going to be open for at least eight hours. They advised travelers to spend the night, as there was no other highway that would get us moving in that direction. Oh, no! Laura needed to make it home, and I didn't want to miss the thirty-minute window of opportunity to see Robert at his home before his dinner meeting. We stopped in a parking lot nearby to regroup. I saw a local standing next to his truck, so I jumped out and asked him if he knew of another route. He nodded yes but had a troubled look on his face: "There's a back road, but it's a rough ride." He wasn't 100 percent certain if it would get us beyond the point of the accident but said it would be worth trying. He also needed to go that way and suggested that we follow him.

We were initially concerned about the dangerous dirt road, and our fear heightened as we realized we were following a guy with a gun rack and had no idea if he was leading us astray or in the right direction. Thankfully, the road got us to the other side of the closure after we'd endured a road that was meant for all-terrain vehicles. Miraculously we were on our way. The tension subsided, although Laura remained upset, and little conversation took place between us. Regrettably, I had to email Robert's assistant and alert her we'd need to cancel lunch. With all the delays, the probability of arriving in time to meet Robert at all was unlikely. During the drive, I resolved in my mind that if it wasn't meant to be, I'd already had the healing experience with the flow of gratitude. Either way would be okay.

As Laura dropped me at the hotel, I felt frazzled and disoriented. After a quick, awkward goodbye, she was back on the road. I checked my map and saw that, fortunately, the winery was only about ten minutes away. Upon check-in, I asked the hotel to call a car service for me. I dropped my bags in the room, changed my clothes, and was back downstairs in a flash.

In a serendipitous alignment of the Universe, I arrived at Robert's private residence right on time. As I walked up to the door, memories from being there almost twelve years prior came flooding back. To calm my mind as I waited for him, I photographed the many beautiful flowers in the garden near the door. Robert was running a few minutes late, which provided the perfect opportunity to collect myself from the chaos of the day.

Robert texted, inviting me to go inside and make myself at home until he arrived, stating that a staff member would attend to me. Sitting in the living room felt surreal. His staff was diligently preparing for the dinner taking place later that evening in the dining room. Anticipating his arrival, I felt slightly nervous and fidgety as I peered out at the stunning vineyard view through the floor-to-ceiling windows. The last time I was in this room, I was his guest, sitting with a group of friends at the table.

No more than ten minutes had passed when the door opened and Robert walked in. At first glance, he looked almost the same as he did years ago: slender, tall, and beaming with enthusiasm. We had a quick, friendly embrace, and he said, "It's so good to see you."

I couldn't stop myself from smiling and responded, "It's wonderful to see you too; it's been so long!"

Acknowledging his staff member, he then turned to me and said, "Let's go into my private living room."

Admittedly, my heart was softly pounding as I sat down in the chair next to the sofa he was sitting on. There was a beautiful moment when I felt intrigued and delighted that we'd come together after all this time. I couldn't wait to hear what was happening in his life, but without pause, he said, "Tell me everything! I want to hear what you're up to."

Knowing he probably had only about twenty minutes at this point, I did my best to be brief, as I was eager to hear what was going on with him. He followed with updates on his family and spoke briefly on business and life before we had to abruptly leave so he could fulfill his speaking engagement to a group of executives meeting in one of the winery chambers. I knew all these details of his schedule from his original email, so I'd been sensitized to being squeezed, literally, into his calendar.

As we stood up to leave, he inquired about my friend, and I mentioned that she had to head home unexpectedly. He insisted that I be his guest at the restaurant for dinner and offered to give me a ride to the winery, which was less than a mile away. Upon arrival, staff members were waiting, and as we exited the vehicle, he introduced me and asked them to take good care of me. As we walked under the arches at the entrance, it felt as though we'd only gotten started catching up. He momentarily paused, turned to me, and said, "I'll come by the restaurant to say a proper goodbye." Knowing his board members would be awaiting his arrival at dinner, I was quick to say he need not worry about doing so.

As I was seated, my awareness went to a romantic table of two on my right and a four-top of couples enjoying themselves on my left. Memories of the terrace and the first trip, where we'd had such a fantastic weekend together, came flashing back. Moments later, I sat looking at my handbag in the empty chair across from me, which ignited feelings of deep despair that I was still single and sitting alone. Although I knew deep in my heart that I was happier to be alone than in a destructive relationship, disappointment set in yet again. I'd been on my spiritual journey for years, doing the inner work that was tapping me into deeper levels of myself, and I felt great about championing self-love. My request remained simple. I longed to attract a romantic match with a man in a similar vibration and awareness to share life experiences. So why wasn't it happening? Now it felt like a slap in the face as I sat there with tears welling in my eyes.

The happenings of the last twenty-four hours had created a roller coaster of emotions with extreme highs and lows. But now, it was starting to feel like one of my worst days. I'd had a brief encounter with the man who'd woken me from a deep spiritual slumber and with whom I'd always wished I'd been able to explore a deeper relationship.

> My friend wasn't there to chat it out or laugh about life's quandaries, and as the depths of loneliness crept in, this seemed to be the theme of my life that I could no longer ignore.

The tears were coming on stronger, and I desperately wanted to go back to my room and cry. I tried to suck it up and enjoy the incredible food and wine, but the emotions kept swelling, and I prayed the drops wouldn't roll down my cheeks for others to see.

Desperate to find a way to distract myself, I called my mom. She'd met Robert years ago when we were dating and knew I was planning to see him on this trip. So it wouldn't be a surprise, and I decided to risk "losing it" in the hope that she would say something to cheer me up. She answered on the first ring, asking how the day went. This led me to share about Laura's early departure, and while I was disappointed, I had Robert's winery tour and lunch to look forward to the next day. She consoled me by relaying her excitement for my arrival in a few days. Just as our conversation paused, Robert unexpectedly swooped around behind me and sat at the table with me. I swiftly hung up on my mom as my headphones continued to dangle from my ear, hoping she'd figure it out and not try to keep calling me back.

Robert made small talk about how much fun we'd had in New York City and reminisced by expressing, "We really had a great connection." This sentiment surprised me. He'd never affirmed this verbally when we were together, but it seemed undeniable while we were dating. Since our relationship had ended a bit abruptly for me, I had tried to convince myself over the years that I must have imagined our connection.

Spirit quickly stepped in and reminded me to share the insights that had surfaced the night prior. While holding his gaze, I said, "I want to share how grateful I am that you came into my life. I wouldn't be where I am today without the impact you had on me." There was a momentary pause as he gently tilted his head, smiled, and softly said, "That means a lot to me." We both seemed to feel appreciated and acknowledged, and I felt complete. Noticing the time, he gestured for a hug as he stood up and expressed that he wished he didn't have to run off so quickly. He'd be leaving the winery early the following day, and I didn't expect to see him ever again.

As I awoke to the sun rising, I was hit with emotion and began crying my eyes out. I wasn't even sure what made me so sad about the situation. *Was it that emotions about everything were piling up? Or was it the fact I had attached such meaning to my relationship with Robert?* It really wasn't warranted, as we didn't date each other for that long. It was nice that he confirmed he'd also experienced a special connection with me, but life goes on. What was my problem?

Maybe it was the heartbreak I'd left behind in Bali that added to my emotions, or the pattern of not-quite-the-one relationships. Or was it simply that I was so f—ing tired of living my life alone? Having built such an incredible life, I was eager to have someone to travel with, explore life, and share in the depths of love I knew I was capable of in relationships. But it just wasn't happening.

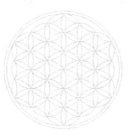

CHAPTER 19

Entrepreneurial Challenges

Arriving back to where I grew up always shined a spotlight on the ideations and programs installed during my childhood. I'd always viewed them as "good ole Midwestern values": work hard, be humble, put your nose to the grindstone, and secure a job or career you think will give you the identity and income that define success. Now I believed something different, as my approach to life had shifted significantly over the last decade through a repertoire of life experiences.

Thankfully my parents had miraculously grown along with me in many ways over the years. While I was in Bali, I talked with them a few times a week around 4:00 p.m. their time, which was 6:00 a.m. mine. In each conversation I'd share the excitement and details from my shop, the healings, interesting visitors, and other random stories about my life. Through it all, my parents have remained my biggest fans, and for that I am grateful. Arriving home this time, I had an even larger number of stories under my belt and an overflowing spiritual toolbox. However, many questions were surfacing that required my deep reflection and honesty.

I couldn't ignore my self-imposed question: "Was I failing as an entrepreneur?" My profit and loss spreadsheet certainly suggested this, as I continued to reflect harshly on my missed sales goals. Yes, I had unleashed my creativity and leveraged my marketing skills, but I wasn't becoming the self-made businesswoman I desired to be. The "fake it until you make it" approach wasn't something that resonated with me either. I was avidly applying the practice of visualizing my goals being achieved and using energy-shifting techniques from innovators such as Tony Robbins and Abraham Hicks. My efforts to straddle life in the mainstream three-dimensional life and an elevated spiritual five-dimensional realm were becoming difficult, especially when I wasn't seeing my returns matching my vision and couldn't get the pivot I needed to accelerate my business.

My life, love, and entrepreneurial experiences had catapulted me forward in many amazing and unique ways. Although a more traditional person might define accomplishments by financial abundance, materialistic gains would most likely frame me as a failure. Google's definition of failure is "a general incompetence, a defect or fault, shortcoming or weakness." None of these descriptors seemed to ring true regarding my entrepreneurial experiences. My desires for Western world materialism seemed to have waned as I gained spiritual wealth from my time in Bali, which felt priceless.

Even though I wasn't interested in acquiring more things in my life, it became increasingly difficult not to have the freedoms and abundance that cash flow provides. Pinching pennies and being frugal was not the energy I wanted to be in. My frustrations increased when my visualizations of abundance were not experienced in my bank account. I had personal standards that I preferred to follow, including owning the home I lived in as an investment, not a monthly rental expense. In addition, I wasn't adding to my savings and retirement investments, which caused some anxiety since I'd been dipping into this more than I was comfortable doing.

> As an entrepreneur, the effort I was putting in seemed endless, but the financial rewards were nowhere near my previous income standards.

Was it black magic holding me back? Hidden limiting beliefs? Lord knows I was doing the work to uncover any beliefs no longer serving me. Was I not focused enough on the right strategies or tactics? Was I pivoting too much, not enough, or too quickly and not staying the course on initiatives I'd worked so hard to implement? Or was it simply not my destiny to help empower pure love and purpose through my products?

The questions hit hard, especially as I had been reminded of Robert's ability to build an empire, which was simultaneously inspiring and deflating. When I was working my corporate job, I'd often felt on top of the world when I came back home to visit my parents, mostly because my relatively stable bank account balance always made me feel secure, and I felt rewarded for all my hard work and accomplishments. Talking about my corporate job was a comfortable conversation, even if I was overwhelmed and overworked, because everyone understood climbing the corporate ladder and what's expected to become "successful."

While I hadn't made a fortune on any of my endeavors just yet, optimism remained one of my strengths, and I resisted going back to traditional ideas and definitions of an accomplished life. This was often difficult, as the external world projected particular ideas about what success looked like, and it was almost 100 percent based on net worth. The reality was that things weren't coming together as I'd initially planned, but had any of *my* plans been *the* plan? What if thinking that I was in control and needed to make things happen was merely part of the illusion? Trusting I was still on the right track, I persevered, believing that things would align, as they often did when I got out of my own way. Knowing that many entrepreneurs experience their most significant wins just as they are about to quit, I was determined not to give up.

Reflecting on my life further brought my attention to my condo back in New Jersey. I'd been living in Bali for about five and a half years and Asia for almost eight. My condo felt like the home I was waiting to go back to, as it was such a special place for me. My life plan of having it as a second home and the dream of sharing it with a future life partner were now in question because some realities were coming forward in my life. Was I going to live in Bali forever? No. My heartstrings were pulling on me as I felt it was time to be closer to my aging parents and my nephews, who were growing up fast.

My questioning continued. Could I afford to move back into my luxury high-rise condo? Not on my current entrepreneurial salary, and I didn't want to use my savings to cover the costs. Did I want to go back to traditional corporate life for income? No. Did I want to live in New Jersey full time? Absolutely not. Enduring the winters wouldn't make me happy, having just come from the tropics. These questions made me realize that my mind was starting to get the best of me.

The more questions I asked and answered, the less clarity I experienced as analysis paralysis set in.

> My logical mind was trying to make sense of it all when I realized going back to my heart center would bring the answers and insights I needed.

How did I *feel* about all these possibilities? What was my heart telling me? Simplifying and prioritizing my desires, it became clear that I wanted to be closer to my family and to live in a warm climate.

A week or so into my visit home, I had an intuitive feeling that the real estate market in New Jersey might be on its way to a downturn. It was 2018, and I was getting an intuitive hit to cash out in an upmarket; I called my realtor to schedule a time to meet upon arriving on the East Coast. If I wasn't going to live in and care for the condo, perhaps it was time to let it go. Almost every year, I had a new tenant. Great ones, luckily, but the property deserved a permanent resident. Frankly, I didn't want to deal with the logistics of managing the property from afar. Logically, selling was probably the best thing, as it would also provide some cash in my checking account. My mind wondered; would not having my condo with a spectacular view of New York City for the future be another failed dream?

It was critical to reframe my entrepreneurial experiences to positively shift the energy. Becoming an entrepreneur had allowed me to build an entirely new set of skills, as I gained significant insights from building a business from the ground up. Being a confident businesswoman, I hadn't been expecting the level of vulnerability I experienced and was feeling uncomfortable about where my business was at. There was no way to hide; creating and running a small business highlighted both my strengths and my areas of opportunities in a way that no corporate job or fancy development program could have touched. When you're a solopreneur with a brick and mortar store, it's a tough job to wear all the hats.

Another aspect that needed shifting was my mindset of judging myself and beating myself up over what wasn't working under the guise of finding solutions. Circuitous loops of thought focused on everything I'd done wrong would not breed success. Of course, it's helpful to know what behaviors and tactics are or aren't serving business goals. But being hard on myself was a part of my upbringing, as I was rewarded for finding faults to fix. This wasn't a bad thing, but there's an energy that comes with judgments, and it requires a healthy balance of discernment, not negativity. This often requires staying in the energy of receiving, which is different from doing and giving. This same type of thinking is reinforced in corporate environments where everyone's trying to jostle to get ahead, often through notoriety for finding faults in others. Instead, I needed to shift to what's working successfully and maximize people's strengths.

It was clear I really needed to stay focused on every little thing that *was* working and the importance of remaining open to receiving. I came to recognize I wasn't intensifying the energy around the small wins, seeing only the big misses, which was impacting my flow of receiving. Doing a happy dance with every customer purchase wasn't my thing, but it was clear that being happy and grateful for every sale, no matter the amount, could shift the flow. When the losses outweighed the wins, staying in this positive vibration became harder.

I was always good at finding another way, a new possibility, brainstorming ideas, and taking action.

> As time went on, I practiced my belief that life is about our ability to make another choice.

I had pivoted a lot and worked harder than at any corporate job, paving new roads with unique strategies and tactics. All through it, Spirit was guiding me to another level of trust that everything was happening for a reason. It was a time that challenged my inner "knowing" that all the threads would eventually come together with meaning and significance.

Taking inspired action and intuitive risks over the years was fulfilling. I utilized this often when designing new products and implementing new business ideas. But the profit and loss always drew me back to a concerning mindset. The reality remained that I was nowhere near being able to sustain myself with my business in its current financial state.

More questions and doubts surfaced. Had I bought into this world of spirituality only to learn that living my dreams meant being the "starving artist" archetype I'd always feared? Perhaps the concept of manifesting wasn't working for me any longer. Was this some kind of cosmic joke, and I'd reached a secret limit of manifestations in a lifetime? I didn't believe this to be the case, but at the same time, I wasn't being shown anything encouraging when it came to big financial wins.

My storefront in Bali was a huge stepping-stone, a dream to pursue, and a way to share my intention of pollinating love through inspirational jewelry, flower photos, and other products, but brick and mortar was never my forever dream. My business capacity was much greater than the daily dealings of a retail store in a country where I could not hire fellow Westerners to support my vision. Fortunately, I had the wisdom and intuition to know when to fold, as it was the perfect time to exit. The store was an incredible chapter in my life, but it wasn't meant to be my life any longer. I would soon recognize that the Universe truly had my back. As I closed the doors for one final time, I found myself reflecting fondly on the many beautiful experiences, connections, and learnings I'd gained. I was blessed to have been able to put my heart and soul into my business, leverage my creativity, and meet people from all walks of life from around the world. I felt complete and relieved at the same time.

Just months after closing the shop, Mount Agung, Bali's largest volcano, unexpectedly became active after being dormant for almost one hundred years. People fled the island since a massive eruption was thought to be imminent. Tourists, expats, and Indonesian workers fled the island in droves, although I chose to stay. At the height of the predicted eruption, the smell of hydrogen sulfide wafted through Ubud. Googling about the danger, I learned this gas could lead to acid rain, and there was already heavy pollution with ash in the air.

This rattled me, and when I called a dear friend, Leticia, she said, "Let's go!" We packed our bags and put her children and Lily in the car. Within two hours we had a driver taking us to the northeast tip of Bali. This appeared to be the farthest point on the island from the volcano, where Lily and I would stay, while Leticia planned to take her children on the ferry across the channel, as it was the only way off the island. Even if I had wanted to leave the island, Lily wouldn't have been able to go because she wasn't microchipped, and a month's lead time was required for paperwork and logistics.

My parents were verging on hysteria. They repeatedly shared that when Mount St. Helens erupted in the eighties, North Dakota, over 1,300 miles away, was covered in ash. The island of Bali spans only ninety-five miles from one side to the other, and it was a serious possibility that many people could die. There was no way I would leave the island without Lily, even when a life-threatening eruption seemed imminent. Silly?

Perhaps, but I trusted that it wasn't our time to part from each other or die in a natural disaster and wasn't going to live in fear of this. Luckily the volcano never fully erupted, and we only suffered a few inches of ash. This was a dramatic experience but allowed Lily and me to spend two weeks waiting it out in a gorgeous little oceanside town.

This event was something no business plan could have possibly accounted for and caused many stores and restaurants to close permanently. If I'd decided to extend my lease, the shop would have been decimated, as no business happened on the island for almost an entire year. The Universe was taking care of me; it had spoken to me, and I had listened. But my disappointment about not meeting my sales projections remained on my mind. Many days I had to give myself a pep talk to avoid going down the rabbit hole of disenchantment as a solopreneur. Nothing I'd done had been a small task. Creating a company internationally wasn't easy, nor was finding my way through all the tenant improvements to build a store and design and manufacture numerous product lines. Launching the innovative *Savvy Insider's Guide* brochure and a radio show were also notable accomplishments. Knowing I had a choice in how I would frame this time of my life, I was determined not to let the ego-mind get the best of me by making comparisons solely based on third-dimensional ideations of how success is determined.

While I was deeply immersed in my dreams, I never knew why they didn't work out. It wasn't until I stepped away and observed myself that I could finally laugh at how seriously I took everything. The wisdom I'd embodied was worth more than any external creation I could have provided to the material world. At the same time, I watched many friends continue to climb through job titles, salary increases, and obtain numerous worldly possessions. For me, the glamor and benefits were not worth more than all the amazing life experiences I'd encountered. I trusted that the future held new opportunities to frolic back into the financial fun of life. I appreciated now more than ever that it was the inward journey that had helped me see the beauty beyond all the beliefs of the world, and

I realized the real magic unfolds when I detach from what
I think I'm here to do or be.

All the while, through all my explorations, the Universe was holding me and teaching me the importance of learning the many lessons
along the way. These years as a "failed" entrepreneur ended up being the
most significant and fruitful years of my life. Focusing on the inner healing work that heightened my awareness and expanded my consciousness was one of the greatest gifts that would serve my purpose in due
time. Without taking all the risks and big jumps, I wouldn't have made
the deeper dives to be where I am today emotionally, spiritually, and
mentally.

During my visit back to the States, these reflections hit me hard; I
seemed to be having new revelations at every turn while in the energy of
the Westernized world. My month in the United States went by quickly,
and my travels to see family and friends would soon end. It had been a
whirlwind in such a short time. And now the final week would be on the
East Coast, staying with Katarina in New Jersey for a few days, checking on my condo, and meeting with my realtor for a coffee chat about
the real estate market. My last stop was with Jessica and her family on
Long Island before returning to Bali out of JFK Airport in New York. It
was always great to have my final hug come from my dearest childhood
friend, especially knowing that no matter what happened in life, she'd
be there for me.

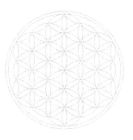

CHAPTER 20

Leaving Black Magic Behind

T OURISM REMAINED AT an all-time low due to the aftermath of the volcanic eruption scare, and the island felt very subdued upon my return. Many of my expat friends had left, although my business owner friends remained optimistic that tourism would start again, wanting to revitalize their businesses. The energy of this situation deepened my conviction that my time to leave the island of bliss was approaching.

My realtor in the US remained diligent and persistent about selling my condo. After much deliberation, I was finally able to settle my mind by deciding I'd only sell it if I could get the price I wanted. If I didn't receive offers meeting my number, I'd hold on to it. The day I saw the photographs on the realtor's website listing, I knew I'd be heading back to the US sooner rather than later. I trusted that the Universe would bring me a buyer who would cherish the home I loved so much. Even though I could not spend much time in that little oasis in the sky, it was still a part of my heart. I knew that selling it would provide closure to another aspect of my life. I was right. I had offers almost immediately.

The next big hurdle was thinking about the logistics of leaving my home, managing my Bali business from afar, and working through the challenges of getting Lily out of the country, as dogs are not allowed to fly out of the international airport in Bali. If I was going to attempt to take her, I'd need to get going on all the requirements for microchipping and completing the paperwork required to pass through customs in the US.

One last session with Tunjung seemed timely to provide insights regarding the big moves coming up. Although I felt proficient in accessing other realms and guidance from my higher self, tapping into guidance from trusted psychic readers, healers, and shamans for validation still provided additional clarity and insights I might not have tapped into on my own. Suspecting it might be a while before I'd be back in Bali, I also wanted to see her because we'd become friendly with one another. As I sat down, we both smiled and started laughing, which helped to lighten the mood before we embarked on our typical philosophical topics.

Moving into the healing segment of our session, Tunjung had me lie on the table. This allowed her to use her crystals on reflexology points on my feet and other key points on my body. When I felt the first poke of the crystals pressing into my skin, I almost passed out from the pain and didn't hold back yelling to let her know. Next, she placed many crystals on my solar plexus, the area around my belly button. Lying there in a meditative state, I relaxed into calming energy, feeling small bursts of air from the large feather she oscillated over the top of my body. I found this interesting, as she was doing things she hadn't done in prior appointments.

As the session ended and I started to open my eyes, Tunjung had an interesting look on her face. She exclaimed,

"I just took *a lot* of black magic out of you!"

I popped off the table, shocked and annoyed. "*What*?! I thought you said not to believe in black magic!" I continued in frustration, "I came to you on my first visit asking about this. Why are you validating this now?"

She explained that she always recommends not giving black magic any energy through thoughts or fear; she also noted that she doesn't always see it until it comes to the surface. She further elaborated that it can only be observed and cleared once the individual is ready for the learning, emphasizing that no one would have been able to help me until I was prepared to release it at a soul level.

"*Unbelievable!*" I said as I sat back in the chair across from her, with the crystal ball (a real one!) in between us.

"Three of them are still actively doing black magic on you." In the next breath, she looked me in the eye and said, "Don't try to figure out who they are; it will only give them more power."

"I don't have to think about it!" I exclaimed. "They are showing up here very clearly—I can see all three of them right now."

Tunjung softly and emphatically replied, "Great. Thank them for the lesson. It's done. Now you need to move on."

In disbelief and concern, I said, "How do you know for sure? Especially if they are actively doing this?"

"Trust me. I've removed the black magic. Do not give it any energy or thought. Do you understand?"

Honestly, I was pissed off because I'd felt this all along and wondered why I would choose to block her from seeing it over the last five years! The three people included Kadek, the silversmith, the Westerner who'd introduced us, and the priestess in her village who'd doused me with water. Now all my unexplainable struggles seemed to make sense. At that moment, something powerful opened within my chest, like a beam of light facilitating a sense of closeness to Source energy that I'd only felt while in deep meditation or a healing session.

On my way home, I broke into laughter, thinking this was the funniest thing I'd ever experienced. It was like when a kid is scared of the boogieman in the closet and then one of their parents opens the door, all the terror miraculously disappears. Now here I was with the door flung open, and suddenly my fears about black magic had vanished! I realized *it is all energy*. Only when we hold on to the thought constructs about it can we be impacted.

Understanding the deeper meaning of the ongoing swirl of the light and dark energies felt like a massive initiation. I reflected on a conversation with the water purification high priestess in which she shared with me that before being ordained, priests had to choose whether they would work with the dark or the light. This blew me away; I couldn't possibly imagine that any Balinese, let alone a priest, would choose the dark side. So much knowledge was converging about these energies and the lessons regarding the balance of how the dark and light work together.

As this was swirling, so were the offers on my condo. A serious buyer was eager for me to accept or counter their offer. Everything was moving quickly in negotiations as I made my final offer, which included all my furniture to sweeten the deal. A week later, we had a signed contract. Emotions flowed through my body at that moment; I felt excited and anxious about selling my oasis in the sky. The inspection was seamless, and a closing date was set.

Now that I had experienced a financial win, a feeling of abundance I hadn't felt in years finally flowed through. This highlighted for me, once again, how impacted I'd been by my scarcity mentality infiltrating my mind since leaving my corporate paycheck and benefits. The impact of the black magic only made the experience of scarcity more profound, as I found it difficult to manifest things that had been easy in the past. Now I would be free of a mortgage and could start my life in the US with some additional cash in my bank account. The most important factor in coming back was to be geographically closer to my nephews and parents. I was excited about spending family time together.

As the days came to a close in Bali, I let go of 90 percent of my furnishings, including my furniture and everything in my kitchen and bath.

Both my households and earthly life as I knew it were about to be gone. Was I ready for this? Spirit said yes, and I willingly and joyfully followed suit, seeing this as an opportunity to scrub my life, practice non-attachment, and energetically free myself.

The first step required the daunting task of getting Lily and myself on an airplane. Avoiding the issue of the ban on flying dogs out of Bali, I hired a special driver recommended by a French woman. She confirmed that he had connections and could secretly get us on the boat ferry and drive us to Jakarta, where we could legally fly out. According to Google Maps, the trip would take twenty-four hours without stops. I planned to arrive five days early in Jakarta to do the necessary health check on Lily and obtain the official customs paperwork that would allow us to fly out of Indonesia and into the United States.

The driver arrived, and both Wayan and Putu were by my side as we loaded Lily and my luggage into the truck. I was nervous because Lily would be confined to a crate shoved into the back of the enclosed truck. There was an air conditioner and fan to keep Lily cool, but I knew she would not like being in this confined space. Being a feral dog, Lily had made it clear to me early on in our relationship that freedom was her number one priority. Now I was trapping her in these confines until we were through the checkpoints at the ferry entrance.

When I realized the driver didn't speak English—my Bahasa was minimal—both Wayan and Putu could see my stress. They both communicated that Lily and I were like family and that he should take good care of us. This made me feel better, but I was anxious to get across the border and hoped Lily would remain quiet while the customs officials checked the car.

After about five hours of bumpy, winding roads in the back seat of a pickup truck, I was nauseous and happy to hear the driver say, in broken English, that we were nearing the ferry entrance. Moments later, the driver turned to me unexpectedly and said, "Get down!" I thought, *What*? Startled, I saw guards walking toward the truck as I lay down across the back seat. No one told me I was going to have to hide! Soon after this checkpoint, I could tell that we were driving onto the ferry as the wheels hit the metal plates, making a loud noise. Within ten minutes, the horn was blaring, and we were pushing off the dock. My heart raced, and I prayed Lily wouldn't whine or bark. It was the longest twenty-minute ferry ride of my life. Upon reaching the other side, we remained incognito until we were about an hour into Java, and then we pulled over to get Lily out of the back of the truck. She was distressed, but we were happy to be in each other's arms.

The trip to Jakarta was worse than I could have ever expected. It took over forty-eight hours driving nonstop, with two other drivers rotating in to give my driver a break. There was a system to the madness, and our few stops to eat and use the restroom were coveted. It was impossible to sleep in an uncomfortable truck at high speeds in nerve-racking traffic. It was 3:00 a.m. when Lily and I checked into our hotel room in the city center of Jakarta. The French woman who'd connected me to the driver had recommended this hotel, as it accepted dogs. The accommodations were horrifying and at the top of the list for the worst places I'd ever stayed! This appeared to be a hotel that accepted hourly reservations, and there wasn't a clean spot in the room.

Exhausted, I kept trying to tell myself to go to sleep. But that was difficult, knowing the place was probably full of bed bugs and more. I put bug spray all over and covered the pillow with a towel and laid my head down while remaining completely clothed from head to toe. All I could do was stare at myself in the ceiling mirror—yes, a ceiling mirror—fuming at the French woman and wondering why I had to endure this. Watching Lily sleeping at my feet, my thoughts turned to gratitude that we'd arrived safely after the tumultuous journey, and I looked forward to laughing about it in the future.

A few hours later, the sun was up, prompting me to go online to look for a pet-friendly hotel. Indonesia, with the exception of the island of Bali, is a Muslim country, which meant dogs were not welcome in most places. After about ten calls, I finally found a home available at the British International School. It was larger than we needed and way over my budget, but I wanted a clean bed, a safe place, and a space that allowed Lily to use outdoor facilities without scrutiny or offending the local culture.

The driver from the school arrived around 9:00 a.m., and in less than an hour, we arrived at a beautiful oasis. Now we were safe, and we had a roof over our heads and a pillow free of bugs. As we let our guard down and settled in, it was time to focus on making sure all the details for Lily's final health check at customs were being finalized. It was a stressful day because I wasn't allowed to be with her during the visit to immigration and customs authorities at the airport. She had panic attacks when veterinarians poked at her, and I knew she'd be anxious and a growling mess. Hesitantly, I handed her over to the professional agency that I paid to handle these details. Thankfully she passed all her tests, the paperwork was complete, and everything was a go. Having a few days to wait, I relaxed into preparing for our departure.

The night of our flight, I became nervous about flying Lily. She'd never traveled in a crate, other than during the traumatic ride in the truck, nor had she experienced the noises or turbulence of an airplane. I knew she'd be frightened during the twenty-four hours it would take for us to arrive on US soil. As the agents placed the "Live Animal" sticker on her crate, my mind froze and fixated on the risk I was taking to have her with me. But leaving her wasn't an option I would consider. I prayed she would make the trip unharmed and without drama, as many friends warned me of horrific stories of transports gone wrong. Upon our arrival at the airport in Jakarta, Lily was in a nervous tizzy due to all the loud noises. Knowing she would pick up on my anxiety, I tried my best to remain calm and hold it all together.

A major issue ensued at the check-in counter: my luggage was too heavy, which caused an hour delay. I pleaded with the gate agent, negotiating an option to pay for the overage as I frantically shuffled the contents of my bags. I had already reached the maximum luggage and weight requirement but eventually encouraged them to break the rules and let me pay exxtra. Completing this task, I reached in to give Lily one last pat on the head. Unexpectedly, she grabbed my hand with her paw and tried to hang on as I closed the door. My heart ached; I tried my best to hold back the tears while I watched the crew load her cage on the luggage belt.

I ran to the gate, boarding in the nick of time but drenched in sweat. Worried whether Lily had made it into cargo below, I frantically spoke to the crew to confirm that she was onboard. After checking, they reassured me that she had boarded, and I prayed she was okay. Exhausted, I planned to sleep and hoped Lily would do the same on our eight-hour flight headed to Doha, Qatar.

The airlines promised that they'd let Lily out to walk, eat, and do her business during our three-hour layover. Stressed that I couldn't receive any updates on her, I finally concluded that I'd need to relax and trust she was in good hands.

As we approached JFK in New York, my emotions started to swell. I would be landing in the US to live, not just to visit; I had Lily with me and a new life ahead that was full of unknowns. As I walked toward the luggage area, I kept my eyes peeled for the kennel with Ms. Lily inside. I waited by the oversized luggage area, hoping to hear her bark, but no sounds came out. All my other luggage was already off the belt, and my heart raced as I waited for her. Eventually, I could see the kennel coming out. I held my breath, hoping she was okay. We locked eyes and all she could do was whimper. She didn't have enough energy to bark and appeared frazzled and anxious. Excited to be reunited with Lily, I couldn't stop squeezing and kissing her on the way to my condo in Jersey City.

I'd negotiated a closing date that would give me one month to sort the last of my belongings and clear out my storage unit in the building. Knowing this would be a quick stop back into my old life, I wondered, *How will I feel? Will I be triggered? Will I regret selling my condo?* Lots of emotions swirled, and I couldn't ignore the fact that I was deeply saddened by the idea of letting go of my little oasis in the sky. Yet I knew this was another moment in life where trusting in the unknown, without attachment, was key.

Lily's first elevator ride to the forty-second floor was a bit traumatic, as she'd never experienced this before. The noises and the feeling of floating upward didn't go over so well for this once rice paddy-running Bali dog. Walking into my old life, it felt strange to have a pup by my side. Lily quickly sniffed the place out, and within moments I felt "home" again. The rush of memories of high heels and designer suits felt familiar, although nonexistent for years. This reminded me of when I first left corporate life and experienced severe foot cramps for over a year until my body adjusted from high heels to flip-flops.

I loved living in nature and being with the animals in Bali, but something about my Westernized space invigorated me. Jersey City was a place where I'd healed heartbreak and started a new life, and it would undoubtedly remain a special place in my heart. I felt connected to Source energy in a different way than in the rice fields of Bali. New York City felt blissful from this high floor, and the buzz of energy flowed across the river. The transition was much easier for me than for Lily; she was petrified by the view, perplexed by the elevators, and couldn't get grounded. I'm sure her first chakra was a mess, as fear and anxiety of the unknowns kicked in. She'd lost her job protecting the villa and had no idea how to navigate the concrete of the big city. I hoped she'd adapt to modernized living and quickly find her way in the West with me. We'd be moving swiftly and only be in the condo long enough to unpack and prepare for the closing at the end of the month.

There was a lot for both of us to integrate, as the energies of our Bali life were very different. As I observed the masses of people swiftly walking the streets on their way to work, it seemed that everyone felt separate, isolated, and lonely and was quietly struggling. There wasn't a feeling of people caring for the community or tribe like I'd become accustomed to in Ubud. No one was waving or tapping their horns in a friendly hello. Everyone was looking down or straight ahead without a glance or a smile; they appeared to be on their own in a world that felt harsh and unforgiving.

The lessons from *A Course in Miracles* and everything I'd learned about flowing in life were being put into practice.

> Undoubtedly, the best times of my life after divorce were when I didn't have a clue what was coming next.

That's not to say I couldn't create a plan but that I knew there already was one, and I simply needed to follow it with gratitude and listen to the intuitive guidance coming through.

As I started visualizing my new life, I knew my radio show would keep me going. I was excited about pursuing several new ideas of how I could take it to the next level. Since launching the show in Bali, I'd had great success with guests, and now my creativity was on high speed. Why limit it to a radio show with only audio when video would be much more dynamic? I'd always envisioned having my own TV talk show, and this would get me closer to that goal. I wanted to create a studio feel that would allow for in-person interviews, eventually rolling out my larger vision, involving a pop-up studio audience. The idea to broadcast out of a mobile vehicle, empowering others to live their life's purpose, was exciting. This was only the beginning phase of the show concept I planned to pitch to producers and sponsors. Maybe the *House Hunters International* production team would be interested in taking on my new concept.

After some research, I purchased a Ram cargo van and planned to convert it into an interview studio to record the episodes. Instead of heading west after the condo closing as initially planned, I built out the van on the East Coast. Since completing this project would take some time, Katarina graciously invited Lily and me to stay with her while I worked on this new endeavor. This resulted in residing with her for a few months, as our departure date to head west wasn't until early November.

I'd recruited my dad to drive with us from New Jersey to Texas. From there, Axel would fly in from California to drive with me to Arizona. I picked a date and bought airline tickets for the guys to show up for their driving and travel companion assignments. I had high hopes of showing my dad some sights along the way. However, blizzard conditions were forecasted, diminishing the possibility of exploring sites until we got to warmer weather down south.

Enjoying some father-daughter time, we were able to have long chats and fun stops with relatives in Atlanta. We also spent an evening in

New Orleans, which was eye-opening for Dad, as he'd never been there. We did the customary walk down Bourbon Street, along with a stop at the famous Café du Monde restaurant. We didn't order any beignets because my dad is very practical and didn't see the point of spending the money on a glorified donut. However, we did pop into a touristy New Orleans restaurant for a crawfish dinner before heading to our hotel on the outskirts of town.

After crossing several states with three overnights, Dad and I reached Texas in time for him to catch his plane back home to North Dakota. My dad is an avid hunter and needed to get home to finish out the deer hunting season. He was always eager to get back into nature and be in the wilderness. Off he went as Axel arrived, and we were on our way, headed west to Arizona. Axel and I had a great time talking about life and discussing *A Course in Miracles*, as we'd done throughout the years.

Arriving in Scottsdale after being on the road for over a week was exciting. Upon dropping Axel at the airport, my anticipation to see my brother's family and hug my nephews grew. We were all thrilled to reconnect, and I couldn't wait for them to finally meet Lily. I hoped she'd immediately get along with their dog, Dakota, a large chocolate Lab. However, the introduction was a little strained as Lily put on her best Bali growl, hoping to scare her. Luckily, Dakota wasn't bothered and somehow knew it was her job to integrate her into Western dog life. Lily needed this playful approach, as she'd struggled to fit in at the dog parks on the East Coast. All she knew from her Bali upbringing was protecting territory, and she didn't understand the concept of play yet.

Thinking I would be in Arizona for a three-month layover, I moved the twenty boxes of my household that I'd brought from Jersey City into a storage unit and began looking for a temporary place to live. Long story short, that plan wasn't meant to be *the* plan either, and I was inspired to sign a one-year lease. Now I'd have to repurchase furniture! But something about it seemed so fitting, as my new home was only fifteen minutes away from my nephews. This was a dream come true, and I looked forward to spending more time together, especially during these most precious preteen years.

Unpacking my boxes uncovered some items I hadn't seen in almost eight years. The few keepsakes and cherished household items I'd kept through all my moves provided the perfect touch of fond memories to incorporate into my new home. My brother's family worked hard to help me set everything up, even hanging photos and mirrors. I appreciated their assistance more than I would have ever imagined. It felt wonderful to have family nearby, and I realized I hadn't had this since college. Setting up a residence here felt so guided, and I was grateful to have listened to the call to be near them. My parents were an easy forty minutes away, and with my brother's family minutes down the road, there would inevitably be numerous opportunities to partake in activities together. Or so I thought.

I loved attending my nephews' lacrosse, soccer, and baseball games and was thrilled to have my mom and dad, my brother, and his family gathering to watch the boys play and compete. Loving my tiny apartment in the heart of Scottsdale, I dreamt of all the things I could do with my nephews nearby. However, within a month or so, I started to see that the excitement I had about spending time together wasn't going to come to fruition.

My requests for playdates were denied because schedules were "too busy." It probably took me longer than most to realize it just wasn't going to happen. I didn't get to help drive them places, hang out, make memories, or have sleepovers—all the stuff I knew my auntie friends were getting to do with their nieces and nephews. It was crushing for me. I looked for opportunities to discuss the situation, hoping more openings would transpire. But sadly, I wasn't successful making any inroads.

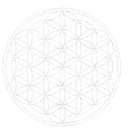

CHAPTER 21

Intriguing Romantic Encounters

Six months into my Scottsdale lifestyle, the heat of the desert summer was taking a toll on me. My parents, being snowbirds, had left in the spring to go back to North Dakota. Not having them around and seeing my nephews for such a limited time left me feeling lonely. I began contemplating the purpose of sitting in the desert heat alone.

Then one day, I unexpectedly received an introduction to a gentleman named Mark. On our first phone call, he shared that he'd immigrated to the US by himself when he was sixteen years old. This piqued my curiosity, and I wanted to learn more. We both enjoyed our conversation and proceeded to make a date for tea at 10:00 a.m. on Saturday morning. I figured morning tea was harmless and easy to leave if we weren't a match.

I arrived early and was standing in front of the restaurant when I saw Mark come around the corner toward me. I was taken aback by his size and stature; he looked like a Roman warrior, although much softer and more approachable. He had dark hair, a beautiful skin tone, and a gorgeous smile. I'd not dated someone quite like this and looked forward to exploring someone so different from my typical "type." Upon sitting down, we talked endlessly and barely touched the food we had in front of us, as it felt less important than all the fun stories we were sharing.

He grew up in the countryside of a small country in the Middle East. Although he'd lived in a few different cities in the US, he'd been a resident of Arizona for over twenty-five years. He'd also traveled the world extensively and spent significant time in Asia, including Singapore. Coincidentally, he was there at the same time I'd lived there, and we could have likely walked past each other, as he had meetings in the same building where I worked. Talking with someone who'd had an adventurous life and was cultured was incredibly refreshing. He came across as a good human, and I was interested in learning more about him. It was apparent that we were both enjoying our conversation as tea turned into lunch after a brief walk in the heat.

Mark and I were from very different upbringings but quickly learned that we had some similar experiences and interests. I shared a lot about my spiritual and entrepreneurial ventures. Mark, being an engineer, was science-based. Although he wasn't familiar with most of my atypical healing modalities and paranormal experiences, he appeared open to topics of spirituality. He viewed things from a scientific background and wanted proof of everything philosophical. This led him to share his interest in the Large Hadron Collider in Geneva. He explained that it's the largest experiment in human history looking at subatomic particles and the origin of the universe. With me being focused on expanding consciousness and all topics being spiritual, there were some interesting links between us bridging science and spirituality. After all, several of my books were on quantum physics, so I could discuss awakening topics from a science orientation.

Somewhere in the middle of all this high-vibe discussion, he reached his arm up around the back of my chair and gently placed the tips of his fingers on my back. The connection between us was undeniable and was accelerated by this simple movement. I could feel the heat radiating through his hands going directly into my spine. This activated me to be more intrigued about our unexpected connection. After we devoured a pizza and finished a bottle of rosé, he leaned over and ever so softly, yet firmly, kissed me on the lips. We continued talking, and several hours later, we were off to a sushi dinner.

Our morning tea had turned into a ten-hour date, and by 8:00 p.m., he was on his way home. This day had gone in a completely unexpected way. Reflecting on our time, I was ecstatic to have romantic interest in a man who could also partake in philosophical and spiritual discussions.

Over the next few months, the intensity grew between Mark and me as we got to know one another better. I had fun introducing him to my friends and family, as it was easy for me to share with others how I felt about him. He'd mentioned that he'd been divorced for a few years on our first date and claimed his marriage had been at a standstill regarding intimacy for several years prior. So I didn't see any sensitivities for us to be moving into a relationship, especially since he'd mentioned that he was looking for a long-term, committed relationship when we met. Several months passed, and he wasn't introducing me to anyone. I understood waiting to share with his teenage children, but it seemed strange that he wouldn't want his friends to know about me. We talked all the time, and he came over frequently, but I was disappointed that he wasn't interested in me being a part of his life.

Since Mark had asked me to be in an exclusive relationship with him in the first few weeks, this led me to believe that he was serious about exploring a potential future together. But he wasn't making me a priority, as he wasn't available on many nights, including some weekends. We were intimately connected when he and I were together and seemed inseparable. Romantically and sexually, he was all in, but I deserved more than being a secret to everyone else.

My work life kept me happily distracted, as I enjoyed taping show episodes inside the van. Interesting people seemed to fall into my lap, and I had almost effortless connections to show guests. I frequently traveled to California to film my interviews since many of my well-known guests lived there. Some of my favorites included Brian Smith, the founder of UGG boots; Hawk Koch, a popular Hollywood producer; and Louie Schwartzberg, a famous time-lapse cinematographer, to name a few. Every episode I filmed impacted my life in some way, and I was grateful for these dynamic conversations.

Louie's interview seemed to happen in Divine timing. I'd admired his work for years, as he was on the cutting edge with time-lapse videography of flowers and nature. He was especially interested in talking about his recently launched documentary, *Fantastic Fungi*. Questions flowed as I learned more about the superhighways of communication and connection to Mother Nature we can all tap into. I had heard of the concept of trees talking to each other via their root systems but never knew the role fungi played in this biological ecosystem.

> Much of what the flowers had been teaching me about allowing and receiving became clear as he described the mycelium network of mushrooms underground.

This superhighway of interconnectedness also represented the aboveground energetic connection we all have to one another and to Source energy.

Louie had a strong relationship with plants and flowers, which led me to inquire about his opinion on magic mushrooms and spiritual medicines. He spoke highly of psilocybin mushrooms, the psychoactive type, and encouraged me to try them in the right set and setting. This piqued my interest, but I wasn't so sure I would jump on the bandwagon of these trendy new-age drugs disguised as "spiritual medicines." I was familiar with magic mushrooms, as they were legal in Bali, but I didn't have a desire to partake in them. Intrigued by everything he shared that day, I left with a greater appreciation for Mother Nature's magic and how humans can interact with it.

As Thanksgiving approached, I'd hoped to spend the day with family. However, I didn't want to impose myself on my brother's family and unfortunately, my parents wouldn't be in Arizona in time. I really didn't want to be alone during the holidays as I'd spent several away from family while living abroad. Since things were moving along with Mark, we made plans to spend it together a week in advance. The night before, Mark alerted me that he'd had a change in plans and wasn't going to be able to spend Thanksgiving day with me. This was a bit upsetting because I thought our relationship meant something more. This last-minute cancellation made it painfully obvious that it didn't. When he asked me to go to the store with him to buy groceries for the dinner he'd planned the next day without me, the relationship was over in my mind. Breaking up would be a logistical formality. Disappointed, I sat wondering if perhaps I'd made a mistake signing a one-year lease in Arizona.

Sitting in my rocking chair on Thanksgiving morning, unshowered and feeling down, I looked forward to the Macy's Thanksgiving Day Parade, thinking it would lift my spirits. Around 11:40 a.m., my phone rang. It was my nephew asking, "Can you come over for Thanksgiving?" I said, "Sure, what time?" He said, "We're eating in fifteen minutes." I told him I'd be on my way but would be a few minutes late. It would take me fifteen minutes to drive there, and I had to collect myself, not wanting to look so disheveled. We had a great meal together, and I was happy we could all spend a portion of the day together. Admittedly, I was sad that I lived fifteen minutes away and yet, over the previous eleven months, we'd spent minimal time together.

Christmas was fast approaching, only a few weeks away. When my friend Leticia, who was living in London, invited me to join her family, I accepted the invitation. On the way, I planned to stop in New York City for a few days to see Jessica and her family before flying abroad. My parents were crushed, but I wasn't going to wait until the morning of, hoping to receive an invitation to watch my nephews open gifts. When asking, they were noncommittal, and I wanted advanced plans for the holiday.

It was overwhelming to have come back to the United States intending to spend time with family only to have it become one of the loneliest periods of my life. By December, only a year after I'd arrived, it was clear that it was time to move out of Scottsdale. I'd been driving back and forth to California once a month, which inspired me to explore moving back there. It seemed the sooner I moved, the better I'd feel. I booked a flight to California in early December to visit my friend Dee and go house hunting.

While driving in Encinitas, we saw an interesting property with a rental sign out front. I immediately called the number, and the owner answered, saying, "I'm here now; please come." Within moments of entering, I was confident it would be my new home. After the walk-through, I said, "I'll take it." Just like that, my life changed, and I was exhilarated to be moving on from my family and boyfriend dilemmas. My trip to London to enjoy the holidays would be a highlight followed by a new home in the new year.

I announced my upcoming move in the new year to my parents, and they were disappointed. After having their dream of me living so close come true, they were not pleased to hear I would be moving to California and would be absent for Christmas. Telling my nephews was the most challenging part for me. I don't think it significantly impacted them, although they were inquisitive about why I was moving less than a year after I'd arrived. This was hard to explain, as I didn't feel it was appropriate to tell them that the limited time constraints were agonizing for me. I positioned it as a desire to be by the ocean, which was true.

A welcome surprise came out of the blue: an email from Robert appeared in my inbox with the subject line, "Where in the world are you?" A burst of excitement shot through me. We hadn't been in touch since my twenty-minute meeting with him at his winery years prior. Where was he? And why would he be reaching out? Was he single? I couldn't wait to find out. The timing of this was incredible. Or maybe I was elated about nothing.

I responded and provided a brief update, sharing that I lived in Scottsdale. He returned the note, mentioned that he was no longer married, and said he was coming to Phoenix in the new year on a business trip. He'd be arriving only days before my scheduled move. Thrilled to have the Universe align us once again, we carved out time for a Sunday lunch with great anticipation of reconnecting.

December was a busy month, as I actively prepared my household for the big move. One of the best parts was knowing I'd only be a one-hour plane ride away, or a six-hour car ride if I wanted to come back to visit family and could easily bring Lily. Despite my disappointment with Mark and our imminent breakup, life was starting to swirl again, and I had many great things to look forward to.

During my time in New York City and London, great memories were created, and a strength within me to move forward was blossoming. While in England, I sent Mark the breakup email that I'd been writing in my head for weeks. It wasn't easy, as the relationship had so much potential. We had a special connection between us, but his inability to treat me like a significant other in his life drove us apart. I desired a man who fully appreciated me and couldn't wait to share his world with me.

The new year came in with a bang, and my lunch date with Robert was approaching. Our excitement to see one another seemed mutual, and we frequently texted in the days leading up to his arrival. However, the thought of seeing him made me a bit nervous. I wondered if we'd still have the same intense chemistry or romantic interest in one another. As I drove to meet him, a jolt of excitement started running through me in anticipation of our reconnection.

Arriving at the hotel, I waited for him in the lobby. It was only a few minutes when I glanced over and saw him walking enthusiastically toward me. A great sense of calm flowed through my body. It was that feeling of familiarity again, which seemed to emanate between us, and my nervousness subsided almost instantly. There was no awkwardness as we jumped into a hired car to take us to our lunch reservation. Robert immediately grabbed my hand, touching it softly as our conversation started up and flowed nonstop through our three-hour lunch date. It was like meeting up with a dear friend I hadn't seen in years.

The chemistry was still zinging between us, and I wondered, yet again, what it all meant to my life. Why were we reconnecting now? My mind wanted to figure it out. It seemed only a flash in time before our encounter was over. He was off to his evening dinner meeting, and I wondered if or when I might see him again. It felt serendipitous how he popped back into my life immediately after my split with Shawn and now after my breakup with Mark. Was he showing up to remind me that I wanted and deserved so much more?

So many things were happening at once. Moving day had arrived, and the hired men were loading my household onto the truck. Thanks to my parents and two of my neighbor friends, everything was packed and loaded in record time. My dad planned to drive the U-Haul, towing my smart car, while Lily and I would drive in the recording studio cargo van, filled to maximum capacity. It was a short trip compared to the three full days we'd spent driving across the US a year earlier.

Approaching San Diego, we witnessed a gorgeous welcome sunset over the Pacific Ocean. My entire body lit up; it felt like I was returning home after having moved from the California coast with Stuart more than eighteen years prior. My dad and I worked super hard, into the dark of the evening, to help the movers unload the vans. Morning came quickly, and we rushed to return the U-Haul and get my dad to his plane to make his evening activities back in Arizona. I spent the next forty-eight hours whipping my new home into shape and finding the perfect place for each piece. I had more space than I'd had in my apartment and looked forward to sprawling out a little. I also couldn't wait to get to the beach.

Although I had clarity regarding my relationship with Mark, I must admit my heart was broken, yet again. My theme of building another home alone continued. I didn't wallow in this pity party long. I had people to meet, places to explore, the ocean breeze to enjoy, and the California sun to frolic in. I had no immediate plans to see Robert again, although we hoped our schedules would align again soon.

I was excited to explore Encinitas; the beautiful cliff beaches and the Pacific Ocean were happy spots for me. The community was eclectic, with a focus on surfing and all things spiritual. It wasn't Bali, but possibly the closest experience in the States, as the endless events would likely introduce me to a plethora of like-minded people. Dee was an hour up the road, Axel was twenty minutes away, and Angelique had moved back from Bali and was fifteen minutes inland. Elated to have a few core friends nearby, I anticipated meeting new people and finally integrating myself into a community. The future seemed optimistic and exciting, and my show's momentum was building with a lineup of incredible guests.

A month later, COVID hit, and everything shut down, including my new business adventure interviewing entrepreneurs in my cargo van recording studio. No events were going to occur, and opportunities to integrate into the community were eliminated.

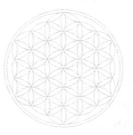

CHAPTER 22

Spiritual Medicines, Psychedelics, and Awakening

I N MID-2019, DEE had been diagnosed with breast cancer, plunging her into another level of inward search for answers and meaning. She'd been introduced to a shaman who administered spiritual medicines to help her understand why she was attracting cancer for a second time. Like me, she was a corporate professional, and drugs had always been a definite no-go. But her deep desire to understand her disease led her to open up to a nontraditional route and try MDMA.

Having no knowledge of MDMA, or ecstasy as it's called on the streets, I googled it. I found out that it's a synthetic substance that increases the concentrations of neurotransmitters like serotonin, dopamine, and nor-epinephrine in the brain. In short, this chemical compound opens the heart and allows feelings of empathy and compassion toward oneself and others to increase. Amazingly, the trajectory of dealing with the cancer diagnosis and double mastectomy changed entirely for Dee in one spiritual medicine session. I listened for hours as she shared the learnings from her session. She'd received guidance and insights about the storylines and emotional underpinnings that brought about the illness.

My zero-tolerance for drugs was something I stuck to and didn't plan on ever breaking. So I was surprised to be having this conversation with Dee about her professionally assisted journey. Eager to learn more, I found that MDMA was being actively studied in proper clinical trials and had been fast-tracked by the FDA to treat emotional disorders, including posttraumatic stress disorder and depression. It came as a surprise to me that the treatment of many other health conditions with various mind-altering substances that have been around for centuries was also being studied.

I saw the impact MDMA had on Dee and began to respect this chemical compound that could profoundly impact intuition and consciousness. I also had a better understanding of why some mind-altering substances are referred to as spiritual medicines and could appreciate them having legitimacy for healing. However, I still wasn't interested in trying them myself. I'd been through so many different modalities of healing and transformation; I wasn't interested in partaking in mind-altering activities that could cause hallucinations, and the word *psychedelics* alone scared me. The last thing I wanted was to undo all the spiritual work I'd done!

As Dee shared about her second MDMA experience, my resistance softened, and I began considering the possibility of partaking in some type of spiritual medicine ceremony. However, I was adamant that I would only do this with an experienced shaman in an appropriate setting. It would have to be either in a private session or with a small group who shared overlapping intentions for the expansion of consciousness. Since I knew about the darker realms of black magic and humans with bad intentions, I was sensitive to the possibility of life cords being hacked, manipulation, and the sucking of energy, to name a few. Let's just say I was very cautious.

Dee wanted to embark on exploring other medicines and had signed up to attend a San Pedro ceremony. She asked me to drop her off, thinking it would be a great opportunity for me to meet the hosts and tour the temple where ceremonies took place. I enjoyed meeting them and had a good feeling about the ceremonies they were leading but didn't think I'd feel called to partake in one anytime soon.

Curious to learn more, I researched this plant medicine and found it to be a cactus indigenous to Peru.

> Some described San Pedro as a key that opens the gates of heaven, while others described it as a "teacher plant."

I'd also read about its healing nature and numerous accounts of "miracle cures" for a wide variety of illnesses, including cancer, paralysis, and emotional issues. I didn't have an illness I needed to cure, but I was interested in learning from this plant's wisdom about other realms of consciousness.

A few months later, Dee called to see if I was interested in participating in an upcoming San Pedro ceremony with her trusted shaman. I told her "I'd think about it", not sure if I was ready to embark on this journey just yet. Serendipitously, I happened to be editing my episode with Louie Schwartzberg. When I listened again to all Louie had to say about plant medicine, the power of nature, and its impact on our connection to Source, it made me eager to explore this opportunity. He recommended I try them in the right set and setting, elaborating on the importance of one's mindset and the physical setting to create a safe environment for the most optimal inward journey. Being reminded of his encouragement, I decided to take the plunge and experience the power of the San Pedro plant. After all, it was simply a cactus ground into a powder and mixed into water, and Peruvians have been partaking in it ceremonially for centuries.

The prep sheet included a specific diet of only plants and no alcohol for one week leading up to the ceremony. This wasn't difficult to comply with as my diet was already comparable to this. Recognizing that many different things could happen, I set clear intentions for my experience in order to reduce any mischief or interactions with unwelcome spirits or energies from other realms.

Arriving at the temple, I felt nervous yet confident that exactly what needed to happen would take place. I didn't know anyone in the group of ten people, and I wasn't interested in making friends other than acknowledging the others with a brief hello. I hoped to prevent any overlap of journeys to avoid any issues or traumas others would be bringing forward. Before heading into the temple, I found a quiet, sacred space where I could go after drinking the medicine and experience the effects for the next six to eight hours.

As we all sat quietly, waiting for the facilitators to start the ceremony, a woman seated to my left looked me in the eyes and gently smiled. I smiled back as she said to me, very quietly, "I always feel like I'm cheating when I do this because I receive so many insights." I was a bit taken back, as it was exactly what I'd thought before she said it. I'd been wondering this myself. Was I cheating? Shouldn't I be able to do this on my own, without the medicine? Then our attention was called to the front of the temple.

After a brief opening, we were asked to share our intention with the group. I'd spent some time in the days prior reflecting, and my intentions were clear:

- Cleanse at a cellular level (cellular soul scrub)
- Clear anything not serving my higher good
- Embody Divine love and light

I stated these out loud as we sat in a circle, creating a beautiful, sacred space, and waited to be served the cactus drink. Moments later, people were sipping and gagging on the drink and chewing ginger candies to avoid becoming nauseous. This didn't seem encouraging. Surprisingly, when I drank mine, I liked its taste. I'm an avid matcha tea drinker, so the bitterness of the cactus didn't bother me.

The shamans encouraged us to drink fast, warning us that the cactus expands quickly in the water, creating a gel-like texture. I guzzled the green goo, and it was gone without a gag. My fellow journeyers weren't all finding it as easy to drink. Some were already belching, but the facilitators requested we keep the medicine in for at least forty minutes. After that, purging anywhere in the gardens was welcomed. Yes, anywhere, except the swimming pool. They also recommended that if we did throw up, we should look at it to see if any messages or insights appeared in what came out. Wow, an even less attractive idea. Throwing up has never been an issue for me, as I've always trusted my body to know when it needs to release what's not serving me. The reality was I hadn't eaten anything for the last eighteen hours and guessed there wouldn't be too much that could come up other than the green cactus sludge.

After everyone drank their portion, we were encouraged to find a comfortable place to sit in nature. Retreating to my predetermined poolside swing, I'd be by myself and not interfere with anyone else. Sitting quietly, my mind raced to determine what was happening to me, if anything. I felt relaxed but didn't think anything was transpiring until the light veil fabric on the back of the swing blew forward, gently touching my shoulder, kissing my skin. I was like, "Oh, oh, okay, Spirit." Still completely aware of myself, I didn't feel drugged in any way. Then a gentle voice from Spirit said, "We're here."

It was subtle and intriguing that this flowing fabric seemed to be connected to the wind while it brought me along into the ease and flow of the breeze. Feeling safe and relaxed made it easier to sit back in wonderment of what was to come. My mind kept trying to kick in and say, "Don't let go. You don't know where this is going to take you; something bad could happen!" Somehow, I knew I had to ignore my mind because turning back now and resisting would be futile. And the next thought was, *I'm going to do this by myself!*

It was a classic case of the ego-mind not wanting to
surrender, not wanting to be out of a job when my higher
self takes hold of the steering wheel.

The voice of the mind returned, saying, "You don't even know these
people, and any number of things could go wrong." My mind continued
to hold on to the idea that I'd feel safe if it was in control. Then my mind
bantered with me for a while as I sat listening to the dialog. *Wait, if I lose
control, that means someone else is in control, right? Do I know them? Do I
trust them?* I wasn't sure if I was worried about the other people on the
journey or spirits in other realms. Now I was wondering who "they"
were!

After some time of quiet reflection, I started to feel nauseous. I moved
to a different spot to have a little more privacy since purging in front of
everyone wasn't of interest to me. I remembered that Dee said she'd tor-
tured herself the entire time, contemplating the feelings of throwing up.
She realized later that she was so caught up in listening to her mind that
it kept her from surrendering to the experience, causing the entire day
to be a challenge. I didn't want to do that and stepped into welcoming
nausea and letting go of any hang-ups around throwing up.

It had been a few hours since the first dose, and the shamans
announced it was time for a second dose. Although this was optional, I
knew without question that I wanted to take it and reentered the temple.
Having spent the last thirty to forty minutes already thinking I might
throw up, the mere smell of the San Pedro made me increasingly nauseous. It was more difficult to drink now that everyone was gagging
loudly as we all drank the second serving. These noises created a truly
unpleasant environment, making it challenging to guzzle this round.

I swiftly headed back to my swing to close my eyes and relax into
whatever was going to happen next. At the same time, I felt the lump of
green goo stuck in my transverse colon, causing discomfort. I decided
to welcome this too, even though my mind wanted to evaluate and think
about its meaning. Finally, the medicinal aspects of San Pedro kicked
in and gave me a break from the thoughts in my mind. Feeling quite

relaxed, the few thoughts I did have were related to my gut.

At one point, I decided that sitting in the rocking chair next to one of the hosts seemed like a good idea. She greeted me and asked a few questions. Strangely, it was as though my jaw was wired shut. I felt like a spy who was sworn to secrecy and wasn't going to disclose anything. It was the weirdest thing, as I typically love to talk and share but felt there was nothing to say. I proceeded to tell her, "I can't talk. I'm not here to talk; I'm not here to share," expressing that I was in conversation with the High Council. I knew in my conscious mind that what I was saying would most likely sound ridiculous. However, she understood and simply smiled while continuing to rock in the chair next to me.

I'd traveled to many different dimensions while not on spiritual medicines, so this part was familiar and it made sense that I was speaking to beings in another realm. It's often challenging to translate information that's revealed from these other dimensions into the English language, as it comes as a vibration. It's telepathically transmitted and becomes a "knowing" that's not always explainable. The concept of thought seems like a lower vibration that doesn't require articulation.

Moments later, I decided to lie on a yoga mat on the ground in front of me as the shaman knelt next to me. I shared that there was a big knot inside my gut, which prompted her to hold her hands in a hovering position over my belly for a few minutes. As she walked away, my eyes closed, and the most beautiful, bright yellow kaleidoscope figures started to swirl. It was a fantastic display of art that I had never seen in this multi-dimensional way. Instead of focusing on the discomfort, I welcomed it and told myself not to fight it.

The next thing I knew, I started convulsing. Oh my God, convulsing massively, yet rhythmically. My whole body shook on the ground, and at the same time, I felt an incredibly comforting feeling—having no fears, no drama, like I was being shaken vigorously yet with great care. I wondered if this is how they felt back in the ashram doing the shaking therapy, moving their life force—chi energy—through their body to open energy blocks. The difference here was that I wasn't trying to shake myself. I was experiencing full-body movements in a rhythm I was not controlling. I was involuntarily being moved by a force much larger than me.

The San Pedro had gone into every cell of my body, releasing blocks and working its way back into my intestinal tract. My whole body was pulsing it out, pumping, pumping, pumping. I had no concept of time, but it felt like this was going on for at least one to two hours, maybe longer. From an outside observer standpoint, it may have appeared violent. But inside, I was experiencing a miraculous cleansing and felt wonderful as I flopped and shook in complete surrender. Toxins continued to move out of my cells toward the big medicine ball in my gut like a magnet. The San Pedro knew what it was doing, moving debris from my body into my intestines and escorting it out.

The shaking and movements started to subside after what felt like several hours. I could hear others beginning to gather down by the pool as they emerged from their journeys. I wasn't anywhere near the point of wanting to talk with anyone but managed to peel myself off the ground and get back into the rocking chair. I slowly reoriented back into time-space reality.

Dee arrived to pick me up and was eager to hear the details from the day as she sat with me in the gardens. Having nothing to say, I wanted to remain still for as long as possible. It wasn't a bad feeling reintegrating with my body; it was just an unfamiliar experience. I hadn't lost my identity, although I experienced a beautiful window into what it feels like not to be a slave to the thoughts of my mind. It was a peaceful pause that couldn't have happened for me in a yearlong meditation practice. Now I knew from experience what it felt like to genuinely stop the suffering of the mind. But could I reach this state on my own?

When I returned home, Lily was eager to see me, and I was happy to see her. I still hadn't released the San Pedro and could feel it all backed up in my GI tract. As the evening went on, I continued to have episodes of intermittent shaking on the floor. Thank goodness Dee was familiar with the medicine and wasn't freaked out, although I'm not so sure she had seen anything quite like this.

I went to bed, and as my head hit the pillow, my ego-mind started waking up as thoughts began pouring back in, questioning and judging, wanting to be heard. It wasn't until that moment that I realized how much the mind had been set aside throughout the day, as I'd truly surrendered to Spirit.

> Perhaps the most memorable ideation I took from the ceremony was the power of the mind and how it runs our lives without us even knowing it.

I recognized that duality is so woven into the landscape of our external environment that it can be difficult to identify the nudging of the soul when the ego-mind is talking all the time. With the assistance of this spiritual medicine, the teachings of A Course in Miracles were now going beyond the intellectualization of the concepts to embodying them. I was beginning to experience my soul inside my body—this complex idea to explain was now solidified in a way I couldn't have learned from a textbook.

A lot happened during my San Pedro journey, and ideas about life seemed clearer. Overall, I felt lighter, but there were two things that happened physically in my body that I couldn't ignore or explain. I had been suffering from severe back pain for years, and it had reached an all-time high, and none of my typical techniques, such as chiropractic care and stretching, were working. As I flopped about on my floor, I realized my back pain was completely gone. All the shaking had released the energetic blocks that were causing the discomfort.

Another fascinating physical change had taken place in my gut. A few months prior, Axel had detected a lump in the area of my transverse colon or abdominal aorta, the same place I felt the San Pedro had stuck. Concerned, I'd gone to the doctor to have it checked out. They immediately scheduled a colonoscopy and endoscopy to see if they could determine what was causing the bulge. Everything appeared normal, except that I had an infection of H. pylori, a strong bacterial strain that can only be eliminated by heavy doses of strong antibiotics.

After the San Pedro journey, this mysterious lump I'd been feeling for months was miraculously gone. I was retested for the bacteria, and it was gone too. I did not expect the San Pedro to heal me of physical ailments, but it did. This meant I was able to avoid taking the aggressive antibiotic regimen. I wasn't sure if or when I'd do San Pedro again, but it seemed the medicine, the plant power, had done precisely what I'd asked it to do: help me cleanse, clear, and embody Divine light.

Reflecting deeper, I realized all I'm ever doing in my everyday life is experiencing a feedback loop and trying to figure out who I am based on what my external environment is telling me. This leads me to a continuous examination and judgment of how I fit in.

> These are facts about how I show up in the three-dimensional world, but when I cut out the external reflections, I can easily experience who I really am as a being of Source energy experiencing oneness through my awareness.

My thought constructs had been clouding the truth, creating a thick veil, making it difficult to see my true self. After this cleansing, I embodied philosophical concepts on an entirely different level.

When an opportunity arose to attend another ceremony, I was ready to go back in and surrender to Spirit and quiet the mind. My goal was to experience more peace and reduce or eliminate the attachments to the external field. I was eager to further unravel my false ideations and beliefs about ingrained thought constructs we all live by. Although many have experienced sustained healing through one session, very few have experienced sustained enlightenment after one dose. I knew that doing the integration work would help make the shifts to maintain higher levels of consciousness by embodying the wisdom that would keep the mind in its rightful place. All our minds can be strong, but mine in particular was fervent to stay in control and intact. Without it, who would I be?

Several months later, I visited my friend Dan and learned that he planned to participate in a Bufo (short for *Bufo alvarius*) ceremony later that afternoon. I was surprised when he described Bufo to me as venom from a toad's back that's crystallized and smoked through a pipe.

It sounded horrific and was not enticing to me at all. On top of this, you immediately pass out! I couldn't see how that made any sense.

Dan had experienced this medicine once before and said it was typical for the ceremony to last around fifteen to thirty minutes, and people were able to drive immediately afterward. This was hard for me to comprehend, especially after my journey on San Pedro, when I'd continued to shake through the night. It seemed too good to be true. What if it was too powerful? Even though there were supposed to be no lasting effects that would impair participants' ability to function in the world, I was not eager to try it. But I was willing to support my friend's journey. Concerned about him going alone, I offered to attend and hold the space during his session.

As we walked in, the environment felt comforting: a soft mat was on the floor with blankets and pillows all around. Everyone in the room seemed at ease, and the meditative music added an element of tranquility. Lily was allowed in the room, and I wondered how she would react to everything, as she is extremely sensitive to energy. We all made small talk, and I asked questions about how everyone had gotten involved with this modality. The team holding the space had such interesting stories. They seemed to be living somewhat normal, conventional lives outside of the fact that they were serving toad venom to people via a pipe. I mean, was I really involved in this? It felt surreal.

The shaman serving the "medicine" had been trained by a licensed psychologist to administer the Bufo. The host was an investment banker at a prestigious bank branch, and the support team had extensive experience with this sacred space. They all appeared very loving, yet serious about administering the medicine. I used to laugh at the term *medicine* as I questioned this as a fancy way to dress up drugs to make it seem "spiritual," but the effect was so deeply profound that "spiritual medicine" now makes complete sense to me.

The shaman asked my friend to state his intention, then read a declaration to invoke the blessings of the Bufo to initiate the ceremony. After Dan took one large puff from the pipe, he immediately passed out, and the facilitators laid him back ever so slowly onto the mat. A few minutes later, he exclaimed, "Holy shit!" and a few minutes after that, he sat straight up and was ready to stand up off the mat. A bit stunned, I waited anxiously to hear more about what had taken place. He turned to me, smiling, and said, "I feel like I just talked to God for an hour."

The reality was that only five to ten minutes had passed. Mind you, this man came from a military background and was currently employed as a pilot on one of the major airlines. He had a lot to lose if he "lost his mind" doing drugs. Seeing that he was completely back to himself but honoring the fact that he had experienced something way beyond this reality, I was intrigued.

Then the question came: "Do you want to go next?" I hadn't planned to partake but was feeling comfortable with the set, setting, and the shaman. Suddenly I heard myself say yes. Looking back, I believe not having much time to think about it contributed to my willingness. If I'd scheduled it in advance, my mind would have tried to talk me out of it. I had just come along to make sure my friend was comfortable and to hold a safe space for him. As I felt into the opportunity, I knew it would open another level of consciousness.

Nervously I sat on the mat, knowing only a puff would knock me out cold in a matter of seconds. As instructed, I read the invocation out loud and took a puff of the toad venom. Immediately my eyes closed, and I started to see vivid visuals and hear sounds I'd never experienced before. The team gently laid me back on the soft mat.

I had a few brief moments, as I went in and out of consciousness, where I thought, *Holy crap, I'm dying. I'm literally dying.* My entire physical body, energy body, and mind were completely vanishing. It was as though someone had poured acid all over me, and I was dissolving into nothingness. I had an instant that felt like a long time, probably only a nanosecond, where I thought, *Okay, I'm going. Yup, this is it. I'm off the planet,*

as I fell into the most incredible experience of peace that surpasses all understanding.

My mind was muted, as I felt completely blissed out and part of the entire cosmos. I was spanning endlessly into infinity. A sensation of ecstasy and a surge of energy came through my body. It felt electrifying, as though I was clearing out every cell and replacing it with the whitest bright light imaginable. It was equivalent to experiencing a full-body orgasm that had nothing to do with my genitals.

As I lay there, my body started a gentle shaking movement, which helped me integrate back into this reality and return my awareness to my physical body, a related feeling to what I'd experienced with San Pedro. All my identity points of who I know myself as started to come back online as I reconnected to my physical body and settled back into awareness here on the earth plane. Many mystics and shamans call this "examining the particulars of your own form identity."

Going into complete ego dissolution of who I was, into nothingness, allowed me to experience the feelings of pure, unconditional love in oneness. The movie *Lucy* demonstrates this in the final scene, where Lucy dissolves into nothing but becomes everything. It's impossible to describe or imagine this experience; it must be felt. The true void of any personal identity and the freedom of being in oneness with God, as a part of God, was astounding. This is something I think many ministers talk about but haven't experienced or embodied.

Unlike my friend, who seemed to pop up so quickly, I took about forty minutes to sit up. When I noticed the thought, *Do I have bad breath?* it was apparent that I was back. It was funny to hear myself think this, as it was symbolic of the mind coming online trying to judge me. Then Lily sniffed my head, and I felt fully grounded back into the awareness of my body. Only about thirty minutes afterward, I was driving home and felt "normal," although it was apparent that something significant had just taken place. An incredible feeling of interconnectedness and gratefulness flowed through me. The veil of illusions had been lifted entirely; I had experienced freedom from the storylines of the mind.

My overarching takeaways seemed to clarify concepts and ideas I'd been learning about through all the healing modalities. Now it felt like

I'd experienced shortcuts to another depth of understanding through my experiences with psychedelics. The following are a few of the many concepts that became more solidified from personal experience, which took me way beyond book knowledge.

ONENESS

Bufo accentuated my awakening. It solidified for me that the true meaning of the phrase "the ultimate reality" is oneness. That we are all manifestations of the same consciousness. We think we are separate from one another although we are actually a spark from the same "Source energy" that sustains all of life. We come here to have a human experience to learn about emotions and feelings through relationships with others and our external environment. As Axel would say, "to become the happiest motherfuckers on earth" and to recognize that no person, place, or thing is responsible for our internal peace. Seeking pleasure from the external world provides only temporary happiness, and mastering the inner space is key. Transcendence to the highest level of consciousness brings us back to embodying the idea that we are a part of the whole of existence.

My previous journeys were leading me there, but I hadn't achieved this phenomenon prior. It's where there's no memory, and the initial idea that there's a fault is gone. A recognition that I am perfect and whole, emphasizing that the goal is to be in this world but not of it. Realizing there was a perceived moment of separation where duality comes into play. Re-membering back to Source brings awareness that there is only this one moment. This eternal home, this eternal "I am" kind of thing. It's like, "Okay, that's reality"—it can't be further described and best to be experienced. Anything else is some form of the illusion that there's another place to go, another state to reach, or something other than being in the awareness of oneness, embodying complete perfection. It means the mind is corrected, all societal and ancestral programming is erased, and sight becomes clear.

My experiences with psychedelics provided the training wheels that assisted me to ride into oneness.

FEAR VERSUS SURRENDER

My fear that mind-altering spiritual medicines would lead me to drug addiction or to choose to leave the earth plane had merit, but I found the opposite to be true for me. Seeing how blissful life could be while out in the cosmos inspired me to bring back the wisdom and integrate it into my life. It can be jolting to go out there, have thought constructs blow up, be shown oneness, and then come back here and try to practice it in this dense vibrational field. I guess that's why some people fall off the rails when they rely on any type of mind-altering drug to take them somewhere instead of doing the work to achieve oneness and universal love in the here and now. Through the natural surrender and release of the concepts of my mind, I realized psychedelics emphasized how important it is to stay grounded here in this three-dimensional world we live in and experience bliss on the earth.

INTEGRATION

Psychedelics are very powerful in assisting humans in expanding their consciousness. However, I saw the importance of seeing them as tools, like any of the other spiritual modalities I've practiced. In yoga, the goal isn't how long you hold the pose but the ability to calm the mind through breathing to stay in position. Then outside the classroom, the student practices by applying these relaxed states to frustrating or stressful experiences, like standing in line at the Department of Motor Vehicles. The practice is to bring oneself back to inner peace and a flow state by using the yogic breath to reduce frustration. I've found that integrating learnings from all modalities, especially psychedelic journeys, requires integration work over a period of time to gently activate and embody the most valuable lessons from the medicines.

NATURE'S INTELLIGENCE

Mother Nature displays the concept of oneness effortlessly, constantly encouraging and guiding us to our power within that connects us to Source energy. I learned that nature is an access point into inner stillness through flower photography. This activity brought me a greater realization of how observing flowers can be a powerful nontraditional meditation tool.

Over the years, nature has been one of my greatest teachers and guides, helping me access other realms and connect to my higher self. When I heard Eckhart Tolle say, "Flowers help us get in touch with the dimensions and depth within oneself," my fascination and experiences were validated even more. I realized the flowers were my first shortcut into the magic of quieting the mind, but there was so much more they came to teach me as representatives of the spirit realm.

> Flowers demonstrate a level of trust in the Source energy that created them, surrendering to Divine timing as they gently open through the power of innate intelligence.

They display the connection to Source that lies within each of us.

SHORTCUTS

It became clear that the ego-mind eagerly wants to be in control, but

> the end game is having the mind work for you by naturally quieting its presence and influence.

The teachings kept me mindful of shifting my awareness to allow Spirit to drive and keep the ego-mind in the back seat. My friend Angelique always reminded me that letting the ego drive is like putting a small child behind the wheel. When this happens, you'll take the long road home. Listening to the mind while it's in the driver's seat will trap you in the trauma, heartbreak, illness, or whatever situation you put forth for your awakening. The shortcut is to have your higher-self navigating so you don't miss the joyride along the way.

Psychedelics highlighted the shortcut of not having to go through suffering to embody bliss. All ideas are simply mental constructs of the mind that can appear very complicated. When we buy an airline ticket, we buy a direct flight, which is taking a shortcut because we don't want to make three stops. There's no guilt in that, so why should there be guilt in finding out who you really are in a psychedelic trip that flips the switch for you? Why should the "easy button" be off-limits?

Getting a North Star, as a compass to help get us through the thought constructs and illusions we've built individually and collectively, catapults our ability to be in this world but not of it. Psychedelics provide a conduit to experience who we really are instead of the particulars of who we think we are. It became clear that we all need to have a sense of what point to hit: communion with our brothers and sisters at minimum, if not oneness. Since we're all on this earth-walk together, why not experience it in harmony?

INNOVATION

While to some, the emergence of psychedelics may seem new, feel foreign, or create concern, it's easy to see they've been around a long time. I was surprised to learn that they've been used by some of the greatest thought leaders of all time who have contributed to some of the most significant advances in humanity (google it). They understood the importance of putting the mind in its rightful place to hear their inner wisdom and guidance from their higher self. This allowed for heightened creativity and facilitated greater clarity.

Many innovators, leaders, and creative artists—including Steve Jobs, who microdosed LSD; the Beatles, whose music was influenced by LSD and psilocybin mushrooms; and the artist Sting, who used psychoactive substances—experienced other dimensions of reality. Even the well-known life and wealth coach Tony Robbins has talked openly about his experience with Bufo on *The Joe Rogan Experience*. With more individuals sharing the profound learnings from their journeys, the negative stigma is changing, amplifying the role of psychedelics in healing, expanding, and correcting the mind back to wholeness.

SUFFERING

With the enormous mental health epidemic, taking shortcuts is even more enticing than taking the "long road." People are often more willing to surrender when their suffering is high, and they know "there's gotta be another way." Clinical trials are underway looking at mental health conditions, neurological disorders, and other brain conditions using various psychedelic formulations. The initial results have contributed to the FDA's decision to fast-track the approval process for MDMA, and it is anticipated to be approved in a few years for the use of depression, anxiety, and PTSD.

At a minimum, we'll have more science than ever before regarding psychedelics' abilities to balance brain chemistry, impact neuroplasticity, and ultimately open our minds. It's exciting to know that we may have options to help us positively impact limiting patterns and beliefs that are stuck in the default mode network of our brains. Psychedelics are helping us train ourselves to leverage the mind and not be a slave to it.

The irony is that these base molecules have been around for centuries but were kept underground as the world went through a revolution of industrialism and materialism. Psilocybin "magic" mushrooms have been identified in numerous works of ancient and religious art, suggesting psychedelics may have been used by some historical, religious icons. Perhaps they are one of the best-kept secrets, as powerful and influential leaders want to keep societies following a narrative that relinquishes freedom of expansion, desiring to keep the masses entrapped in the ideations and illusions the external world projects as societal norms.

NOT FOR EVERYONE

With that said, I don't think psychedelics are the answer for everything or everyone. It's important for individuals to feel called to spiritual medicines, as they are life-changing, and not everyone is ready for change. For me, psychedelics unexpectedly solidified many awakening concepts I'd been introduced to through various modalities and a myriad of spiritual teachings and practices. I've discussed some of them here in the book, including quantum physics, breathwork, Family Constellation, yoga, and hypnosis, to name a few. Through this spiritual toolbox I've built through the years, I've been able to break through the veil and experience my connection to higher realms. These practices have helped me to integrate and enhance my understanding of how to release the suffering of the mind, achieve expanded states of consciousness, and embody my natural birthright of bliss.

AWAKENING

I realized that blissful states of oneness are accessible simply by not being willing to be separate in any way. Granted, maintaining a blissful state is tested repeatedly with relationships and our external environment. This is when it's essential to stay grounded, welcome the emotions, and allow ourselves to observe the triggers that stimulate us so we can find our way back to a blissfully neutral state. That's the work in everyday life, and it's never-ending.

> The key was realizing that as soon as I turn my agenda over, it connects me into the peace of God, Source energy, also known as my higher self.

And I don't mean that in a religious sense. That's the real trip, and it doesn't require outside stimulus; it's an inward journey to the wisdom that's always available. It's ultimately about learning how to do it in the here and now, without any psychedelics or spiritual medicines.

I finally understood why gurus suggest the hardest thing anyone will ever do is just be yourself. We're often focused on trying to be somebody and figure out who we are and how to fit in. Your only job is to be you in your purest form. I'm still working on this daily by bringing awareness to having my soul in the driver's seat and staying on the joyride instead of the rollercoaster of the mind.

Everything I've written about contains stories that held so much relevance for so many years until I simply stopped going into the storylines and embodied the idea that everything is a projection of my mind. I intellectually understood the concepts of the holographic universe from my quantum physics books, but now it's integrated in a way that I would have never expected. All of this led to the recognition that all the characters were chosen by me, for me, on my path of awakening to experience this character, Beth Bell, here on earth. The relationships and experiences that didn't feel good often have the juiciest nuggets to learn from. I hope that throughout the book you've been able to identify the characters in your life that have brought the greatest gifts to you.

Minimizing the path of examining cause and effect is an ongoing practice, as it requires getting out of the stories we create. It's when we take the characters, such as the boyfriend/girlfriend, an idol, or whoever we're focused on, completely out of the picture because it's not about them. It's about knowing they're all angels we call in to help us awaken. These were all instances where I was giving beauty, power, loveliness, and charm to someone or something else so I could go chase it in the illusional world, not remembering that everything I need is already within myself. Realizing they're fragments of myself being mirrored back to me, I could access the wisdom from within and cherish the beauty, charm, and power within myself.

It became clear my ex-husband was an angel I'd called in to help me break free from many programs. Robert was a beautiful projection of my mind, helping me to see another fragment of myself. So was the devil in India, along with the fireman in Bali and all the incredible characters who showed up to help me learn more about myself. Of course, through all this learning and detachment from the stories, the dynamics of my relationships changed. Mark was calling, professing his love, as he'd had a massive shift and wanted to be together. Robert was only a text message away, and I continued to wonder what I had set myself up for with him. Would I see either of them again, or would someone new be coming into my life? I decided to live in the magic of non-attachment to the outcomes and see what was in store for the future.

CONCLUSION

M Y LIFE IS my path, which is different from other people's paths. Axel would often quote Jesus saying, through *A Course in Miracles*, "There's thousands and thousands of ways to get back to God. But this is the one that's been designed for you, by you, and the shortest hack you could ever possibly make is knowing you're already there."

I've been called to release many people from my life at a time when our soul contracts were complete. Along the journey of awakening, people fall away, some more surprisingly or dramatically than others. I've learned it's imperative to allow them to leave, especially when I wanted to hang on. Being faced with significant decisions, shifts, and changes has provided opportunities to trust it's happening for my higher good. Sometimes it requires baby steps and other times tremendous leaps of faith. Either way, my only task is to remember Source by dismantling all the distractions and roadblocks I've created for myself. Allowing these opportunities to expand my consciousness accentuated my awakening and shifted me into knowing the powerful being I've always been.

It may sound odd, but it's liberating when you finally realize *no one is coming for you*. **No lover, no parent, no friend can save you from the suffering of your mind.** Why? Because you created all of them to support you on your journey of awakening. That's the mind mess we all need to work through. The sooner you can laugh about it, the faster you can overcome the insanity by unraveling the mind to unveil the illusions and know the truth of who you really are.

* * *

For additional information and insights regarding modalities for the awakening journey, please visit my website at BethBell.me

Beth Bell. *me*

Check out additional books & products
Learn more about healing and awakening
Join the tribe in "Pollinating the Planet with Love"

GRATITUDE NOTES

Mom, I don't know how you put up with all my crazy ideas over my life-time. I'm sorry for every gray hair and worry wrinkle I may have caused. Without your undeniable love that could only come from a mother, I wouldn't have survived this world. I love you and look forward to many more lifetimes with you "out there" somewhere.

Dad, You warned me at my high school graduation that "There's a lot of nuts out there." I want you to know that you prepared me perfectly with the never-ending, unconditional love you shared with me, even when you disagreed with what I was doing. Your belief in me is priceless. I love you and can't wait to see which planet we end up on together next.

To my brother, You helped me have the best childhood that any human could ever want. I looked up to you and have always admired your integrity, devotion, and desire to support family. Thank you for believing in me amongst all of life's twists and turns, even when you had no idea what I was doing.

Dear Jessica, Your friendship and never-ending love that began at the tender age of three (me) and four (you) provided the foundation I needed to bare my soul. Thank you for always supporting me, even when I came back beat up! You are a godsend. I can't wait to see who we are together in our next lifetime, as this one's been quite the trip.

Dear Jane, Thank goodness for remedial college math; it bonded us together. You've grounded me through some of my darkest times, and without your wisdom, I don't know where I'd be! I appreciate you more than you may know. I look forward to many more swirls around the sun.

Dear Katinka, Thank you for being my rock in some of my most difficult times. Thank you for not judging me and shining the light brighter just when I needed to see through to the next step. Your giving heart and selfless contributions to our friendship will be cherished for many more lifetimes to come.

Dear Stuart, Thank you for all the great life experiences we had together. I apologize for the things that I may have missed along the way to better understand your feelings. We were young and finding our way through life's experiences for our individual awakenings. I hope you learned as much as I did from our time together and all the revelations afterward.

Dear Robert, Thanks for playing along with me in such a fun way through the years, popping in just when I needed you. I'm grateful for all the inspiration you gave me to go for the sparkles in life.

Dear Axel, Where would I be without your words of encouragement and divinity just when I needed them most? I wouldn't be upright today without your incredible body and mind work, which kept my human vessel strong throughout the many wonders on my journey. Thank you for your never-ending commitment and service to humanity. You are the one. I am the one. To you and your sunshine girl: ILYSFM! See you again in a New York minute.

Dear Lei, Thank you for providing me with an incredible safe haven with your friendship and home at some of the darkest and most shattered times in my life. I am grateful for all the amazing memories and look forward to making more!

Dear Klaus, Thank you for introducing me to the depths of darkness that I was too naive to think I would encounter. I hope that our story will inspire many others to understand that they can and will survive sleeping with their devils. And most importantly, I hope it assists others in taking their power back from darker forces, enabling the great awakening. Thank you for all the lessons. I am wiser as a result.

Dear Angelique, Thank you, earth angel, for guiding me through so many dimensions. I am grateful for the white, bright light you shine and the space you held to assist in opening my eyes to so many realms. You made coming back to earth and integrating a lot of fun!

Dear Dee, Thanks to Darrin for saying hello at Elephant Café in Bali so that we could meet, only to find out we grew up three hundred miles from one another in the middle of the North American continent! I am grateful for your love, light, and support through my many projects, triumphs, and tribulations. I appreciate the gentle nudge you provided to explore spiritual medicines. What an incredible set of adventures in life we've had, and there are so many more to come!!!!

Dear Barbara, I am so grateful for the Bali magic that swirled us together as friends to navigate the insanity while having fun doing it. Thank you for listening to my endless ah ha moments and deeper revelations as I edited this book. We've written a million self-help books through all our in-depth discussions! I appreciate your friendship and support more than words can say.

Dear Fred, Thank you for loving me with your heart and soul. Your encouragement to get out of my "cocoon" along with my innate stubbornness to live my destiny created the perfect storm. It turned my deep inner flame on high to get this book out into the world to help humanity awaken. Letting me go to do this work is true love.

Dear Erik, Thank you for your ongoing support for this book and my journey. I am grateful for you and appreciate your dedication to our friendship over the years.

Dear Brian, You are a blessing. I am beyond grateful that our paths crossed and have been able to share so many life journey stories. Your wisdom has inspired me!! Your phone call saying, "It's a winner!" after reading the book made me jump up and down as the energy and excitement came pulsing through. Thank you for your ongoing support and for being such a great example of a beacon of light for others to follow.

Dear Lisa Fugard, I am grateful that you came into my life as my writing coach and editor when you did. It was your graceful yet honest way of giving me feedback that fueled my spark to get this book ready for readers. Your first set of comments came on the heels of a breakup with my boyfriend, who emphatically told me I would fail. Without your words of support and encouragement, I'm not sure where this book would be.

To my higher self, God, the creator of all that is, I loved the journey of re-connecting with you and look forward to all the adventures I have yet to experience. Most importantly, I'm excited about being right here, right now, in this moment.

PERSONAL ACKNOWLEDGMENTS

Special thanks for reading and providing extensive comments on the manuscript:

Jennifer Vizina, Catherine Holtz, Stephen Cook, Patricia Crowell, Erik Hawkinson, Dawn Kopseng, Susan Brown, Susan Shelton, Brian Smith, Danielle Schlegal, Delilah Panio, Yamin Wang, Gail Tennison, Sherry Lynn, Mike Huss, Erin Kelly, Ute Meinel, Heba Abu Musaed, Stephanie Salt, Jeff Sandgren, and Gary Stuart.

Friends, Healers, High-Vibe Earth Angels, I have immense gratitude for your healing work and gifts to humanity:

Axel Anderson, Paula Shaw, Deb Lily, Victoria Simoneaux, Julz Smith, Ida Reise, Paul Derks, Meriam Marie Jose, Julie Lowenstine, Tunjung Crystal, Sandhi Spiers, Hillary Black, Dr. David Yoder, Chet Collins, Putu Hutari, Dr. Darrin Walters, Dr. Sujatha Kekada, Shelly Reef, Nykki Hardin, Erika Johansson, Sue O'Callahan, Jean Sheehan, John Steele, Dr. Shawn Warwick, Dona Fleet, and Dr. Joe.

Additional Friends, Family, and Professional Acknowledgments:

Jilly Healy, Cindy Hayes, Patty Howard, Heather Dixon, Tara Sinclair, Stefen Oelrich, Leslie North, Cathy Byrd, Caroline Gargulio, Edio Zampaglione, Nenzy Zambrano, Geoff Bailey, Niki Coleman, AVM, David Balk, Leticia Cidade, Adele DiBari, Stephen Faraday, Jen Henkel,

Lisa Fugard, Kathleen Herrala, Randall Hayward, Phoenix Love, Susan Macdonald, Tina Nalis, Carmelina Capasso, Kurt Pederson, Swathimaa, Anna Quinn, Dennis Hauswirth, Iwona Korzeniewski, Evana Valle, Rika, and Fred Rezaei.

CPSIA information can be obtained
at www.ICGtesting.com
Printed in the USA
JSHW021918241022
32052JS00003B/10

Shape poems

Dennis

D
E
N
N
I
S

Denis is the ice
cream man – He drives
about in his ice cream van
You always know when he's around
Because: a) you can hear
that little tune he plays
from miles away –
and b) everyone
runs outside
screaming
'Hey, it's
Dennis
!!!'

James Carter

Cats can

Cats can s t r e t c h

And cats *can curl*

Cats can p o u n c e

t   t
w   w
And   i   i
r   r
l   l

s   z
Cats can i t   z
z

And eats can laze

And pu r r r into

A sleepy haze.

Coral Rumble

Undersea Tea

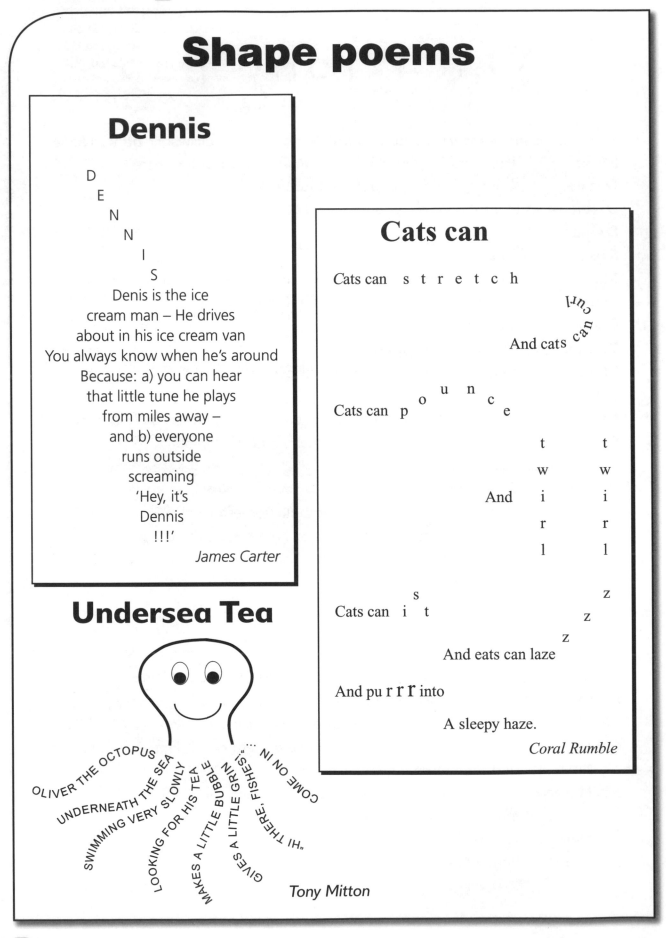

OLIVER THE OCTOPUS
UNDERNEATH THE SEA
SWIMMING VERY SLOWLY
LOOKING FOR HIS TEA
MAKES A LITTLE BUBBLE
GIVES A LITTLE GRIN
"HI THERE, FISHES"...
COME ON IN"

Tony Mitton

PANDA

The Giant Panda is perhaps the best-known and the most loved of all rare animals. About 1000 of them survive in the rainy hills of south-west China, in the provinces of Sichuan, Shaanxi and Gansu. Here the pandas feed on various sorts of bamboo which grow in dense thickets on the hillsides.

WHAT ARE THE DANGERS FOR PANDAS?

Every ten or fifteen years the bamboos which the pandas eat all flower at once and then die off after they have produced their seeds. This leaves the pandas with very little to eat until new bamboo plants have grown. In the past, the pandas would move to other areas to find bamboo that was not flowering. In recent years, though, people have cut down so much bamboo, to make spaces for their homes and their crops, that many pandas die of starvation.

In addition, pandas are sometimes trapped for their skins, which can be sold for very high prices, or are accidentally caught in snares which poachers have set for other animals

IS ANYONE HELPING PANDAS?

Yes. The Chinese Government has made it illegal to kill them, and has turned most of the areas where they still live into national parks and reserves. Since 1980 the World Wide Fund for Nature has worked with the Chinese Government to try to find out more about the pandas' habits so that they can be better protected.

ARE EFFORTS TO SAVE PANDAS SUCCEEDING?

Up to a point. The population is not decreasing, in fact it has remained the same for ten years now. However, scientists worry that this population size may not be big enough to ensure that the breed survives. Pandas prefer to live solitary lives, their courtship rituals are long and complicated, and the female usually only has one cub. This means that the pandas which die from starvation, trapping, or simply old age are not replaced very rapidly. There is a lot more work to do before anyone can say for certain that the panda is safe.

Judy Allen

Writing instructions

Dear Auntie Jane

During your stay with us you said you wanted to see the shops. When you're shopping I wondered if you could post the letter I've left here at the main Post Office in town. Here are instructions on how to find the Post Office and the shops.

To find the post office:
1. Turn left out of the front door and right at the crossroads.
2. When you get to the T-junction turn left and carry on until you reach the traffic lights.
3. Go over the traffic lights.
The Post Office is on your left just past the chemist shop and in between the Chinese take away and the vegetable shop.

To walk to the main shopping centre:
1. Cross the zebra crossing outside the Post Office
2. Turn left and then second right.
The shopping area is all around here.

Have a good day. See you later

Emily

Neela Mann

50 LITERACY HOURS FOR LESS-ABLE
LEARNERS : Ages 7 to 9

SCHOLASTIC

How valleys form

As a river flows downhill it picks up pieces of loose rock which grind against the river bank, wearing it away and carving out a V-shaped valley.

The Grand Canyon

The Grand Canyon in the USA is the largest and deepest gorge, or valley, in the world. It was formed by the Colorado river flowing over the ground at 50kph, carrying small rocks and stones. The Canyon is over 1,524 m deep and 20 km wide in some places. It gets wider and deeper each year.

Some valleys are shaped by the action of glaciers – large, slow-moving rivers of ice.

Glaciers occur when snow from high up in a mountain range turns to ice and flows smoothly downhill, often following a valley shape left by a river.

As it travels along, a glacier picks up debris such as rocks and stones. These gradually grind down the valley floor, changing its shape from a V to a U.

Anita Ganeri

50 LITERACY HOURS FOR LESS-ABLE
LEARNERS : Ages 7 to 9

Hey you! Yes you!

Where are you going?

We're all going to **Smith's Sizzling Summer Sale** –
The best prices in the west for BBQ bargains
Coals and lights, tools and equipment, camping and hiking
Prices going up in smoke! Bargains to light up your eyes!

Today, tomorrow and Sunday
Smith's, High Street, Bangertown

So…

Where are you going?
To **Smith's Sizzling Summer Sale** of course!

Free cookbook
with all
purchases
over £50

See you
there!

Neela Mann